PERGAMON MODERN LEGAL OUTLINES
General Editor: W. A. J. FARNDALE

The Administration of Civil Justice in England and Wales

OTHER TITLES BY C. F. SHOOLBRED

LOTTERIES AND THE LAW

THE LAW OF GAMING AND BETTING

THE ADMINISTRATION OF CRIMINAL JUSTICE IN ENGLAND AND WALES

The Administration of Civil Justice in England and Wales

by R. W. VICK, B.A. (Cantab.)

of the Inner Temple, Barrister-at-Law, Deputy Chairman of the Middlesex Area Quarter Sessions of Greater London

and C. F. SHOOLBRED, B.A., LL.B. (Cantab.)

of the Middle Temple, Barrister-at-Law, formerly Clerk of the Peace for the Middlesex Area Quarter Sessions of Greater London

FOREWORD BY RIGHT HON LORD JUSTICE SELLERS, M.C., P.C.

PERGAMON PRESS

OXFORD · LONDON · EDINBURGH · NEW YORK
TORONTO · SYDNEY · PARIS · BRAUNSCHWEIG

Pergamon Press Ltd., Headington Hill Hall, Oxford
4 & 5 Fitzroy Square, London W.1

Pergamon Press (Scotland) Ltd., 2 & 3 Teviot Place, Edinburgh 1

Pergamon Press Inc., 44–01 21st Street, Long Island City,
New York 11101

Pergamon of Canada Ltd., 207 Queen's Quay West, Toronto 1

Pergamon Press (Aust.) Pty. Ltd., Rushcutters Bay,
Sydney, New South Wales

Pergamon Press S.A.R.L., 24 rue des Écoles, Paris 5^e^

Vieweg & Sohn GmbH, Burgplatz 1, Braunschweig

First edition 1968

Library of Congress Catalog Card No. 67–31508

Printed in Great Britain by A. Wheaton & Co., Exeter

08 103690 6 (flexicover)
08 203690 X (hard cover)

Contents

Foreword

In the course of every term there are many visitors from both home and abroad to the Royal Courts of Justice, Strand. Some also visit one or more of the four Inns of Court. Of those visitors who call on me I find that they take a real interest in watching and hearing the work of the various courts and many have remarked that they would like to know much more of the history of the courts, of the manner of the administration of justice, its procedure and practice, the nature of the litigation and how it is allocated and performed. The more interested and inquisitive visitors have been anxious to read about the subject. They do not want a book of technical detail but a broad comprehensive book which combines conciseness with accuracy. The two authors of this work come from separate fields of practice and experience in the law and they are well qualified to work together on a general survey such as this book achieves.

In the future I am afraid I shall have to keep a copy of the book by me and make it available to the more enthusiastic of my visitors.

The authors have included information on the Liverpool Court of Passage. This is not the only local court with a busy civil jurisdiction but it is, I think, by far the most important. I have been tempted to refer to it as I had the benefit of practising there as a junior in the days of that outstanding judge, Sir Francis Kyffin-Taylor, K.C. (later Lord Maeman) who was its presiding judge for so many years. A number of the juniors in Liverpool (and some from Manchester) who appeared frequently in his court eventually reached the High Court and county court benches and each would acknowledge the splendid example of his judicial manner and wisdom.

There is I think less general knowledge than there should be amongst our citizens of how our law both civil and criminal is administered, and this work should bring reliable information to those who seek it whatever their occupation or activity.

Royal Courts of Justice
London.

FREDERIC SELLERS

Editorial Foreword

HERE is a most useful and interesting book describing the administration of civil justice, including the composition and jurisdiction of the county courts, civil work of the magistrates' courts (also described in the earlier volume on *Administration of Criminal Justice* by C. F. Shoolbred), and of the High Court of Justice. It also refers to many rules of procedure involving both solicitors and barristers. With this in mind the authors have set out to explain in simple language the main elements involved when litigation is undertaken.

The information given in this book is of a very practical nature and much more so than in many a textbook. It will, therefore, be of great value to law students and newly qualified practitioners both solicitors and barristers. For example, it will be found that a detailed explanation is given for the benefit of students as to the steps, together with the academic standards that are required in order that students may qualify themselves either for admission as a solicitor or for call to the Bar as a barrister. In both instances, a brief outline is given of the ways in which they can carry on their respective practices. The disciplinary powers with which the Law Society and the four Inns of Court are endowed in order to deal with any lapses by members of either branch of the profession are briefly described. This and similar information will also be found invaluable to students in other professions studying "general principles of law" in preparation for their intermediate examinations. In addition to law students, this book is recommended for schools and colleges, as it gives many interesting details in respect of becoming a solicitor or a barrister, and summarizes many of the current examination and other regulations of the examining bodies concerned. Any young person reading this book may well feel stimulated and interested in the career of a lawyer, and we shall be very pleased if it is instrumental in guiding some young people into a legal career and helping them by wise advice on their way.

The book begins by tracing the historical origins from which our modern courts have emerged. The work of the courts of necessity requires the assistance and co-operation of advocates, and as already indicated the reader is informed in detail how the status of a solicitor or of a barrister is acquired. Consideration is then given to the various strata of courts, namely magistrates' courts, county courts, the High Court of Justice including its several divisions, and the appeal facilities that are available to litigants right up to the House of Lords and the Privy Council.

There is separate reference to the various administrative tribunals and inquiries which of recent years have tended to become more widespread in administering the many rights and remedies that are legally open to the citizens of this country and of the Principality of Wales.

Costs, which from the litigant's point of view must be an all-important matter for consideration, are dealt with in connection with the different courts in which they are liable to be incurred; and due regard is given to the question of legal aid and advice which, as the years go by, tends to become more and more widely available.

It is perhaps not without interest at this stage to note that, whereas the Judicature Act, 1925, enacted a maximum number of thirty-two judges to be appointed to the High Court bench, this number was increased from time to time until in the Resale Prices Act, 1964, the maximum figure was increased to fifty-six. In other words, during the last four decades Parliament has found it necessary almost to double the number of puisne judges in order to be able to keep the various courts in London as well as on the circuits of assize up to date with their work. It should, however, be noted that the increase in the civil work of courts was not the only reason for requiring the services of more judges; the large increase in the number of criminal cases that have to be dealt with was also largely responsible. The interlocutory proceedings which are a necessary preliminary to a trial in the High Court, are taken into consideration when the divisions of the High Court are reviewed by the authors.

Both the authors are barristers-at-law with additional responsibilities. Mr. R. W. Vick is deputy chairman of the Middlesex Area Quarter Sessions of Greater London. He also has had a wide experience of all courts both civil and criminal as a practising barrister prior to his present appointment, especially in the High Court and on the South-eastern circuit.

Mr. Shoolbred is well known for his administration of the work at the Middlesex Quarter Sessions. For many years the Quarter Sessions have been in the Middlesex Guildhall which is situated immediately opposite the House of Commons. Mr. Shoolbred is clerk of the peace for these sessions, having been associated with them for some 30 years. The office carries with it many duties and results in his advice being sought by all and sundry, including the chairmen of the courts, solicitors, barristers and even on occasions from persons who are undergoing sentences in prison resulting from their appearance at the sessions.

Mr. Shoolbred is already an author of an earlier and successful volume in the series on the *Administration of Criminal Justice*.

Both these authors therefore have a wide and intimate knowledge of all aspects of the administration of justice. They are well qualified to write a book on this subject and I welcome this sequel from their joint pens.

Members of the public who may be involved in litigation would do well to have a copy of this book as it would help them to understand the operation of the law and the duties of the members of the legal profession and of the courts with which they may come into contact. I believe that lay people are interested in the background to lawsuits, and this book provides them with a most useful and interesting introduction to the various aspects of the administration of civil justice, as does the earlier companion volume on *Administration of Criminal Justice*. In addition, our many visitors from abroad would find that they would gain a better understanding of the English legal system through reading this book. It is also hoped that the legal profession to whom this book is initially addressed would recommend it to their clients as giving the sort of information which an intelligent client may wish to be told.

The authors of this book, Mr. Vick and Mr. Shoolbred, are to be congratulated in presenting such detailed and practical information which will be of great value to lawyers, clients and students.

London, 1967 W. A. J. FARNDALE

Preface

THE publishers on accepting the manuscript for the *Administration of Criminal Justice in England and Wales* put forward the suggestion that a companion work dealing with *Civil Justice* would be an appropriate follow-up. Whilst readily agreeing with this proposition the author of *Criminal Justice* did not feel qualified to tackle this very much wider field of our law on his own, and therefore sought the assistance as co-author of someone with practical experience in this aspect of our legal administration. Mr. R. W. Vick, Deputy Chairman of the Middlesex Area Quarter Sessions of Greater London who, prior to his appointment, had enjoyed a considerable practice and experience in this field of law, readily agreed to join in this joint venture.

The main objective underlying the intention of this book is akin to that in the earlier one on criminal law, namely that the authors have set out to explain in simple language, without going into too much detail, the whole field of civil jurisdiction as practised in the various courts in the land, from the magistrates' courts, on the one hand, to the House of Lords and the Privy Council, on the other. In doing so they have sought to make each department a separate and complete entity on its own. For example, in Chapter 5, which deals with county courts, the authors have endeavoured to cover the whole field so that those who practise in these courts will, they hope, find guidance in general to cover the majority of questions which might arise when conducting cases on behalf of their clients in these courts.

It will, of course, be appreciated that in a work of this nature it is only possible to refer to some of the most important types of action that are dealt with in the various courts. The work would, however, fail in its object to be of assistance to practising lawyers and students without full reference being made to the many statutes which affect our law; on the other hand, it is not within the purpose of this book to refer to cited cases. A trial in the High Court is of sufficient importance to warrant a separate chapter, in which every stage of such an action is traced from the issue of the writ right up to the final judgment of the court.

When referring to magistrates' courts, the three main civil functions of those courts are set out, namely adult, domestic and juvenile courts. In connection with county courts the increase in their jurisdiction which has come about of recent years comes under consideration, as well as the important question of the transfer of actions to or from the High Court.

The book starts in Chapter 1 with a brief historical introduction from which the reader will be able to see the roots from which our present day courts have developed. Chapters 2 and 3 deal respectively with solicitors and barristers, and trace briefly the means by which a student can emerge from his studies and become qualified to operate as a practising member of either of these two main branches of the legal profession.

Having thus shown the means by virtue of which students become fully fledged advocates, the next natural step is to refer to the various courts in which they will be required to appear as advocates on behalf of their respective clients. The next six chapters, therefore, are devoted to setting out the whole of this field beginning in Chapter 4 with magistrates' courts describing their civil jurisdiction in relation to adult, domestic and juvenile courts. Chapter 5 moves on to county courts, dealing with the practice and procedure in these courts, including the important aspect of their jurisdiction in regard to the transfer to or from the High Court of cases triable in the county court.

The High Court of Justice, including its several divisions, is the subject of Chapter 6 where reference is also made to many of the chief offices that go to make up the constitution of the High Court. In order to complete this phase of the book, Chapter 7 takes the reader through the various stages of the appellate jurisdiction of these courts starting with appeals from a master or registrar to a judge in chambers and concluding with the House of Lords and the Privy Council. A more detailed account of a trial in the High Court is given in Chapter 9, including the interlocutory proceedings that are required in order to get an action set down for trial. Chapter 10 is concerned with the trial itself.

The jurisdiction which is exercised by the Palatine Court of Lancaster and the Liverpool Court of Passage being somewhat apart from that of the other courts that are the subject matter of this book, a brief reference is made to them in Chapter 8. In modern times tribunals and inquiries, which are the outcome of various Acts of Parliament, have tended to occupy a more and more important place in the administration of the legal rights and remedies that are statutorily available to the citizens of England and Wales, and Chapter 10 deals with this aspect of our procedure.

The final chapter of the book, Chapter 12, covers the all-important question of costs which, when all is said and done, remains a factor of the highest significance to all who are engaged in carrying on litigation or who desire to exercise any of their legal rights. This chapter deals with this aspect court by court and also includes a survey, without which no modern work would be complete, of the increasingly important subject of free legal aid and advice; which it will be seen has assumed as great an importance in connection with civil administration as it has with criminal matters.

The authors wish to express their sincere thanks for the valuable advice and assistance that has been extended to them in their various spheres by Mr. Harold B. Williams, Q.C., Mr. L. A. C. Pratt, Clerk to the Justices of the Edmonton Petty Sessional Division of the Middlesex Area of Greater London, Mr. G. M. Somper, Solicitor, Master I. H. Jacob of the Queen's Bench Division of the Supreme Court, His Honour Judge T. Dewar and Mr. Richard Cave, Principal Clerk of the Judicial Department of the House of Lords and taxing officer of judicial costs. They would also like to express their thanks to the Incorporated Council of Law Reporting for England and Wales, to Dr. W. A. J. Farndale, not only for writing an editorial preface but also for the great help he has rendered the authors throughout. Our grateful thanks are also due to Mrs. P. Ducker for her painstaking editing of the text. And, finally, to the Right Honourable Lord Justice F. Sellers, M.C., P.C., for kindly consenting to write a foreword to this book.

R. W. V.
C. F. S.

Table of Courts having Civil Jurisdiction in England and Wales

Court	Bench	Court official	Matters dealt with
Magistrates'	Chairman and lay justices or stipendiary magistrate	Clerk to justices	
(*a*) Adult court			Hearing of complaints: Civil debts Contribution orders Abatement of nuisance Ejectment
(*b*) Domestic court			Affiliation Matrimonial proceedings Guardianship of infants Consent to marriage of infants
(*c*) Juvenile court			Adoption Care and protection Schoolattendance
Quarter Sessions	Chairman and lay justices	Clerk of the peace	Appeals from magistrates' courts including appeals from decisions of licensing and betting committees

Table of Courts—*cont.*

Court	Bench	Court official	Matters dealt with
County Court	County court judge or registrar	Chief Clerk	Actions in which amount claimed does not exceed Judge £500 Registrar £30
High Court of Justice (*a*) Queen's Bench Division	Lord Chief Justice and puisne judges	Associate of the High Court	Civil actions without restriction as to amount claimed
(*b*) Chancery Division	Lord Chancellor and High Court judges	Registrar of High Court	All causes and matters in respect of which the former Court of Chancery had exclusive jurisdiction
(*c*) Probate, Divorce, and Admiralty Division	President and High Court judges	Registrar of High Court	All matters in connection with proof of wills and intestacy All causes, suits and matters matrimonial All maritime actions including prize court
Assize Courts	Lord Chief Justice and High Court judges	Clerk of assize	Civil actions
Divisional court of High Court of Justice (*a*) Queen's Bench Division	Lord Chief Justice and High Court judges of the Queen's Bench Division	Associate of the High Court	Appeals from masters and judges of the High Court Cases stated on points of law from magistrates' courts and Quarter Sessions

Table of Courts—*cont.*

Court	Bench	Court official	Matters dealt with
			Certiorari, Prohibition and mandamus
(*b*) Chancery Division	Judges of the High Court Chancery Division	Registrar Chancery	Appeals from county courts in bankruptcy. Settled land and land registration appeals
(*c*) Divorce Division	President and Judges of Divorce Division	Registrar of Divorce Division	Matrimonial appeals from magistrates' courts
Appeal Court of High Court of Justice	Lord Chief Justice Master of Rolls President of Probate Divorce and Admiralty Division Lord Justices of Appeal in ordinary	Associate of the High Court	Appeals from High Court judges, county courts and divisional court. Bankruptcy settled land and land registration
House of Lords	Lord Chancellor and law lords	Registrar of Clerk of the Parliaments	Appeals from Appeal Court of Supreme Court
Privy Council	Lord President of the Council, Lord Chancellor, Lords of appeal in ordinary, and others duly qualified (see Chapter 7, p. 146)	Clerk of the Council	Appeals from Channel Islands, Isle of Man, Commonwealth countries, also, in England, ecclesiastical courts and from Admiralty Court in prize matters.

CHAPTER 1

Historical Introduction

Shire court — Hundred Moot — Norman courts — King's courts — Courts of Common Pleas and King's Bench — Assize courts — Court of Exchequer Chamber — Court of Admiralty — The writ system — The growth of equity — Chancery procedure — The ecclesiastical courts: Divorce; Probate — The common law — Statute law — Construction of statutes — Doctrine of judicial precedent — The modern doctrine of judicial precedent — The Law Commission.

THE purpose of this volume is to introduce the reader to the system of courts and tribunals by which civil law is administered in England and Wales today, to trace the pattern which has emerged over the years, and to describe the law administered therein and the persons responsible for its administration.

The present system of courts and tribunals has been developed largely by statutes enacted in and since the year 1873, and therefore we may ask why it is necessary to consider the earlier history of our courts. The answer is that our present legal system is not the result of a tidy logical growth, nor is it a codified system as in some other countries. At no point of time can one say that this was the moment when our legal system took on its present form. Similarly, one cannot say that the Supreme Court of Judicature Acts, 1873 and 1875, simply took a new broom and swept away all the existing institutions, replacing them with fresh ones. Rather, the process was one of rebuilding and refashioning the functions of the earlier courts by making use of much that was good, and much that was not.

The approach was thus a practical rather than a doctrinaire one, trying to make use of that which was well tried and proved, and discarding what was out of tune with the public needs of the time. But this means that the functions of the modern courts cannot be fully understood without some knowledge of the functions of the institutions which they replaced. Our law therefore has a complex history of growth and development.

We have little knowledge of the laws which existed in pre-Norman England. From such sources as are available, for example, the Anglo-Saxon Dooms, it appears that the principal purpose of the civil law was to regulate the use and ownership of land. Justice, such as it was, took a rough and ready form; there were few established communities to lead to the establishment of a recognized and recognizable code of conduct. But it would be quite wrong to think that the seeds of a form of justicial law were not present. Long before the advent of the Normans and the growth of the manorial system, distinct communities had developed in the form of the vills, a number of which combined to form a hundred, which in turn combined to form a shire. Hence it was from the shire that we acquired one of the most ancient offices in the country—the sheriff or shire-reeve as he was then known, who presided over the shire court just as his lesser brother, the hundred reeve, who has since vanished, presided over his court of lesser jurisdiction.

Tradition ascribes the origin of shires, now called counties, to a division of the country by Alfred the Great. This, however, may have no foundation in fact, since some of the counties, e.g. Kent and Sussex, have their origin in the former independent kingdoms. Others, like the northern counties other than Yorkshire, cannot be said to have existed before the Norman Conquest. Elsewhere, e.g. Wessex, where the traditional division by Alfred is more possible, the counties probably originated in the dioceses of bishops, and it is possible that counties existed in Wessex as early as the reign of Ini. It seems certain that the whole of southern England was divided into counties substantially the same as at present as early as the reign of Edgar, and in Wessex as early as the reign of Ini.

Shire and *reeve* are Anglo-Saxon words. The shire-reeve or sheriff was the king's representative in the county, and was generally nominated by the king.

SHIRE COURT

The law administered by these courts was derived from local custom and was by no means uniform throughout the country. Communications were poor and the requirements of areas and communities varied greatly. Trial was primitive in form: there were no rules of evidence as we understand them today, and trial by ordeal was a feature of the system.

The courts themselves were based on administrative areas, just as the modern county courts are today. They dealt with administrative matters, and essentially local disputes over land, cattle, and personal rights, apart from their even more important function in the sphere of criminal law. Villages, towns, hundreds, and shires were left to deal with their own offenders, after the community itself had been punished, usually by fine, for the wrong doing of its inhabitant. There may be something to be said for this system of shared responsibility, but it undoubtedly led to false allegations between neighbours and to other abuses.

HUNDRED MOOT

The lesser court, the hundred moot, was presided over by the "hundred man" and consisted of the representatives of each of the local communities, each of which provided a senior official (or reeve, as he was known), and four men. Above this stood the shire moot having a county-wide jurisdiction with the shire-reeve presiding. This court was composed of the reeve and four men from each community, the principal men in the county and the parish priests. Here again justice was administered according to custom, remembered but not recorded, and in accordance with the discretion of the court.

NORMAN COURTS

With the advent of the Normans under William I, two major factors emerged to influence the growth of our legal system. Firstly, the Curia Regis was introduced from Normandy; secondly, the introduction of the feudal system of tenure of land brought in its train the manorial courts.

It is difficult to express precisely the effect of the Norman Conquest on the legal system of the time, but it is right to say that while the Conquest was a turning point, it was not a starting point. William did not regard himself as a conqueror, but rather as the rightful successor of Edward the Confessor, whose laws he preserved. He was the first of a line of strong kings under whose rule a rapid growth and development took place and to whose reforms we owe the common law of England.

In this way the system of manorial courts and a modified feudal system limited to land tenure rather than government which was centralized in the Curia Regis, came into being. Substantial use was made of the old courts of the shire and hundred, but the *Curia Regis* was not established on a firm basis until the time of Henry I, who also established the Exchequer and retained and strengthened the county and hundred courts: "No man durst misdo against another in his time." Henry I appointed officers of the Court as Sheriffs, and while he did not originate the circuit system there were judicial journeys of the justiciar and other royal justices which may have prepared the way for the reforms of Henry II.

In England the king has never in theory succeeded in establishing his position above the law. Nonetheless, when one scrutinizes the growth of the central administration at the expense of private rights, however beneficial the results may have been, one cannot but wonder how the reality can be made to accord with the theory.

The Curia Regis, or King's Court, was not exclusively or even primarily a court of law. Its members consisted of the highest officers of State and such other men as the king might call upon to advise and assist him. It was, in fact, the core of the central government—governing, making laws, administering them, and also providing the judges to try suits.

If, indeed, there was ever any truth that Montesquieu's theory of the separation of powers could be applied to the functions of the legislature, the executive, and the judiciary in England, it was certainly not so in the Norman era.

At first the King's Court was more concerned with its other functions than in trying cases. The holding of courts to redress grievances between persons was regarded as a private right closely allied to the right to take the profit from the fees charged to litigants, by the holder of the right, and not a public duty as it became later.

Alongside the older customary courts of hundred and shire were the manorial courts, established as part of the feudal system. Inevitably much of the land fell into Norman hands and the lord of the manor was entitled to hold courts for his own tenants, which he did, exercising jurisdiction over them in civil matters.

KING'S COURTS

The death of Henry I was followed by the reign of Stephen, largely occupied by a period of civil war lasting for 11 years, and during this time the king made no attempt to observe his own or any of his predecessors' charters. As a result the development of any system of justice became disorganized.

His successor, Henry II, was thus compelled from the outset of his reign, to devote himself to creating and consolidating a strong central government which controlled the whole of the financial, judicial, and military business of the country. It is perhaps a singular coincidence that a period of anarchy was followed by the reign of one of the ablest kings who has ever occupied the English throne.

No doubt there were visitations of some or most of the southern counties early in the reign; but from 1166, following the Assize of Clarendon, there was regular visitation of all the counties by the justiciar and other justices. These "Eyres" as they were called, and the later assizes dealing with both civil and criminal business, left a lasting mark on the system of justice in England. Indeed, in 1176, by the Assize of Northampton, the provisions of the Assize of Clarendon were extended to deal with tenure, wardship, fealty, reliefs, and other feudal incidents.

The process of extinction of the local courts was a gradual one, and the methods used were indirect and in many instances not deliberate. The emergence of a better system of administering justice by the King's Court, coupled with the use of its legislative powers by the same body, led to the local courts falling slowly into desuetude. In particular, mention should be made of the Statute of Gloucester of 1278 which, while restricting the jurisdiction of the king's courts to a minimum of forty shillings, had the practical effect of destroying the jurisdiction of the customary courts where more was at stake, and thereby vitally reduced their value.

The jurisdiction of the feudal courts was attacked more deliberately by statute from time to time. For instance the Statute of Marlborough, 1267, relieved all freeholders from their duties as judges in their manorial courts, save in specified circumstances; and the vitally important *Quia Emptores* of 1289–90 very effectively reduced the number of suitors to the manorial courts by providing that the grantee of an interest in land should be deemed to hold the land not of his immediate grantor but of the Crown.

In this way, by statutory discouragement on the one hand and the provision of wider and better facilities for litigation on the other, the growth of the King's Court was fostered and encouraged at the expense of the lesser courts.

The process was a gradual one. The judicial functions of the King's Court became separated from its functions of governing and administering, and first one court and then others were established to deal with litigious matters.

As will be seen in Chapter 6, the first royal court of justice was the Court of Exchequer in the reign of Henry I. It was established to supervise the royal accounts and to decide disputes affecting the king's revenue. Meanwhile, from time to time, the king appointed officials under his royal commission to visit certain parts of the realm to inquire into various matters which were specified in the commission. At first the commissioners had little to do with the administration of justice. Their early visits, or eyres as they were known, were concerned principally with fiscal matters in which the king had an interest, and an early result of their activities can be seen in *Domesday Book*. Gradually, however, these officials began to be used as judges to hear and determine civil disputes as well as to try the more serious crimes.

The twelfth century saw rapid growth of a common law throughout the kingdom. In the reign of Henry II the first royal court of justice was set up, and trial of civil actions by jury was introduced. In addition Glanvil wrote the first book on English law, *Tractatus de legibus angliae*, and the writ system was introduced.

The texts of the documents by which the reforms of Henry II were instituted have not all come down to us—if they ever existed. It is most probable that, as Pollock and Maitland have suggested, "a few words written or spoken to his Justices might establish a new mode of procedurc". But there is no doubt that in this reign trial by the Grand Assize, the Possessory Assizes of Mort d'Ancestre, Novel Disseisin and Darrien Presentment, and the Assize Utrum were instituted. This period saw an end of the days when "every Lord had a court", a clear limitation of the jurisdiction of the county and hundred courts; though the county could still entertain matters of such importance as the writ of right, and an institution of regular procedure in the king's courts. Granvil, in his *Tractatus de legibus*, gives the actual text of the majority of the writs in use under Henry II and of the law so administered. It is probably due to Henry II that the writs of pone and justicies were instituted. By the writ of pone matters proceeding in the local courts were removed to the King's Court, and by the writ of justicies trifling matters in the King's Court were sent to the local courts for trial.

That all this is due to Henry II is perhaps clearly and picturesquely illustrated by a comparison with the manorial courts of earlier times, when every lord had jurisdiction in "sac and soc, toll and team, and infangtheof". These are dark and obscure words, but they do serve to illustrate the state of the time. "Sac and soc", so far as we know, merely implied jurisdiction—the right to hold a court and hear pleas in it; "tol" implied the right to tallage one's villeins, and "team", apparently, the right to call a stranger to warranty in one's court. "Infangtheof" was the right to hang a thief taken "hand-having or back-bearing" on one's land. The rare "utfangtheof" was the right to hang such a thief wherever taken.

The first royal court to deal exclusively with the administration of justice was composed of five men learned in the law and holding the royal commission to decide disputes. They replaced the commissioners of eyre and were required to travel with the king wherever he went, hearing and deciding disputes, referring only those of exceptional difficulty to the king and his inner council, and acting as a kind of appeal court.

Prior to the setting up of this court the litigant had either to have recourse to his local court if the amount involved was small, or to the Court of Exchequer, or to the king if he was successful in finding his court as it travelled about the country. With the new court it became the practice for it to sit at Westminster from time to time even when the king was elsewhere.

COURTS OF COMMON PLEAS AND KING'S BENCH

From this practice two distinct courts developed: that which usually sat in Westminster and whose official record of the proceedings (Roll) was marked "de banco". This became known as the Court of Common Pleas. The other accompanied the king. Its official record was marked "Coram Rege" and it became the Court of King's Bench.

At first the two courts remained part of the *Curia Regis*. The judges were appointed from the king's advisers and officials and might sit in one court or the other, but no certain line could be drawn between the jurisdiction of the two. However, in the year 1215 there became, with the signing of Magna Carta by King

John, a much clearer distinction between the two courts: it was provided that common pleas (i.e. civil actions) should thereafter be heard at a fixed place, which in time came to be at Westminster.

As has already been seen, in 1278 the Statute of Gloucester reduced the jurisdiction of the lesser courts to disputes involving not more than forty shillings, with the result that all cases of any substance had to be heard in one of the royal courts at Westminster.

ASSIZE COURTS

Going to Westminster often caused considerable inconvenience and expense to litigants, their witnesses, and the jurors, and in the latter part of the thirteenth century this situation was eased by the development of the system of assize courts. An action could then be set down in one of the courts at Westminster, whilst the evidence was heard by one of the king's commissioners when he visited the local town to try criminal cases. Judgment in the action, however, was given at Westminster. The assize system, although much altered and improved, still exists today, and forms an important part of the functions of the common law judges.

Alongside the increase in the part taken by the three common law courts, there was a growing tendency for the judges of these courts to be drawn from the senior ranks of those who practised in them, and for the judges to withdraw from the political sphere. This process continued until 1607, when Coke C.J., in a case of prohibitions, refused to permit the king to sit in court, so that today an Act of Parliament is required to overrule the decision of the highest court.

Thus by the end of the fourteenth century there can be seen the emergence of a system of law throughout the country based on precedents set by judgments given on similar points; in short, common law. Unfortunately, the system, excellent though it was in producing uniformity, had its defects, the greatest of which were its rigid formality and attention to dogma. If a litigant could not bring his case within one of the accepted causes of action he might well find himself without a remedy at law, however just his cause.

COURT OF EXCHEQUER CHAMBER

Before considering the writ system and the evolution of the Court of Chancery, mention should be made of the other common law courts which existed before 1873.

The Court of Exchequer Chamber was first set up in the fourteenth century to hear appeals from the Court of Exchequer. At different times there have been four courts bearing this title and exercising appellate jurisdiction from the common law courts, until the court was abolished in 1873 and its jurisdiction assigned to the modern Court of Appeal.

COURT OF ADMIRALTY

To an island community such as ours, piracy at sea was always a vital concern. Our history is deeply bound up with that of bands of traders such as the Merchant Adventurers and others of their kind. How were their enterprises to be protected if their merchandise was lost at sea; who was to compensate them? Prior to the reign of Edward III, jurisdiction over incidents which occurred on the high seas was assumed by the King's Council, the common law courts, and the Chancellor.

The Court of Admiralty first appeared after the victory of Edward's ships at the battle of Sluys in 1340 which put his fleet in a commanding position on the high seas. Thereafter acts of piracy and civil causes concerning the high seas or overseas were frequently tried before the Admiral of the Fleet or, if none was appointed, by a board of admirals. The common lawyers permitted this encroachment on their preserves, which was perhaps fortunate for it encouraged a healthy and vigorous development of commercial law in this country. As England developed its trade with foreign countries, merchants from abroad increasingly attended our fairs and markets. Even today, one of the first concerns of traders who contract with others abroad is to ascertain the law to be applied to their contract, and the tribunal which will exercise jurisdiction in the event of litigation. The same was true in the fourteenth and fifteenth centuries. Trade was international even then, and the merchants themselves had developed their own customs by which they were prepared to be bound. In some instances these were codified, as, for example, in the Laws of Oleron, which originated in France. It was these laws and not the common law of England which were administered in the Court of Admiralty. It was civil law or the law of nations or Law Merchant, akin to the *jus gentium* of the Roman law.

As might be expected in such a tribunal, the rules of procedure were less rigid than those of the common law courts. It was recognized that the function of the court in civil matters was to enable merchants to obtain a just decision with the minimum of delay and expense. At first the admiral himself presided over trials. As the court's business increased at the expense of the common law courts and the older courts administering the Law Merchant, such as the Courts of Pie Powder and the Staple Courts, trained lawyers were appointed to discharge the judicial functions.

The lawyers who were appointed were drawn principally from the ranks of those who practised in the ecclesiastical courts. This was not surprising, as they were doctors of civil law trained in Roman law, and formed a distinct body apart from the common lawyers.

Unfortunately, piracy on the high seas was followed in the sixteenth century by piracy on land. When the Tudor common lawyers realized what an opportunity they had missed in allowing the flourishing commercial business conducted by their Admiralty brethren to slip from their grasp, they began to usurp the functions of the maritime court. The measures used were devious but nevertheless effective. The use of the prerogative writs, such as prohibition, directed to the Admiralty Court forbidding it to hear a case on the ground that it had no jurisdiction to do so was one; the use by the King's Bench of its special supervisory powers was another. The common law courts, moreover, acquired jurisdiction by the simple expedient of allowing the plaintiff who desired to bring his action in the common law court, where the cause of action arose at sea or overseas, to assert that the place where it arose was in England, and refusing to allow the defendant to deny that this was so.

By these means, and by using their not inconsiderable influence in Parliament to secure legislation to enhance their powers at the expense of the maritime court, the common law courts succeeded in reducing the powers of the Admiralty Court, first by depriving it of much of its commercial work and then of its criminal jurisdiction. Eventually, the Admiralty Court was left with only the reduced but still important business of piracy, collision at sea, prize and salvage, wreck, and stranding, to mention a few.

Fortunately the process of competition made common law judges and lawyers realize that to compete successfully for custom among the merchants, procedure must be simplified and speeded up, and suitable rights and remedies offered. The Law Merchant became part of the common law of England and, indeed, part of the international custom of merchants was incorporated in the Sale of Goods Act, 1893, and other statutes. An important part in this transition in the seventeenth and eighteenth centuries was played by great judges such as Coke and Lord Mansfield, who had the courage and power to apply the doctrine of judicial precedent to the established custom of merchants. As a consequence, a custom once judicially established became part of the law of the realm.

As will be seen later, the class of work thus acquired by the common law courts led in 1895 to the setting up of a commercial court as part of the Queen's Bench Division, presided over by judges experienced in commercial litigation.

THE WRIT SYSTEM

In its early form the writ was no more than the king's command in writing directed to an official or to a private citizen commanding him to do or to abstain from doing something under threat of punishment if he failed to obey. Clearly it was an inefficient and often unjust system. The unfortunate defendant had no opportunity of disputing in advance the grounds upon which the writ was granted, and was left to the costly and burdensome task of prevailing upon the king to withdraw his writ.

In recognition of this unsatisfactory state of affairs, the form and purpose of the writ was altered. If addressed to an official it would direct him to inquire into the issues. If directed to a defendant it would require him either to admit the plaintiff's claim or to appear and show cause why judgment should not be given against him. In this way it became the accepted practice for all actions in the king's courts to be initiated by the issue of a writ from the King's Chancery which would be served upon the defendant. The Chancellor and his office thereby became an important instrument in the field of litigation, which was to have considerable effect when equity began to emerge in competition with the common law.

At first the system worked quite well. Forms of writ were devised to meet the usual complaints. The writ of detinue was used for the recovery of goods unlawfully withheld, or their value; the writ of covenant was used for breaches of any agreement under seal; while the writ of debt was for the recovery of liquidated sums owing.

By far the most important was the writ of trespass which was introduced in the reign of Edward I. It was founded upon the doctrine that any breach of the king's peace was a criminal offence against the king and punishable as such.

In this way the royal courts acquired jurisdiction to try cases where trespass was alleged, although the substance of the dispute was a civil action between private individuals. An individual could thus obtain redress for trespass to his land, *quare clausum fregit*, or to his goods, *de bonis asportatis*, or to his person. The preamble to the writ would include the words "vi et armis contra pacem domini nostri regis", but the medieval judge would not be misled thereby into believing that he was to try a criminal charge. He would ignore the allegation of force and arms and proceed to deal with the real issues between the parties.

By the beginning of the thirteenth century the writ system was well under way, and the common law courts were fast acquiring the work of the manorial courts. At first it was the practice for the Chancellor's clerks to issue writs only in a form already approved by the king or the royal council, but in that century they devised new forms to suit the grievance alleged. This attitude provoked opposition from the barons and the council.

In 1258 the Provisions of Oxford were enacted, whereby no new form of writ was allowed to be issued without the permission of the king. It seemed that the future development of our common law had been brought to a halt by one stroke, but that was not to be.

A period of slower development followed—a period where the common law judges established their authority to refuse to recognize new causes of action or to hear cases on the ground that the cause was not one known to the law. The position was improved somewhat in 1285 by the Statute of Westminster II, which provided that new writs might be issued if they closely resembled the accepted forms in existence.

This was interpreted as meaning that an applicant who could show that his allegations were similar to those on which a writ had been issued before would be granted one. Of more importance was the aid of the judges in extending the use of the writ of trespass to actions on the case, i.e. where the damage suffered was not the direct but rather the consequential result of the injury which was the subject of the complaint.

Even so, without something further to spur it into activity, the common law might have failed to develop as it did. The spur came from an unexpected quarter in the persons of the King's Chancellor and his officials.

THE GROWTH OF EQUITY

From being the king's principal clerk and adviser, the office of Chancellor had by the thirteenth century become one of the highest importance.

Even if the king could no longer direct the judges to do justice in a case where he saw injustice, he could still effectively prevent a miscarriage of justice by ordering that his officials should not enforce the judgment. Intending litigants were not slow to avail themselves of this remedy where they thought that the common law courts would not give them justice, and would petition the king for relief.

As the king acted through the Council, and the Council was far too busy to deal with disputes between private citizens, the practice grew of handing petitions to the Chancellor. As the Chancellor's office, the Chancery, issued the common law writs, he would know whether there was a form of writ to cover the petitioner's case, and, if so, he would tell the petitioner. On the other hand, he was an ecclesiastic and was therefore concerned with questions of conscience. This fitted him well for the role he was to play in mitigating the rigidity and harshness of the common law.

At first the Chancellor, with or without the aid of members of the King's Council, investigated the complaints contained in the petition. He reported his views to the Council who would then make their order. But by the end of the fifteenth century he was himself investigating cases and giving the final decisions in the king's name. The Court of Chancery had become established.

CHANCERY PROCEDURE

Under the common law the principal threat to a man was dispossession of his land. By the late fifteenth century, however, a new class was emerging—a merchant class which was not dependent on the land for fortune or subsistence. It was to this class as well as to the landowners that the Chancery jurisdiction appealed.

The procedure was simpler than at common law—a party would not lose his case simply because as plaintiff he had chosen the wrong form of action or had failed to plead his case correctly in writing. Above all else the Chancellor would require the defendant to attend in person and answer on oath each allegation made by the plaintiff and submit to cross-examination. This latter test was not imposed by the common law courts at that time.

It has to be remembered that even at an early stage in its evolution the powers of the Court of Chancery were supplemental to those of the common law courts. Their purpose was to reinforce and, if necessary, to check by the dictates of conscience the powers and sometimes the shortcomings of the more materialistic tribunals. In this they succeeded although by the time that fusion of law and equity was achieved the equity courts had become as formalized and dogmatic as the common law courts.

One of the most important challenges given by the Chancellor was to the feudal system of tenure which gave the lord of the manor rights over the land of his tenants. The Chancellor recognized and enforced the rights of third parties to the ownership of land of which they were not in possession. In order to avoid the rights of the lord of the manor, uses (or trusts as they are now called) were created whereby the tenant could pass his ownership to another to hold for the use of himself and his heir, thus depriving himself of his paramount title and his landlord of his dues. But the tenant in equity could secure the enjoyment to himself of the property during his lifetime and to his heirs upon his death. Attempts were made to defeat this device, but as it accorded with both common sense and natural justice, they failed.

Perhaps the Chancellor's greatest strength was that his remedies were exercised against the person rather than his property. Hence he would, where equity demanded, grant an injunction restraining a person from doing an act on threat of imprisonment if he were to disobey the order, even refusing him the right to enforce a judgment obtained in the common law courts. Conversely, the Chancellor would order specific performance of contracts where conscience demanded it. He would also order rectification of documents which were manifestly inaccurate, to express the true intention of the parties to them, would order attendance of witnesses by means of subpoenas and enforce the production of documents.

Inevitably there was some conflict between the Chancellor and the common law judges. Equity looked to the intention rather than the form of documents and, from time to time, the judges would resist a particularly flagrant interference with one of their judgments.

Matters came to a head in the seventeenth century in a dispute between the Chancellor (Lord Ellesmere) and Chief Justice Coke when the Chancellor intervened to prevent the enforcement of a judgment obtained in Coke's court by deceit (the Earl of Oxford's case). Such was the heat of the quarrel that the Attorney-General, on the advice of Sir Francis Bacon, personally intervened and decided that where the rules of law and equity conflicted the latter should prevail. Apart from a period during the seventeenth century when the political conflicts between the Crown and Parliament lowered the influence of the Chancery Court, because of its historical connection with the king's conscience, the courts of common law and equity pursued their courses in reasonable amity until in 1873 when the rule that equity should prevail was given statutory recognition by the Judicature Act.

THE ECCLESIASTICAL COURTS

As already seen, judges and legal practitioners in the Admiralty Court were drawn from the ranks of those who practised in the ecclesiastical courts and received training in Roman law. These men were quite distinct from the common law practitioners. They were Doctors of Civil Law, which meant that they were versed in Roman law and the law of the Church or canon law as it is known. They had their own headquarters, known as Doctors' Commons, and it was to one of them that an intending suitor in Probate, Divorce, and Admiralty would go for advice and the help of an advocate, and not to a member of one of the Inns of Court or of the Chancery Inns. It also followed that those promoted to the judicial bench of these courts were drawn from the ranks of these civil lawyers.

Like the Chancery Inns, Doctors' Commons have vanished, as

have the Doctors of Civil Law, and the work in the three courts is now carried on by members of the Inns of Court. Sometimes they are specialists in one or more of the branches of law, but frequently they are common lawyers.

The ecclesiastical approach has not, however, been lost in divorce and matrimonial matters. Such matters are not "inter partes" in the sense that they concern the protagonists alone. Divorce is still regarded as a matter of public concern, and the judge is still required to conduct the hearing of a matrimonial suit with due regard to the interests of public morality in general, as well as to the interests of the parties. The first Matrimonial Causes Act in 1857 which deprived the ecclesiastical courts of their matrimonial jurisdiction and vested it in a civil court known as the Court of Divorce and Matrimonial Causes, expressly provided in section 22 that the courts should follow the principles and rules of the ecclesiastical courts as nearly as possible.

Before the Norman Conquest there were no courts exercising exclusively ecclesiastical jurisdiction, and this is understandable as the division between the secular and the religious spheres was by no means as distinct then as it became later. Among those who presided over the courts of the shire and the hundred, were church dignitaries, varying in rank according to the standing of the court, and hearing and adjudicating upon matters both secular and ecclesiastical. But in the reign of William I this position was changed. William deprived the secular courts of their jurisdiction in ecclesiastical matters and set up courts expressly to deal with disputes which were regarded as the particular province of the Church. Matters which affected the clergy and Church property affairs, private and public morality, heresy, and a host of other matters of a kindred nature, all came within the jurisdiction of these new courts.

From an historical point of view, the most important areas in which these courts acquired exclusive jurisdiction were in divorce and matrimonial disputes and in the administration of the estates of the dead (or "probate" as it is commonly called). Probate was certainly a most important source of revenue from the Church's point of view: a dying man receiving the last rites would not infrequently show his gratitude to the Church and his penitence for past sins by bequeathing to it part of his estate.

Divorce

The matrimonial jurisdiction did not attain real importance until after the Act of 1857 when, for the first time, it was possible for a person to obtain a decree of divorce which enabled the parties to remarry. Prior to that a decree of divorce was no more than our modern decree of judicial separation, entitling the suitor to live apart from his spouse, but not to remarry.

The only way in which a person could obtain the right to remarry while his spouse was still alive was by persuading Parliament to pass a statute to that effect—an expensive and laborious procedure.

The student of history will remember that it was not unconnected with this that Henry VIII became the head of the newly established Church of England, and the ties with Rome were severed. In this way the ecclesiastical courts became the king's courts, but they still retained their ecclesiastical practice and procedure.

Probate

In 1857 jurisdiction over the administration of estates of deceased persons was lost to the old courts. By the Court of Probate Act of that year a civil court known as the Court of Probate was set up to deal with the proof of wills (probate) and the administration of estates of persons who died without leaving a will (intestacy).

By the Judicature Acts of 1873–5 the jurisdiction of the three courts fused into one division of the High Court known as the Probate, Divorce, and Admiralty Division, and they remain so despite many suggestions that the probate side should be passed to the Chancery Division and Admiralty to the Queen's Bench Division.

Today divorce provides the bulk of the work of the Division, and indeed, so heavy are the lists of undefended divorce cases that the county court judges are called upon to sit as divorce commissioners in order to dispose of the lists. This has prompted people in high places to suggest that this part of the work of the High Court should be passed to the county court, leaving the High Court judges to hear defended suits only. The suggestion is under consideration at the present time. If approved this would be a serious blow to the Bar as it would then be possible for solicitors, that is advocates who have the right of audience in the county courts, to conduct such cases without having to brief counsel.

THE COMMON LAW

In the earlier pages of this chapter frequent use has been made of the terms "common law" and "common law courts". The time has come to examine these expressions more closely and to explain what they mean.

The term "common law courts" means just that; namely those of the king's courts in which before the Judicature Acts, 1873–5, the rules and principles of the common law were followed. These were distinct from the chancery courts in which equitable principles were administered. Likewise in its narrowest sense the term "common law" is the law and custom of the realm as distinct from equity. This is the meaning of the term in this chapter unless otherwise stated in the text, and it is the meaning in which most lawyers would probably have used the term before the Act of 1873 provided that the rules of both equity and common law should be used in all the royal courts.

Local custom had its part to play in the development of the common law. As the judges of the three courts or commissioners specially appointed for the purpose travelled the countryside holding courts of assize, they would hear of varied local customs, some of which were deemed worthy of general application and were therefore adopted into the common law of the land; others were allowed to continue in operation locally, whilst others were overruled and discarded entirely.

Traces are to be found also in our law of the influences of the church and of Roman law and, of course, the kings themselves and their counsellors in the Curia Regis had a part to play in originating and decreeing laws.

A second sense in which the term "common law" may be used is to describe the law established by the decisions of the judges—or "case law" as it is often called to distinguish it from statute law, i.e. law enacted by Parliament. This meaning has assumed much greater importance in more recent times, particularly since the emergence of the welfare state. There is ever-increasing incursion of the legislative and administrative branches of government into the judicial and quasi-judicial spheres by means of tribunals and other bodies established by statutes and rules and orders to regulate the rights and duties of private individuals in relation to the State and in relation to each other. In this sense "common law" embraces the authoritative decisions of all the superior courts of common law and equity.

As the subject of tribunals is such an important one it will be given special consideration later in Chapter 11.

Finally, the term "common law" may be used to distinguish the system of law which has evolved in this country over the centuries from those systems which trace their origin from the law of Justinian (Roman law). As might be expected the common law was carried to countries which were colonized by the English. One finds the common law accepted as the basis of the legal system in the United States of America and many of the Commonwealth countries.

In this sense the expression is used to describe the whole of the English legal system and the principles upon which the law is founded and justice is administered. It will not be used in this sense again in this volume, as a comparison of the two systems merits separate consideration by any reader who wishes to pursue the subject.

STATUTE LAW

The term "statute law" is used to mean all laws enacted by Acts of Parliament as distinct from the law contained in the reported decisions of the judges. In early times this meant laws made by the king and the Curia Regis. With the establishment of Parliament, the term came to mean laws enacted by Act of Parliament, that is, laws made by the monarch with the approval and authority of the Lords and Commons, and it has that meaning today.

The part played by statute in the development of our law was comparatively small before the nineteenth century. Although by the sixteenth century the judges were accepting Parliament's authority to make law by statute, they did not recognize the paramount authority of Parliament in this connection. As a result of the struggle between the Stuart kings and Parliament for supreme power in the realm, the courts accepted the dominant position of Parliament and thus accepted as law anything enacted by Parliament.

Until then, the general view of the judges was that the system of judicial decisions which they and their predecessors had evolved over the centuries represented the true common law, and that anything Parliament sought to introduce into their system tended only to confuse an otherwise clear picture.

Hence they felt at liberty to disregard the terms of a statute if it did not accord with the accepted view of the common law. Indeed, until the nineteenth century they continued to interpret statutes in accordance with the common law wherever possible. The natural result of this was, of course, that the words of the statute were strained to make its intention agree with the common law, and the statutes became so hedged about with case law that the original intention of Parliament often became obscured.

The modern position is that the validity of an Act of Parliament cannot be challenged in any English court. Parliament is supreme and the function of a judge in relation to a statute is to make certain of the intention of Parliament from its wording, and by his judgment to give effect to that intention.

CONSTRUCTION OF STATUTES

The basic modern rules of construction of statutes demand first of all that the courts should presume that Parliament knows the law and intends a statute to prevail over the common law where the two conflict. Secondly, they require that every word in a statute must be given its ordinary and grammatical meaning unless this would lead to some absurdity, inconsistency, or repugnance with the remainder of the Act. In the latter event the court should give such meaning to the words as will avoid this repugnancy, absurdity, or inconsistency, and give effect to the presumed intention of Parliament.

It should be stressed that these are the basic rules only; there are others of considerable importance which the practitioner will have to know before he can advise anyone on the construction of a statute. The subject is a very important one today as so much of our law stems from statute in the form of regulations, rules, and orders, and delegated legislation made pursuant to statutes.

DOCTRINE OF JUDICIAL PRECEDENT

The important part played by judicial precedent in modern times is dealt with in the final paragraphs of this chapter, but for a proper understanding of the doctrine it is necessary to have some grasp of the manner in which it evolved and why.

As already seen, existing communities before the Norman Conquest tended to be isolated and to lead their separate corporate existences and to develop their own set of rules and customs to suit the special requirements of each locality. With the emergence of the king's courts after the Conquest the rules of law followed throughout the land gradually acquired a measure of uniformity. It is to the three early common law courts that one must look for the roots of the doctrine of judicial precedent.

It was principally the judges and secondly the lawyers who practised in the courts who evolved the rules and principles which became universally accepted, and from which there developed a system of case law for the guidance of judges, practitioners, and suitors alike.

The mode of trial had an important bearing on the development of the system. Trial by ordeal evolved into trial by jury, but the essence of the procedure in both civil and criminal matters was the same. The proceedings were held in public, a day was set aside for the suitors and their supporters to attend court to state their charges and allegations. The judge presided impartially over the proceedings and ensured that they were conducted fairly. Moreover, in civil matters it was the practice of the common law judges from quite early times to deliver the judgment of the court; that is to say they would summarize the issues in the case—pinpoint the facts which they considered were material to these issues; give their findings on those facts and the principles of law which they considered applied to the facts as found.

In this way, while there were as yet no printed or even written reports, judges would become aware of the decisions of their brother judges. Both by discussion and by the citation of other judicial decisions, advocates would seek to persuade one judge that he should follow the course taken by another on similar facts, having extracted from the earlier case that part of the judgment which was strictly necessary for the decision in law of the points in issue; i.e. *ratio decidendi* as distinct from expressions of opinion by the judge which were *obiter dicta*, or not directly on the points in issue. The *ratio decidendi* has been defined as the rule of law upon which the decision is founded.

In the early history of the Chancery Court the doctrine of precedent played no part as the equity judge was concerned only with the moral issue involved in the suit before him. With the passage of time Chancery acquired a set of rules and principles of its own which, by the end of the eighteenth century, were followed in much the same way as in the common law courts, if not so strictly.

One does not have to seek far for the reason why judicial precedent has played such an important part in the English system. Clearly it was then and still is in the interest of judges, lawyers, and litigants alike that there should be as much consistency as possible between judges in their findings so that a reasonably accurate forecast could be made regarding the outcome of an action. In the Roman law system codification provided the solid basis of uniformity, and in the common law system the basis was to be found in the decisions of the judges which were contained in the reports of cases which had been tried and decided.

It should not be thought, however, that the earlier judges in either the common law or equity courts felt themselves bound in any way to follow strictly the decisions of their brethren, even of superior courts, although they would treat them with respect and as of high persuasive value. Nor, as will be seen later, did they regard the enactments even of the king and his Council as sacrosant. Statutes were construed in accordance with the common law and, if repugnant to common sense and the common law, were disregarded.

The king's judges regarded themselves as the makers of the law and were jealous of any invasion of their territory by the king or, later, by Parliament. As we shall see, it was not until the nineteenth century that the modern doctrine of binding precedent evolved.

THE MODERN DOCTRINE OF JUDICIAL PRECEDENT

The doctrine applied today is one of absolutely binding precedent, where the decision in law of a superior court binds all inferior courts until it is overruled by a court superior to that which made it. This doctrine could not develop fully without accurate reporting and the publication of reliable law reports. A proper system of law reporting and the general use of properly authenticated and approved reports is obviously essential to a system of law based largely on case law. It was not, however, until 1865 that a recognized body within the legal profession, the Incorporated Council of Law Reporting, was established. In the following year the first volumes of the Law Reports were published under the control of the Council. Until then cases had been reported and published in a haphazard and sometimes slipshod manner, and although many of the older reports are admirable, the reliability of others are highly suspect. The history of law reporting is worthy of further mention, and is dealt with in more detail in Chapter 7.

A further factor which led to the more rigid use of judicial precedent in the courts was the rationalization of our system of superior courts by the Judicature Acts, 1873–5. The power was then given to all the judges to exercise the rules of both law and equity in any case before them.

It is both interesting and important to note that on 26 July 1966 the Lord Chancellor announced on behalf of himself and the Lords of Appeal in Ordinary (House of Lords), that they proposed to modify their previous practice of treating former decisions of the House of Lords as absolutely binding, and instead proposed, while treating such decisions as normally binding, to depart from a previous decision when in the interest of justice it appeared right to do so.

This announcement is of such importance that it is worth quoting in full:

> Their Lordships regard the use of precedent as an indispensable foundation upon which to decide what is the law and its application to individual cases. It provides at least some degree of certainty upon which individuals can rely in the conduct of their affairs, as well as a basis for orderly development of legal rules.
>
> Their Lordships nevertheless recognize that too rigid adherence to precedent may lead to injustice in a particular case and also unduly restrict the proper development of the law. They propose therefore to modify their present practice, and, while treating former decisions of this House as normally binding, to depart from a previous decision when it appears right to do so.
>
> In this connection they will bear in mind the danger of disturbing retrospectively the basis on which contracts, settlements of property and fiscal arrangements have been entered into and also the especial need for certainty as to the criminal law.

This announcement is not intended to affect the use of precedent elsewhere than in this House.

Whilst, as indicated, this statement is intended to apply only to the House of Lords, and in no way affects the rigid application of the doctrine in all courts below the Lords, it could possibly be the first step toward a return to the more liberal view of judicial precedent taken by the earlier judges.

THE LAW COMMISSION

On 15 June 1965 the Law Commissions Act, 1965, came into force. This statute establishes a Law Commission for England and Wales, with which this book is concerned, and a Scottish Law Commission.

The duty of the Commission under the Act in general is to promote the simplification and modernization of the law. In particular its duty is to keep under review all the law with which it is concerned with a view to its systematic development and reform, including the codification of such law, the elimination of anomalies, the repeal of obsolete and unnecessary enactments, and the reduction of the number of separate enactments.

This Act is referred to in this chapter because of the effect that some of its provisions may have on our present system of law. Much of the complexity of the existing law is due to the fact that judges are, at least in theory, bound by the doctrine of judicial precedent (*stare decisis*). They are obliged to follow legal principles established by case law, much of which is ancient and out of line with modern life and requirements.

The theory does not always accord with the practice because a judge may be able to distinguish the facts in the case he is trying from those in the earlier cases, and it would be an unusual and unnatural judge who would not do so if he could thereby avoid an unjust result, but this sometimes adds to the complexity of the law. Lawyers are familiar with instances of two lines of reported cases, the facts of which are almost if not entirely identical, but decided differently.

The Law Commission has a herculean task to perform. It has already undertaken a heavy programme of reform and it will undoubtedly take many years to bring our law up to date. The use of the word "codification" in the Act is both interesting and important. If codification is intended, and there is no reason to doubt that it is, we may well see an approach to the continental system of law in which the codifying instrument defines the law and case law is used to interpret it. If the Law Commission and Parliament adopt this approach, it seems logical to expect that much established case law will cease to have binding effect and be replaced by statute law. This in turn may lead to a change in the judicial function. The judges' role of law maker may diminish and they may instead find themselves concerned principally with the interpretation of statutes and the application of the words of statutes to the facts of the case before them.

Recent private pronouncements of Mr. Justice Scarman, the learned and distinguished Chairman of the Law Commission, seem to suggest that he envisages the possibility of these changes in our legal system.

CHAPTER 2

Solicitors

The Law Society — Education and examinations — Articles and training — Roll — Practising certificates — Discipline — Duties to client — Branches of work — Partnership — Retainers — Compensation fund — Remuneration of solicitors — Costs — Commissioner for oaths and public notary — Legal aid.

THE legal profession in England and Wales is divided into two main branches—solicitors and barristers. It is proposed to deal with solicitors in this chapter and with barristers in Chapter 3. It will become apparent that, whilst barristers have a right of audience in all courts, solicitors are more restricted as regards their right to represent their clients personally in court. It will also become apparent that, apart from certain specific exceptions a lay client is unable to appear in court in the dual capacity of appellant or defendant, as the case may be, and that of advocate.

The normal process is that the lay client has to instruct a solicitor, placing the full facts of his case in his hands. The solicitor will pass on these instructions to a barrister in the form of a brief. The barrister will then appear in court and his duty will be to act as mouthpiece for the lay client. The solicitor's duty will have been to ensure beforehand that his brief to counsel (as barristers are generally known) sets out the lay client's instructions in full. It will also be his duty either to attend court in person or to make sure that he sends a competent clerk to attend the court hearing. This will ensure that counsel is kept fully in the picture and that the lay client is properly looked after throughout the hearing of his case. The solicitor will also in the meantime have made sure that all the witnesses who are required for the case are available in court when they are wanted, to give evidence on behalf of the lay client, as well as any documents or other exhibits to which it may be necessary to refer in the course of the case.

Having thus very briefly summarized the respective roles of the two main branches of the legal profession, it is now proposed to turn to a consideration of the education and training which must be undergone by a student who wishes to qualify as a solicitor. Before, however, dealing with these essential factors, we should consider the governing body which is responsible for controlling the admission of persons to act as solicitors and to review briefly their powers in this matter.

THE LAW SOCIETY

The governing body for the admission and control of solicitors is the Law Society. It is responsible for determining the education and setting the examinations which have to be passed before a person can be admitted as a solicitor.

The Law Society is in fact a body corporate endowed with a common seal incorporated under a Royal Charter of 1845 and a series of supplemental charters of later dates. No limit is placed by these charters on the number of members who form the Law Society, and any solicitor of the Supreme Court in England, whether he is practising or not, is eligible for membership of the Society.

The Law Society has a governing body which consists of a president, vice-president, and a council. The president and vice-president are elected by members of the Law Society and hold office from the date of this election until the appointment of a successor. Membership of the Council is a necessary qualification for nomination for either president or vice-president.

The Council consists of members who are elected from solicitors who are practising in England, and consists of not more than seventy or less than twenty members. Members of the Council hold office for a period of 5 years and are eligible for re-election.

Any member of the Law Society may be nominated for election to the Council. England and Wales is divided into twelve constituencies for the purpose of electing members to the Council, and the numbers representing these constituencies vary in accordance with the numbers laid down in the by laws of the charter.

The Law Society is empowered to make regulations which define the requirements for the admission of any person as a solicitor. These regulations are made with the concurrence of the Lord Chancellor, the Lord Chief Justice, and the Master of the Rolls, and they prescribe three main requirements, namely:

(*a*) service under articles;
(*b*) attendance at a course of legal education; and
(*c*) the passing of examinations.

It also has to be borne in mind that as an admitted solicitor is an officer of the Supreme Court, the Law Society has in addition to being satisfied about the passing of the necessary examinations, to be satisfied as to the moral fitness of any person seeking admission as a solicitor.

It is the Law Society that issues the necessary certificates concerned with the passing of the examinations and those enabling an admitted solicitor to carry on a practice in the courts.

Further, the society is endowed with disciplinary powers and can take steps to prevent a solicitor from carrying on practice in the event of misconduct on his part if this is proved to their satisfaction.

EDUCATION AND EXAMINATIONS

These two headings are so closely linked that it is proposed to refer to them under a joint subheading. As already mentioned, the examinations which qualify a student to become an admitted solicitor are held under the direction and supervision of the Law Society. The examinations consist of two parts and are held twice yearly in London, Birmingham, Bristol, Leeds, and Manchester.

Unless the Law Society so determines, no person is entitled to give notice for Part I either as a whole or for any subject in it, unless he has enrolled as a student in accordance with the provisions of Part II of the Students Regulations, 1962. It is also a necessary preliminary to enrolment that he has either (*a*) passed a university degree examination or been awarded a degree as approved by the regulations, or (*b*) has been called to the Bar in England, been a faculty of advocates for Scotland, called to the Bar in Northern Ireland, or become a solicitor in Scotland or Northern Ireland, or (*c*) has held a permanent commission in H.M. Forces and completed not less than 5 years' continuous service, or has retired from a post in the Colonial Civil Service after completing not less than 5 years' service, or (*d*) has, since attaining the age of 18 years, been a bona fide clerk to a solicitor and has been engaged throughout that time in the normal practice of a solicitor's office and has produced to the society satisfactory evidence of his service, or (*e*) has satisfactorily completed attendance as a law school student at a recognized course of legal study.

It is possible for a student, if he has attained certain qualifications as laid down in the regulations, to claim exemption from the whole or part of the qualifying examination. The application for exemption has to be lodged with the Law Society on a particular form and be accompanied by the necessary certificate.

The subjects which have to be passed in connection with Part I of the qualifying examinations, which are known as the Intermediate Examination, are as follows: 1, Outlines of constitutional and administrative law; 2, Outlines of the English legal system; 3, Contract; 4, Torts; 5, Criminal law; 6, Land law.

Any candidate who has passed on the same occasion in at least three subjects is allowed to pass the remaining subjects singly or in a group or groups.

Entry forms have to be obtained from the Law Society, and a student must give at least 56 days' notice of his intention to attempt the examination. This rule is obligatory and cannot be waived in any circumstances. A fee of £3 3*s*. 0*d*. per subject is payable for each subject of which notice is given.

ARTICLES AND TRAINING

After having passed the Intermediate Examinations a student will receive a certificate. He will then proceed to the next stage towards qualifying, which consists in serving for a specified period as an articled clerk in a solicitor's office. Apart from certain stated exemptions, every articled clerk must spend an uninterrupted period of at least 2 years under articles in the office of his principal. This period is known as "the obligatory term" and the articled clerk must have passed or have been granted total exemption from Part I of the examinations before he can embark on it. He will not be allowed to attempt Part II of the examinations until this period has expired, but, as will be seen later, the full period of articles normally amounts to a period of 5 years (see, however, p. 41).

The articled clerk can then take Part II, which is known as the Final Examination and is divided into two main parts; the first consists of compulsory subjects, whilst the second includes optional subjects, one only of which has to be attempted. The conditions governing entry are similar to those to which mention has already been made in connection with Part I: at least 56 days' notice and payment of a fee of £3 3*s*. 0*d*. in respect of each subject of which notice of intention to attempt the examination has been given. The compulsory heads in Part II are: Conveyancing, Accounts, Revenue law, Equity and succession, Commercial law, and Company and partnership. The optional heads are Family law or Local government law or Magisterial law.

A person who has passed all the necessary examinations and satisfactorily completed his service under articles may then apply to the Master of the Rolls through the medium of the Law Society for admission on the roll as a solicitor. Notice of this application may be given before the expiring of his articles, or before the result of the examinations are known, but unless otherwise permitted, application must be made at least 6 weeks before the date on which he wishes to be admitted.

ROLL

The roll which is kept by the Law Society is a record of all the names of persons who have been admitted as solicitors, irrespective of whether they have taken out practising certificates or not. The names are entered in alphabetical order and the roll is open to inspection by any person at any time during office hours without payment. On production of a signed admission certificate, and after payment of the appropriate fee, the Law Society enters the name of the person appearing on the certificate on the roll. The fee payable which is at present £11, shall not exceed £15 (Second Schedule, Solicitors Act, 1965), and if the name of a solicitor has been struck off the roll, a further fee of not more than £15 must be paid in order to have the name replaced. It is the signature of the Master of the Rolls on the admission certificate, or that of any judge of the High Court acting on his behalf, which is the final factor in qualifying the applicant to have his name entered on the roll. This signature will not be forthcoming until the Law Society have sent a certificate to the Master of the Rolls stating that the requirements of the Society have been complied with; and this has to be done not less than 4 days before the admission date.

PRACTISING CERTIFICATES

No person shall be qualified to act as a solicitor unless he fulfils the following requirements:

(*a*) he has been admitted as a solicitor;
(*b*) his name is for the time being on the roll;
(*c*) he has in force a certificate issued by the Society in accordance with Part I of the Solicitors Act, 1957, as amended by the Solicitors Act, 1965. Every practising certificate shall expire at the end of the 31st day of October next after it is issued (section 10, Solicitors Act, 1957, as re-enacted by section 4, Solicitors Act, 1965).

Every person so qualified may practise as a solicitor in the Supreme Court, in any county court, or in a magistrates' court.

Practising certificates, which are issued annually, cover the practice year, which now runs from 1 November to the following 31 October. The provisions of section 4 of the Solicitors Act, 1965, which came into operation on 28 July 1966, and which re-enacted and amended sections 9–11 of the Solicitors Act, 1957, together with the Practising Certificate Regulations, 1966, which came into operation on 1 October 1966, now regulate the procedure for the issue of these certificates to solicitors.

The main distinction between the new procedure and that which it superseded, is that a solicitor no longer has to attend at the Law Society's Hall, either in person or by his agent, in order to apply for a practising certificate.

According to the present procedure the Law Society during the month of October send by post an application form (known as PCR 1) to cover the following practice year to every solicitor who was the holder of a practising certificate for the current practice year. Should any solicitor not receive this application form by the following 7 November the onus is placed on him to make application to the Law Society for a PCR 1 form to be sent to him.

The application form must be correctly completed and accompanied by the necessary fees which at the present time are £11* for the practising certificate and £8 contribution to the compensation fund. These must then be delivered at the Society's Hall either by post, in person, or by an agent 21 days before a practising certificate can be issued. As will be seen later, however, under the sub-title of "Compensation Fund" (see p. 44), a newly admitted solicitor does not have to make full contributions to the compensation fund during the first 6 years of practice.

The practising certificate when issued by the Law Society is then sent by post to the first address shown on the application form unless otherwise advised of another address by the applicant

*The maximum amount was raised to £20 as from 17 August 1965 (Second Schedule, Solicitors Act, 1965).

or of the fact that he wishes to call for the certificate in person.

The information which has to be given on the application form is the applicant's full name, place or places of business, and his date of admission together with such other particulars as are prescribed by the regulations. The form has to be signed by the solicitor in person, subject to the Society's right to waive this at their discretion in the case of illness, absence abroad, or on any other ground that is considered by them to be sufficient, in which case permission is given for the form to be signed by some other competent person (i.e. a partner). It is necessary, however, for an application to have the form signed by a person other than the applicant to be made by a statutory declaration; and if illness is the reason, the declaration must be accompanied by a doctor's certificate.

There are, however, certain cases where an application has to be made 6 weeks before a practising certificate can be issued (section 12, Solicitors Act, 1957, as amended by section 6, Solicitors Act, 1965). The principal cases covered by this rule are those where a solicitor is applying for his first practising certificate. Since 24 August 1965, however, the Council of the Law Society have issued an order that where the application for a first certificate is within 12 months of the date of the applicant's admission, 6 weeks' notice is not required. Other examples are where a period of 12 months or more have passed since the applicant last held a certificate; where he is an undischarged bankrupt or has obtained his discharge in bankruptcy; is a patient within the meaning of section 101 of the Mental Health Act, 1959; or if he is the subject either of a writ of attachment or of a committal order.

In the event that a solicitor's practising certificate should become suspended, the Law Society shall cause notice of suspension to be published in the *London Gazette*, and a note is entered against the name of the solicitor in the roll.

A solicitor practising without a practising certificate is an unqualified person and renders himself liable to a fine not exceeding £50, the previous maximum of £10 being raised to this sum by the Second Schedule to the Solicitors Act, 1965. This generally is recoverable by the Law Society with the sanction of the Attorney-General, by action in the High Court or in any county court (Solicitors Act, 1957, section 18). It follows, therefore, that a solicitor whose practising certificate has been suspended is an unqualified person (section 86 (i), Solicitors Act, 1957). An adjudication in bankruptcy or an order of the disciplinary committee of the Law Society suspending a solicitor from practice has the effect of suspending his practising certificate.

DISCIPLINE

The disciplinary powers of the Law Society are carried out through the medium of a Disciplinary Committee. The members of this Committee are appointed by the Master of the Rolls and the appointments are made from among members of the Council and such former members of the Council as are practising as solicitors in England. The Council must consist of not less than three nor more than nine members as the Master of the Rolls may from time to time think fit (section 46, Solicitors Act, 1957).

The Disciplinary Committee, with the concurrence of the Master of the Rolls, is empowered to make rules for regulating the hearing and determining of applications and complaints.

The jurisdiction and powers of the Disciplinary Committee include the hearing of any application:

(*a*) by a solicitor to procure his name to be removed from the roll;

(*b*) by another person to strike the name of a solicitor off the roll or to require a solicitor to answer any allegation contained in an affidavit.

On the hearing of any application or complaint made to them the disciplinary committee are empowered:

(*a*) to remove from or strike off the roll the name of the solicitor to whom the application or complaint relates;

(*b*) to suspend that solicitor from practice;

(*c*) to order payment by that solicitor of a penalty not exceeding £750 (Second Schedule, Solicitors Act, 1965, which raised the previous limit of £500 to this sum); in which event the sum so ordered to be paid has to be passed on to the Exchequer by the Law Society;

(*d*) to order the payment by any party of costs (section 49, Solicitors Act, 1957).

A right of appeal to the High Court lies at the instance of the applicant or complainant, and any such appeal has to be made within the prescribed time and in the manner as laid down by the rules of court.

DUTIES TO CLIENT

The relationship of solicitor and client is a very personal one and all communications, whether oral or written, between solicitor and client for the purpose of giving or receiving professional advice are privileged. Consequently a solicitor cannot be compelled in the course of legal proceedings, to disclose communications between himself and his client, always provided that such communications are not made in furtherance of fraud or crime, unless the client chooses to waive this privilege.

The handling of any monies received by a solicitor from a client are subject to strict rules of procedure (Solicitor's Accounts Rules, 1945, as amended by the Rules, 1959). In consequence of these rules it is incumbent on solicitors to keep separate accounts which are known as client accounts, and into which they must pay without delay any monies held by them on behalf of their clients. The Council of the Law Society may, however, specifically authorize a solicitor to withhold client's monies from a client account. Unless he has been given such specific authority a solicitor may only draw from a client account (i) money properly required for a payment to or on behalf of a client, (ii) money properly required for a debt due to him, (iii) money drawn on the client's authority, and (iv) money properly required for payment of his bill of costs. A solicitor who has money which he has received from a client can be ordered, on application to the High Court, to pay over money to the client or into court after deducting any costs due to himself.

A solicitor owes a high degree of skill, knowledge, and learning to his client, and should he, through want of such knowledge or care, be guilty of negligence, this may well give rise to an action for damages brought against him on behalf of his client. The client must, however, be in a position to prove that the want of skill or care on the part of the solicitor amounts to a breach of contract. The measure of damages in such cases will be the full amount of the pecuniary loss which the client has suffered or the amount which the client might have recovered in the action had the solicitor exercised due diligence.

BRANCHES OF WORK

It will be appreciated that the work of a solicitor's office covers a very wide field, and although many solicitors carry on a general practice without claiming to be experts in any particular line, others, as is also the case with certain barristers, prefer to specialize in a particular branch. It may well be that the old family solicitor who acts as adviser and "father-in-law" to families drawing up wills, doing conveyancing work and generally dealing with non-contentious matters, will make but rare visits, if any, to the courts.

On the other hand, heavy commercial cases which require a great deal of correspondence involve many attendances in court in connection with interlocutory proceedings, and of necessity take up a great deal of time and effort in preparation for trial. When the trial does eventually take place it may last for weeks rather than days before it is finally disposed of. Such cases are usually the prerogative of solicitors who specialize in this type of work.

A divorce practice may well take up most of the time that is available to some solicitors, so that they decide to specialize in this form of practice. Others may deal almost solely with criminal practice. A solicitor has a right of audience when appearing in a magistrates' court, and it is quite a common practice for a defendant who elects to go for trial at Quarter Sessions or at Assizes to be represented by a solicitor at the lower court and for counsel to be briefed to appear at the trial in the higher court. The advantages to be derived from a solicitor or his firm, as the case may be, in specializing in one type of work are obvious. It is an advantage for him to be known to the judges and magistrates who sit on the various benches before whom he has to appear. This may well prove to be an asset to his client as well.

Another possible line of specialization is in connection with work in the county courts. As we shall see in Chapter 5, the jurisdiction of these courts has been considerably enlarged in recent years. Here again solicitors have a right of audience and can appear in the role of advocate for their client.

We have touched on some of the main possibilities by which solicitors may become known as specialists in particular types of legal work. It has to be remembered, however, that any solicitor may find himself in the position of having to advise a client on a matter which is outside the normal scope of his work; in such a case he will probably instruct counsel with a view to obtaining a written opinion from him. Should the matter eventually turn out to be more serious than at first appeared, the solicitor will be safeguarded by an opinion given by competent counsel.

However, specializing or not, the ordinary routine work of letterwriting on behalf of his clients and generally dealing with ordinary everyday matters will still call for attention. Some of the bigger firms of solicitors in which there are several partners, may, of course, be able to carry on more than one form of specialized practice, with partners specializing in differing types of work.

PARTNERSHIP

A solicitor may carry on practice on his own but it is more usual to find two or more solicitors acting in partnership. Indeed, some of the larger firms consist of a number of partners. The effect of a partnership is that each partner prima facie binds the firm with whom he is in partnership when, in the ordinary course of business he gives an undertaking or is guilty of negligence, fraud, or misconduct.

No person can qualify to become a partner in a firm of solicitors unless he is a qualified and certificated solicitor. It is, however, necessary to refer once more to the question of qualification to explain how an articled clerk fits into the picture *vis-à-vis* the solicitor who engages him for this purpose. A period of service as an articled clerk is a necessary requirement except in the case of a barrister called to the Bar in England who has obtained from two benchers of the Inn of Court to which he belongs or belonged a certificate to the effect that he is a fit and proper person to practise as a solicitor and that he has been in practice as a barrister for a period of not less than 5 years; or, that he has been in employment as a non-practising barrister for a similar period, in which case he will be exempted from service under articles and from Part I of the qualifying examination and will not be required to enrol as a student with the Law Society. The normal period for serving articles is 5 years, subject to certain reductions in specific cases which are set out fully in the First Schedule to the Students Regulations, 1962, as amended by No. 4 Regulations which came into force on the first day of August 1965. The length of the period of service in relation to these exceptions varies from 2 to 4 years.

The articles have to be in writing and are almost invariably entered into by deed in which the clerk undertakes faithfully, honestly, and diligently to serve the solicitor during the term of the articles and the solicitor undertakes on his part to teach the clerk and, at the end of the service of the articles, to assist the clerk's efforts in becoming admitted as a solicitor.

Whether a premium is paid or not is a matter for negotiation. Finally, as a matter of prudence, a provision should be inserted into the articles authorizing the solicitor to dismiss the articled clerk for misconduct during his period of service;

otherwise dismissal can only become effective by gross or habitual misconduct.

Articles have to be registered with the Law Society within 6 months of the date on which they are entered into, and it is the solicitor's duty to see that the articles are registered. For the purpose of articles the solicitor is referred to as "the principal". On registration (i) it is necessary to produce satisfactory evidence that the clerk has passed or has been exempted from the preliminary examination, (ii) a statutory declaration in prescribed form, (iii) the Law Society's written consent to the clerk's entry into articles; and (iv) a fee of £3 has to be paid to the Law Society.

RETAINERS

It is obviously of the utmost importance that the relationship of solicitor and client should be firmly established so that both parties know where they stand in relation to each other. When a client authorizes or employs a solicitor to act on his behalf, this amounts to the making of a contract by the client for the solicitor's employment, and is known as a retainer. Though a retainer need not be in writing, it is generally desirable that it should be both for the sake of the client and the solicitor in order that the terms of the retainer may be made absolutely clear and beyond dispute. It is open to the court to imply the existence of a retainer from the acts of the parties in the case which is under consideration.

A married woman may retain a solicitor either on her own behalf or for her own benefit. She may also pledge the credit of her husband for costs reasonably incurred by her in respect of proceedings for dissolution of marriage or for a judicial separation. Any costs recoverable from the husband must, however, be reasonably incurred, especially in a case where the wife has been an unsuccessful party in the proceedings. A husband still continues to be liable in respect of goods supplied to his wife after a separation order if they are supplied by a person to whom the wife had been held out as having authority to pledge his credit.

This liability continues until the person supplying the goods is made aware of the judicial separation by advertisement or other means.

Solicitors may be retained not only on behalf of individuals but also by corporations, companies, or other bodies. Generally speaking, a solicitor, when retained by a client, undertakes to deal with the business for which he has been retained to its termination; and it is a part of the contract that the client should pay him for his services on the completion of the business. Special circumstances may, of course, arise in which a specific period is put on a retainer and a solicitor may be retained to act for a term at a fixed sum. A solicitor is not, however, bound to carry on a retainer if, for example, he finds that he is being asked to do something dishonourable.

A client has the right to terminate his retainer at any time and change his solicitor when he so desires. In connection with litigation in the High Court, however, termination of a retainer must be done in accordance with the relevant rules of the court.

COMPENSATION FUND

In order to provide for possible defalcations by solicitors or their clerks or servants, section 32 of the Solicitors Act, 1957, enacted that a fund to be known as "Compensation Fund" should be maintained and administered under conditions laid down in the second schedule to the Act. The object of the fund, subject to prescribed rules and conditions, is to enable grants to be made to persons out of the Compensation Fund for the mitigation of losses incurred by them through dishonesty on the part of any solicitor, or any clerk or servant of a solicitor, in connection with that solicitor's practice as a solicitor, or in connection with any trust of which the solicitor is a trustee.

The schedule lays down that the fund is to be maintained and administered by the Law Society. The fund is maintained by contributions from every solicitor who has to pay a sum determined by the Council of the Law Society, but not exceeding £10.

On each occasion on which a practising certificate is issued to him, this fee, known as "the annual contribution", and at present fixed at £8, is paid by the solicitor. The only exceptions to this rule are that a solicitor shall not be required to make these contributions on the issue of the first three certificates to him after his admission, and that the fourth, fifth, and sixth certificates are only subject to one-half of the annual contribution.

Section 15 of the Solicitors Act, 1965, empowered the Law Society to make grants out of the Compensation Fund in cases of hardship. These are known as "hardship grants" and such payments are subject to at least 8 days' notice in writing to the defaulting solicitor (except where he has died), requiring an explanation from him of the circumstances to which the complaint relates. Further, if the solicitor has either failed to comply with the notice or the Law Society are of the opinion (and have so notified the solicitor in writing) that his explanation does not constitute a sufficient assurance that the money will be accounted for in a reasonable time, such "hardship grant" shall not be made. The full conditions under which a "hardship grant" may be made are set out in section 15 of the 1965 Act.

The Law Society have investment and borrowing powers, subject to an aggregate sum owing on loans at any one time not exceeding £100,000. The schedule also authorizes the Law Society to insure with any person authorized by law to carry on insurance business within the United Kingdom.

Paragraphs six and seven of the schedule lay down in more detail the sources from which contributions are to be made, and the purposes for which the fund may be used.

In order to receive a grant out of the Compensation Fund, a person has to deliver a duly completed form in the prescribed manner setting out the facts fully, and stating whether any steps have been taken to institute a civil remedy or to launch any criminal or disciplinary proceedings in respect of the alleged dishonesty. This notice has to be delivered within 6 months, or in special circumstances, within 2 years after the loss first came to the knowledge of the applicant.

When the notice is delivered an application for a grant has to be submitted to the Secretary of the Law Society. This application is made by the delivery of a statutory declaration setting out certain prescribed facts.

REMUNERATION OF SOLICITORS

The work of solicitors is divided into two main categories: non-contentious business and contentious business. In the case of the former, remuneration for professional work by a solicitor for a client is governed by statute and orders. A committee consisting of the Lord Chancellor, the Lord Chief Justice, the Master of the Rolls, the President of the Law Society, a solicitor who is the president of a provincial law society nominated by the Lord Chancellor to serve during his tenure of office as president, and the Chief Land Registrar appointed under the Land Registration Act, 1925, was set up under the provisions of section 56 of the Solicitors Act, 1957, to make general orders prescribing and regulating the remuneration of solicitors for non-contentious business.

It is still, however, open to a solicitor and his client, either before or after or in the course of the transaction of any non-contentious business to make an agreement as to the solicitor's remuneration, subject to the provisions of section 57 of the Solicitors Act, 1957. Section 58 of the Act provides for the remuneration of a solicitor who is a mortgagee.

A client who receives a bill of costs in connection with non-contentious business has a right, provided that the bill has neither been taxed nor paid, to require the solicitor to obtain a certificate from the Law Society certifying that the sum charged is fair and reasonable.

In conveyancing and other non-contentious business the amounts payable to solicitors are laid down in specified scales which are to be found in the Solicitors Remuneration Orders, 1883–1959. Speaking generally, these orders provide two different methods of remuneration, either by an *ad valorem* charge which does not include out-of-pocket expenses (such as counsel's fees, travelling expenses, telephone calls, etc.) or by a gross or lump sum charge which must be fair and reasonable, having regard to all the circumstances of the particular business to which it relates. The first of these two methods is applicable to sales, purchases, mortgages, and leases. Work done by a solicitor in connection with Land Registry matters is governed by a prescribed scale of fees. These fees are lower than those for work done on unregistered land, but the client is himself liable for payment of the land register fee. As more areas in the country become subject to compulsory registration at Her Majesty's Land Registry and more district land registries are set up, the bulk of solicitors' conveyancing work will be in respect of registered land.

It sometimes happens that a solicitor who practises in the country wishes to undertake professional business in London of either a non-contentious or contentious nature. In this case he may employ a firm of solicitors who practise in London to act as his agent, but he remains liable for any negligence on the part of his London agent since there is no relationship of solicitor and client between the London agent and the client. It follows, therefore, that the country solicitor is responsible to the London solicitor for his costs which would include any out-of-pocket expenses incurred.

This custom of agency, however, does not extend to Scottish, Irish, Dominion, and Colonial solicitors.

When a solicitor is retained to conduct contentious business, he may make an agreement in writing with his client regarding his remuneration in respect of such business (section 59). The effect of such an agreement is that the solicitor's costs will not be subject to taxation (section 63) nor will the agreement be subject to the provisions of section 68 (action to recover solicitor's costs).

In order either to commence an action in his client's name, or to appear for and represent him as defendant in an action, or to take part on his behalf in any proceedings, the solicitor must have a special authority. Such an authority is not retrospective; thus any admissions made by a solicitor prior to the granting of the authority cannot be taken advantage of in subsequent proceedings.

Having already dealt with the subject of retainers in an earlier heading, it is now proposed to turn to consideration of costs which are closely related to the question of remuneration.

COSTS

As we have seen, a solicitor is at liberty to make an agreement with his client regarding his own remuneration in connection with any contentious business. Where, however, his remuneration for such business is not the subject of an agreement, the solicitor's bill of costs may, at the option of the solicitor, either contain detailed items or be a gross sum (section 64, Solicitors Act, 1957). Section 67 of the above Act extends the power of the High Court to make orders for the delivery by a solicitor of a bill of costs to include actions heard in the county court.

Section 68 enacts that (subject to the exceptions referred to therein), no action shall be brought to recover any costs due to a solicitor until one month after the bill for them has been delivered as required by the section. These requirements set out that the bill must be signed by the solicitor, or, if due to a firm, by one of the partners of the firm; and that it must be delivered to the party to whom it is to be charged, either personally or by post, at his place of business, dwelling-house, or last known place of abode.

Section 69 makes provision for the taxation of a solicitor's bill of costs. Every order for the taxation of a bill of costs requires the taxing officer to tax not only the bill but also the costs of the taxation, and to certify what is due to or by the solicitor in respect of the costs of the taxation.

Section 70 provides for the taxation of a solicitor's bill of costs on the application of a third party who has either paid or is liable to pay the bill. And, finally, section 73 contains special provisions with regard to contentious business done in the county courts.

These sections of the Solicitors Act, 1957, are the main statutory provisions which affect the taxation of solicitors' costs. It is now proposed to consider more specifically the practical effect of these statutory powers. Since, however, it is contentious business that is affected it may be as well first to refer briefly to non-contentious matters. In dealing with leases and agreements the solicitor's remuneration is regulated by a special scale based on the rent payable. In the case of business in connection with sales, purchases, and mortgages, the solicitor is remunerated by the terms of a scale fee laid down in the Solicitors Remuneration Orders, 1833–1959. In any taxation in relation to these bills the principles of taxation are determined by reference to the prescribed scales of charges for such business; in the event of a lump sum they are related to the fairness and reasonableness of the charge. The main factor to bear in mind is that, in connection with proceedings in the High Court, the amount of costs to which a solicitor is entitled is determined by the taxing officer whose duty it is to make allowances according to the Supreme Court Rules, 1959. The general considerations which the taxing officer will bear in mind are the skill, labour, and responsibility involved in the business done by the solicitor.

The general principles which apply to the payment that a solicitor is entitled to receive for business done by him are laid down in the Solicitors Remuneration Order, 1883, schedule 2. Remuneration is limited to such sum as is fair and reasonable under the circumstances of the case under consideration with particular regard being made to the complexity of the matter, the skill, labour, specialized knowledge, and responsibility involved on the part of the solicitor, the number and importance of documents to be prepared or read, the place where the business is transacted, the time expended by the solicitor and, where property or money is concerned, the amount or value and the importance of the matter to the client.

There are two main types of bills of costs which solicitors have to deliver, namely solicitor and client bills and party and party bills. A bill of costs between a solicitor and client speaks for itself as this is the account rendered to the client by a solicitor in return for work done on the client's instructions. Such bills are generally itemized accounts, but they may be in the form of a gross sum. Unless previously agreed with the client, such a bill is liable to taxation at the request of the party chargeable or the solicitor, or of a third party or other interested person. The normal rule which is subject to certain exceptions is that if one-sixth of the amount of the bill is taxed off, the solicitor must pay the costs, otherwise the party chargeable must pay them.

Such costs, when payable by an adverse party or out of a fund in which the client has no interest, are allowed on a more generous basis to the party for costs actually incurred. If, however, they are payable out of a fund in which the client and others are interested, they are assessed at what is considered to be fair and proper—taking a liberal view.

Apart from proof of fraud or undue influence, no order for taxation can be made after the expiration of 12 months from the payment of a bill of costs.

The other type of bill of costs consists of those costs which are payable to a party to proceedings by another party to those proceedings. Such bills have generally to be taxed on a party and party basis.

The main principle to be applied here is that the successful party should be indemnified against the costs he has reasonably incurred in prosecuting or defending the action. In party and party bills there are two scales—a higher and a lower—which are prescribed by the rules. Normally the lower scale is applicable, but the higher scale applies if the court or a judge so allows because of special circumstances. In any event, a solicitor is entitled to the statutory percentage increase on his profit costs in accordance with the rules, and the taxing master is allowed a very wide discretion.

A solicitor may institute court proceedings for the recovery of the amount of a bill of costs; but such a step cannot be taken until after the expiration of one month from the delivery of the bill to his client. In the High Court this procedure is by way of specially endorsed writ and he may apply for summary judgment. If the client disputes the amount, the bill is referred to the taxing master. As already indicated, this procedure applies also to a county court, in which case the registrar is the taxing officer.

COMMISSIONER FOR OATHS AND PUBLIC NOTARY

An additional qualification which a solicitor can acquire is that of commissioner of oaths. The appointment is made by virtue of the provisions of section 1 of the Commissioner for Oaths Act, 1889, which enacts that the appointment is open to "practising solicitors or other fit and proper persons". In practice, in spite of the wording of the Act, it has been the practice of the Lord Chancellor to appoint only solicitors of at least 6 years' standing.

The appointment is made by the Lord Chancellor, and if a solicitor wishes to be appointed he has to leave a petition for his appointment at the Lord Chancellor's offices, setting out certain specified facts. This petition must be accompanied by a certificate of fitness signed by two practising barristers, two solicitors, and six householders or persons paying rent of offices.

If the petition is approved by the Lord Chancellor, the applicant has to stamp the petition with a £10 stamp. Finally, on receipt of the certificate of appointment it has to be registered with the Law Society and a further fee of £2 is then payable. The certificate remains valid so long as the solicitor continues to practise.

The purpose of this appointment is to permit the solicitor so appointed to administer oaths, including affirmations, declarations, and affidavits. The fees payable to the solicitor for this are laid down by statutory rules.

Any duly qualified solicitor may, subject to his being duly sworn, admitted and enrolled, also practise in all matters relating to applications to obtain notarial faculties (section 2, Solicitors Act, 1957). A notary public, which is an office of great antiquity, is a duly appointed officer who amongst other duties draws, attends, or certifies deeds and other documents. Any person practising as a notary without being duly authorized is liable to a fine not exceeding £100 on summary conviction.

General notaries are appointed under the Public Notaries Acts, 1801–1949. A duly certified notary public is a person who either has in force a practising certificate as a solicitor and is duly entered in the court of faculties, or has in force a practising certificate as a public notary issued by that court. A practising solicitor therefore has only to take out one certificate at the office of the Master of Faculties. Every notary admitted to practice must forward his annual practising certificate every year to the Clerk of the Crown for registration at the Crown Office.

LEGAL AID

The onus of making arrangements available for the provision of legal aid and legal advice in accordance with Part I of the Legal Aid and Advice Act, 1949, is placed on the Law Society, who are required for this purpose to make arrangements in accordance with a scheme approved by the Lord Chancellor with the concurrence of the Treasury.

As a general rule, a person who is receiving legal aid has the right to choose whom he will employ as his solicitor. The provisions cover legal aid in respect of civil matters and actions in the High Courts and county courts. Before, however, a solicitor can be assigned a legal aid certificate it is requisite for him to have his name, or in the case of a partnership, that of his firm, placed on a panel with an indication from him that he is willing to undertake such work.

To complete the picture it is necessary to refer briefly to legal aid for persons who are charged with criminal offences, either summarily in the magistrates' courts or at Quarter Sessions or Assizes. Section 1 of the Poor Prisoners Defence Act, 1930, laid down that any person committed for trial for an indictable offence is entitled to free legal aid in the preparation and conduct of his defence at the trial and to have solicitor and counsel assigned to him. A defence certificate may, subject to the provisions of the section, be granted either by the committing justices or by the judge or chairman of the trial court.

Section 2 of this Act empowers a magistrates' court to assign a solicitor under a "legal aid certificate" (or, in the case of a charge of murder, solicitor and counsel) to assist a defendant in the preparation and conduct of his defence.

If a person who has been convicted by a magistrates' court wishes to appeal to Quarter Sessions against conviction or sentence, a magistrates' court may assign a solicitor to the defendant under an "appeal aid certificate". As the solicitor does not have a right of audience at Quarter Sessions he will then be able to brief counsel to appear on behalf of his client at the appeal hearing.

A solicitor who acts on behalf of a client who prosecutes in respect of criminal proceedings will receive his costs under the provisions of the Costs in Criminal Cases Act, 1952. Such costs are paid out of local funds by authority of a court order after the bill has been duly taxed.

Neither a magistrates' court nor Quarter Sessions has power to grant legal aid in appeals arising out of affiliation proceedings. Appeal aid applications in such cases have to be made under the provisions of the Legal Aid and Advice Act, 1949. This process sometimes results in delay in the hearing of the appeal while the question of legal aid is still under consideration.

Magistrates' courts cannot assign legal aid either in proceedings under the Guardianship of Infants Acts, 1886 and 1925, or in proceedings under the Small Tenements Recovery Act, 1838.

All legal aid assignments are subject to taxation, and it is the duty of a solicitor who has conducted such a defence on behalf of a client to render a bill of costs setting out his charges relating to his services. The bill will include any out-of-pocket expenses, such as travelling fares, counsel's fees, etc. It is the duty of the solicitor in criminal cases, after the bill has been taxed and he has received payment, if that payment includes counsel's fees, to pass on to counsel such fees as have been approved on taxation. In civil matters, however, counsel's fees are paid direct to counsel by the Law Society.

Apart from this preliminary reference to legal aid and legal advice as they affect the practice of solicitors, the subjects will be dealt with more exhaustively in Chapter 12.

CHAPTER 3

Barristers-at-law

Origin of terms "barrister" and "bar" — Serjeants-at-law — Education — Examinations — Inns of Court — Call to the Bar — Pupillage — Chambers — Clerks — Outer Bar — Queen's Counsel — Etiquette — Discipline — Judicial appointments.

WE HAVE given a short summary in Chapter 2 of the way in which a student can qualify to become a solicitor and referred briefly to the method by which an admitted solicitor carries on his practice. The present chapter describes the steps that must be taken by a student who wishes to be called to the Bar in order to carry on a practice as a barrister-at-law.

It has been shown that the Law Society is the governing body for solicitors and that no person can practise as a solicitor until he has passed certain qualifying examinations and been duly admitted. The governing bodies which control the admission of persons seeking to become barristers are the four Inns of Court, namely Lincoln's Inn, the Inner Temple, the Middle Temple, and Gray's Inn. Before, however, dealing with the modern aspect of this matter, it is necessary to give a brief résumé of the historical introduction of the "Bar". The reader will then be able to appreciate how the modern concept of the Bar has developed from those early beginnings.

ORIGIN OF TERMS "BARRISTER" AND "BAR"

The terms "barrister" and "the bar" almost certainly originated from the system of educating the apprentice advocate which was practised by the Inns of Court as early as the fourteenth century.

It was largely of a practical nature, and one of the most important features of the training was that the members of the Inn were required to attend mock trials (or moots as they were called) before they were permitted to practise. These moots usually took place in the hall of the Inn or the library. The senior members of the Inn presided over the trial, and were known as masters of the bench or benchers, as indeed they are known today.

Across the hall there would be placed forms to constitute a bar. Those who argued the points sat outside or "uttermost" on the forms comprising the bar, and became known as outer or utter barristers; whereas other members of the Inn who sat inside the same bar and took a lesser part in the proceedings were known as inner barristers. The practice whereby a barrister is called to the Bar by the benchers of his Inn also seems to have originated from the practice of holding moots at which call would take place.

The development of the Bar as a branch of the legal profession, distinct from that of the attorneys, is closely linked with the growth of a strong independent judiciary. The connection between Bench and Bar is due largely to the emergence in the fourteenth and fifteenth centuries of the Inns of Court as the dominant institutions which provided and regulated the legal education of their members, governed their admission to practise, determined matters of discipline and etiquette, and provided accommodation for them.

The Inns therefore fostered a corporate existence for its members and a strong bond of fellowship which has persisted to the present day. By the middle of the fifteenth century the four principal Inns of Court were firmly established. As their prefix "The Honourable Society of . . ." suggests, each Inn is an association of members who are required to qualify themselves for membership by proof of academic and legal ability, and of honour and integrity.

SERJEANTS-AT-LAW

Of higher degree than the utter or outer barristers were the serjeants-at-law, who were chosen for their ability from the ranks of the outer bar, and possessed the exclusive right of audience in the Court of Common Pleas. The rank of serjeants-at-law was a necessary qualification for the office of judge of the superior common law courts until the Supreme Court of Judicature Act, 1873, and the Supreme Court of Judicature (Consolidation) Act, 1875, were passed. But since 1875 no serjeant-at-law has been created and the rank has disappeared, as have their inns, which were known as Serjeant's Inns.

It will be seen, therefore, that from these early times a hierarchy was established within the Inns. The student advocate received his training from the more experienced members of the profession within the society to which he belonged, and rank was established from which the judges of the higher common law courts were selected. Except that the rank of serjeant has disappeared, the position is similar today.

The right of exclusive audience in hearings in open court in the Supreme Court of Judicature, which includes the Court of Appeal and the High Court of Justice is enjoyed by the Bar, subject to the right of a litigant to elect to conduct his own case. This privilege rests on no more solid foundation than the practice of the judges to refuse to hear solicitors in their courts. It is, however, a sufficiently solid foundation to have secured for the Bar exclusive right of audience in the higher courts for hundreds of years.

EDUCATION

A summary has been given of the early history of the Inns and the system of education employed in them. It was a practical system by which the student was taught through readings and moots to master the niceties of pleadings, the complexities of status, and how to argue cases. Judged by today's standards, the period of apprenticeship was of long duration. The member of the Inn was required to be of 7 years' standing from admission before he could be called to the outer bar, and he was even then required to continue to take part in moots and other practices for a further 3 years in order to retain his status. He was not entitled to appear in the courts as an advocate until that period, or at one time 5 years, had elapsed. It is also interesting to observe that the early student was required to take part in exercises in one of the Chancery Inns as part of his training.

Unfortunately, by the early nineteenth century the practical exercises whereby the Inns had trained their members in the law had fallen into disuse, and no substitute had arisen to take their place. The privilege of call to the Bar required no more than that the applicant should be a student of the Inn, have eaten the requisite number of dinners in the hall of his Inn, and thereby "kept" twelve terms, and paid the appropriate fees.

The only training required was that he should read in chambers with a barrister. This unsatisfactory state of affairs continued until 1852, when the Council of Legal Education was instituted by the four Inns, and a joint enterprise made of restoring a proper system of legal education within the profession. This was followed in 1872 by the introduction of examinations for the aspiring barrister.

EXAMINATIONS

We will now examine in closer detail the examinations which have to be passed to qualify a student to become eligible for call to "the Bar". As already indicated, these examinations are conducted under the supervision and direction of the Council of Legal Education in Lincoln's Inn. The examinations consist of two parts: Part I consisting of the following subjects, (1) Roman law, (2) constitutional law and legal history, (3) the law of contract and the law of tort, (4) the law of land and criminal law.

Part II, which is commonly known as the Final, consists of (1) common law, (2) equity, (3) procedure, (4) the law of evidence and company law, and (5) any two of the following subjects: practical conveyancing, divorce (law and procedure) including the matrimonial jurisdiction of magistrates' courts, conflict of laws, and public international law. A student must pass in each part unless he is exempted either by already having passed certain examinations or on account of illness.

A fee of £1 is payable for each subject in Part I and this fee is payable even when a student is exempted. A fee of £1 5*s*. 0*d*. is payable for each subject in Part II.

The completion of the new building for the Inns of Court School of Law in Gray's Inn has enabled the Council of Legal Education to reorganize its system of teaching and to remedy certain defects which the Council considered to exist in the structure of Part I of the Bar Examination.

The Council has therefore made changes in Part I which came into operation as from the beginning of the academic year which began in October 1967, and which apply compulsorily to all students who joined an Inn of Court after 1 September 1967.

The main alterations in subjects are that a general paper in Roman law is no longer a section of Part I, whilst the law of contract and the law of tort are now separate subjects instead of being taken as a combined paper. Constitutional law, which used to be a separate paper, now becomes a half-paper and is joined with administrative law; whilst the former half-paper on legal history has become a paper on the history of the legal system and of English law.

At the same time the Council took away the former right of sitting for Part I in one subject at a time. The papers for Part I, as from the commencement of the academic year in October 1967, consist of six in number, and are divided into two groups of three papers each; all three papers of each group have to be taken at the same examination. Further, candidates must satisfy the examiners in each of the papers taken in either group A or group B; a student failing in more than one section must sit again for the examination in all three sections of that group.

A candidate (unless permitted to do so by the Council), may not sit for the sections of group B until he has passed or been exempted from the examination in each section of group A. This permission is usually only given in the case of a university candidate.

Finally, a student is not entitled to attempt the examination papers in either group A or group B on more than four occasions, except with the permission of the Council, and that will only be granted in exceptional circumstances.

Part I, as from the commencement of the academic year in October 1967 has therefore consisted of the following subjects:

GROUP A

Section I: The law of contract.

Section II: The law of tort.

Section III: Criminal law.

GROUP B

Section IV: Constitutional and administrative law.

Section V: The history of the legal system and of English law.

Section VI: (*a*) The law of land or

(*b*) (with the permission of the Director) either the general principles of Roman law and the Roman-Dutch law of obligations or two of the following:

(i) Hindu law

(ii) Mohammedan law as applied in India or Pakistan

(iii) Mohammedan law as applied in Africa and elsewhere except in India and Pakistan

(iv) African law—general (i.e. legal and judicial systems of Commonwealth Africa)

(v) African customary law.

The introduction of these changes in the subjects for examination necessitated certain transitional arrangements for students who had already started to read for a degree at a university, which includes Roman law or constitutional law and legal history; such students were allowed to exercise options in regard to the choice of subjects as laid down by the Council of Legal Education. Whilst students who had joined an Inn before 1 September 1967 can still take the sections singly, they also have an option as to Roman law and the first halves of the two new papers in constitutional law and administrative law, and in the history of the courts and of substantive law instead of two full papers in these subjects.

INNS OF COURT

The first choice which a student has to make is to determine which of the four Inns of Court he wishes to join. Having made up his mind on this point, he then has to make the necessary application for admission. This cannot be done, however, until he has passed at least one of the examinations as set out in the first schedule to the consolidated regulations of the Council of Legal Education.

An applicant for admission must produce separate certificates from two responsible people resident in the United Kingdom who have known him for at least one year, and who have had an opportunity of judging his character. Further, an applicant, unless he is exempted under certain regulations, has to complete and sign a Declaration and Undertaking, the main effect of which is to declare that he is not a member of certain professions nor is engaged in certain occupations. The Declaration also includes confirmation that the candidate is not either an undischarged bankrupt, nor that he has been convicted of any criminal offence.

A fee of £1 1*s.* 0*d.* is payable for the application form. This is followed by an education fee of 25 guineas which is payable to the Council of Legal Education. Students of the Inn of Court of Northern Ireland are issued the application form free of charge and have only to pay 9 guineas education fee.

Up to 30 September 1967 an admission fee of £85 6*s.* 0*d.* was payable to the Inn of Court by a student if he was a member of a university. An additional deposit of £100 was payable by all other students. Since 1 October 1967 the admission fee has been raised to £102 6*s.* 0*d.* and the deposit reduced to £77. The fees payable on call, to which reference will be made later, are deducted from the deposit money, and in the case of university students are payable before call.

Before he can be called to the Bar a student has to keep a minimum of eight dining terms unless he is a holder of a Certificate of Honour, when six terms will suffice. If he is called after keeping this number it will qualify him for practising as a barrister outside England and Wales; but before he can practise at the English Bar he must have kept a minimum of twelve dining terms, four of which he may keep after his call to the Bar. A student who is the holder of a certificate of honour need only keep ten terms before he can be called to the Bar.

In order to keep a term a student has to dine in the Hall of the Inn of Court that has accepted him as a student on at least three separate days in that term, and on each occasion he must be present when the opening grace is said and must remain until the closing grace has been said. He must also sign the attendance book at his Inn on each occasion that he attends in order to dine in hall. It is usual for terms to be kept contemporaneously with a student sitting to take the qualifying examinations. There are four dining terms, each consisting of 23 days' duration in each year, and known as Michaelmas, Hilary, Easter, and Trinity. Terms have to be kept in person unless authority is given for one or more terms to be kept *in absentia.*

It may be as well at this point to explain the exact make-up of the four Inns of Court. There are three classes of members who belong to the Inns. First are the masters of the bench, who are generally referred to as the benchers. They consist of barristers of distinction including Queen's Counsel and members who have been appointed to the judicial bench. The second class are the barristers, and these include both members of the outer bar as well as Queen's Counsels who are not benchers. Finally there are the students.

The benchers form the governing body of each Inn, and the elevation of a barrister to become a bencher is the highest honour that an Inn can bestow on one of its members. In addition to their governing powers, the benchers are also empowered to take disciplinary action against any member of their Inn. These powers include the right to expel a student or to suspend or disbar a barrister.

CALL TO THE BAR

If the requisite number of terms has not been kept prior to the date on which the student is called to the Bar, it will be necessary for him to undertake in his Call Declaration that he will make up any outstanding difference in order to bring his total number of terms kept up to the prescribed number.

As qualifying examinations have been passed and the correct number of terms have either already been kept, or an undertaking given to complete them, we can now follow the student to his call to the Bar. Up to 30 September 1967 the call fee payable by a student was £50, which was increased to £75 as from 1 October 1967.

Calls to the Bar take place once in every term on the 21st day of each dining term. The first points to be borne in mind are that no student is eligible for call under 21 years of age and, as we have seen, he must have kept the necessary number of terms and passed the examinations. He must also have completed and signed the Call Declaration. This declaration is so important that it is worth the while setting out its terms here:

> To the Masters of the Bench of the Honourable Society of . . . I . . . being desirous of being called to the Bar by the Honourable Society of . . . Pursuant to Regulation 37B do hereby declare and undertake that if called to the Bar:
>
> (*a*) I will not while in England or Wales in connection with any litigation in England or Wales do any act not proper to be done by a Barrister practising in England or Wales.
>
> (*b*) I will not while in England or Wales conduct any litigation in England or Wales other than the case or cases specified in the certificate referred to in Regulation 37B (*d*), and any other case or cases in which I may be briefed by a Solicitor of the Supreme Court in England or Wales and which I may be specifically authorised by the Executive Council to conduct.
>
> (*c*) I will never, whether in England or elsewhere, rely on the fact that I am or have been a member of the English Bar for any purpose

whatosever other than for the purpose of conducting such case or cases as aforesaid in England and Wales.

(*d*) I will within 21 days of the conclusion of the last of such cases apply to withdraw my name from the list of members of my Inn and to be disbarred.

(*e*) If I fail within the time aforesaid to apply to be disbarred I will not, if called upon at any time thereafter to show cause why I should not be disbarred, seek to show any such cause.

And, finally, his name and description must have been screened for call in the Hall, Benchers' Room, and Treasurer's office of his Inn 8 days in the term in which his call is to take place. The name and description of every student who is to be screened for call has to be sent by the Under Treasurer to each of the other Inns for similar screening.

PUPILLAGE

The next stage through which a student passes is reading as a pupil in a set of chambers. No person can practise at the Bar in England or Wales who has not been a pupil in chambers for an aggregate period of less than 12 months. This period may be completed either before call or after, or partly before call and partly after. No barrister is entitled to receive a pupil into his chambers unless he is himself of more than 5 years' standing. It is also necessary for him to notify the masters of the bench of his Inn that he intends to take a pupil and there must be no objection from them. The intending pupil must also notify the masters of the bench of his intention to become a pupil.

A barrister cannot accept instructions or conduct any case in any court until he has completed 6 months of his pupillage. It is obviously vitally important for a barrister to choose the right set of chambers in which to undergo his pupillage, and his choice will be guided by the type of practice which he hopes to acquire. If he hopes to practise in the criminal courts he will seek entry in criminal chambers; or if he hopes to acquire a practice in the county courts and eventually in the High Court he will enter chambers that deal with that type of work.

CHAMBERS

On being accepted as a pupil into a set of chambers, a barrister or student, as the case may be, will find that he has to pay a fee of 100 guineas to the barrister to whom he has been assigned as a pupil, and a further fee of 10 guineas to the barristers' clerk who is attached to that set of chambers for a full period of 12 months pupillage, or 50 guineas to the barrister and 5 guineas to the clerk for a 6-month period. He will learn about the paper work which has to be settled in chambers. If he is in criminal chambers he will learn how to settle indictments and will most probably be asked to read the papers in the cases in which the barrister for whom he "devils" is engaged; and he will be expected to make notes. Then he will accompany his master in court while the case is being dealt with and thus accustom himself to court procedure. At the same time he will take his own note of the witnesses' evidence as it is given in court.

It may well happen that as soon as he has qualified by doing his 6 months' pupillage, his master will start to get him on to his feet in court by asking him to call a formal witness. To be a pupil in a busy set of chambers may well lead to unexpected early briefs on his own account.

Should the chambers of his choice be common law ones he will similarly learn all about pleadings and interlocutory proceedings. He will be able to trace the course of a case from the initial issuing of the writ down to the final judgment, and if there is an appeal, through the various appeal tribunals. In a nutshell, the more useful a pupil can make himself to his master the more likely he is to gain some real advantage from his pupillage. Whilst we have referred only to common law or criminal chambers, there are, of course, other branches of law in which a pupil may want to specialize when he has completed his training as a pupil, but the principles are the same.

After his 12 months as a pupil have been served, a barrister has then to decide on a set of chambers in which to embark on practice on his own. It may happen that there is a vacancy in the chambers where he has been a pupil. This has obvious advantages as he will already have become known to the solicitors who deal with those chambers; and if he has impressed them he will most probably begin to receive some of the smaller work for himself. Should there be no vacancy in those chambers he will have every help in getting settled into another suitable set of chambers dealing with the type of practice which he hopes to pursue.

It has to be remembered that while many of those who are called to the Bar with a view to practising choose chambers in one of the four Inns of Court, there are also a number of local Bars in the provinces. A student who has the advantage of a local connection may prefer to practise from chambers which are situated near his local connections.

CLERKS

The day-to-day business of every set of chambers is conducted by a clerk who, if it is a busy set of chambers, may well have one or more junior clerks to assist him. Each set of chambers in London is held under a tenancy from the Inn and has a head of chambers who is usually also the tenant and is responsible for payment of the rent and other outgoings in connection with the running of the chambers. Each member of chambers pays a proportion of the rent and gives an undertaking to the head of chambers that he will pay a quarterly rent which is worked out so as to include a fair proportion of rent and chamber expenses being shared by each member.

The method of remuneration of a barristers' clerk may vary according to the terms agreed between each master and his clerk, but it is usual for the clerk to receive either "shillings on the guineas" and the clerk's fees marked on the brief or instructions, or alternatively 10 per cent of the total fee including the clerk's fees. Every brief which is delivered to a barrister also carries a separate fee for the barrister's clerk. In High Court actions this amounts to $2\frac{1}{2}$ per cent of the fee paid to the barrister, but in the House of Lords this may be much higher.

A barrister cannot sue for his fees. It is the duty of his clerk to keep a note of all fees that are owing to each and every one of the tenants of the chambers for which he acts as clerk. The clerk is the agent for collecting fees on behalf of the barristers in his chambers, and it is he who has to write and ask for payment from the respective solicitors. Each fee has also attached to it what is known as a clerk's fee. Thus, whilst the minimum fee which can be paid to a barrister is 2 guineas, the actual sum which has to be collected is £2 4*s.* 6*d.*, the extra halfcrown being the clerk's fee.

That it is not only expedient for a practising barrister to have professional chambers and a breach of etiquette not to, but is in any case obligatory, has been made abundantly clear by a recent ruling of the Bar Council. This follows from the fact that a barrister cannot negotiate his own fees, and unless he is in chambers he will not have a clerk to undertake this necessary duty for him.

The next most important duty a barrister's clerk has to undertake is that of fitting in his master's work. He has to accept briefs from solicitors and must then arrange the work that has been delivered to his chambers so that, if possible, the barrister chosen by the client is available to conduct the case. The clerk will try to ensure that all the barristers in his chambers are kept engaged in such a way that no briefs have to be returned to solicitors because he has no suitable barrister free on the crucial day when any particular case comes up for trial. This obviously is no easy task, and even with the co-operation of those who arrange the lists for the various courts, it cannot always be achieved.

By far and away the most important duty of a barrister's clerk in the early days of a barrister's practice is to obtain for him work which is suitable for his skill and experience. There can be no more valuable aid to a young junior than a loyal and experienced clerk; such a clerk will not try to engage his master for work for which he is not ready; he will at the same time foster his practice and encourage his clients to stay with him as he progresses, and will decide when an increase of fees is justified which will not discourage the client from seeking the professional services of his master in the future.

Although there may be a number of barristers in a set of chambers, the relationship between each member and the clerk is a personal one, and the clerk will look to each master for payment of his fees.

OUTER BAR

Earlier in this chapter we pointed out the qualifications that are required by a student prior to his call to the Bar, and we have referred to his pupillage and residence in chambers. We shall now examine in a little more detail some of the factors which, obvious though they may seem to those engaged in the profession, may yet be of some help to the young barrister who has just been called to the Bar. Hope springs eternal in the human breast, and thoughts of a lucrative future may not unnaturally be foremost in the minds of those who enter this profession. Provided that a student has completed 6 months of pupillage prior to his "call" he can appear in court as an advocate the day following the night of his call. He must therefore have procured for himself by then a set of robes. This consists of a stuff gown (only a Queen's Counsel wears a silk one), a wig, a set of bibs, some butterfly collars, and a blue brief bag with his initials on it as well as a tin box, with his name painted on it, in which to keep his wig.

It should be noted that the brief bag must be a *blue* one. The red brief bag will in all probability follow in due course, but it is the prerogative of a Queen's Counsel to present it to his junior, and unless so presented with a red brief bag no junior member of the Bar is entitled to have one. It is not obligatory for a "silk" to present a red brief bag to each and every junior who appears in a case with him. As a general rule, the presentation is in the nature of a gesture from the "silk" to his junior in return for his assistance in a difficult case.

QUEEN'S COUNSEL

If a member of the junior Bar finds that he is acquiring a heavy and lucrative practice, he will probably consider making an application to the Lord Chancellor to be considered for "silk", which is the name given to Queen's Counsel by the junior Bar. Before taking this most important step he will doubtless seek the advice of his clerk, who will be able to judge from his experience whether the barrister is really likely to be successful in the role of a leader. He may advise him to defer the application for a year or so. It is always a tremendous risk for a barrister to leave the comparative safety of the junior Bar and launch out into the unknown domain of becoming a "silk". His promotion will of necessity place on him a much heavier burden of responsibility.

Apart from the higher status enjoyed by a Queen's Counsel, the position limits the class of work he may do. For instance, he will no longer be permitted to draft pleadings, give written opinions on evidence, and carry out written work in general except in conjunction with a junior on the cases he conducted himself as a junior. Likewise, the client who wishes to obtain his services in future will find that he has to employ a junior also to whom until October 1966 he would have had to pay a fee of two-thirds of the "silk's" fee except where that fee exceeded 150 guineas; since October 1966, however, the two-thirds rule has been abrogated, and a junior's fee is now negotiated on the basis of what he would get if he did the case himself. This rule has been agreed to as an interim measure. If he has been practising in one of the provincial cities he will have the additional expense of acquiring chambers in London even if he intends to continue practising in the provinces, as this is a requirement of his new dignity.

One further limitation which formerly applied has, however, vanished. As the name suggests, Queen's Counsels were originally appointed to conduct cases for the Crown in addition to their ordinary work and had to apply for a licence to appear against the Crown in any case. But in 1920 a general dispensation was granted and now any "silk" can appear against the Crown. Should, however, his clerk be able to endorse the application, the barrister will then be in a position to make his formal application to the Lord Chancellor. It is interesting to note that no qualification for the appointment is laid down, although by convention 10 years from call is the recognized minimum plus a high degree of success as a junior. It will be realized that not all those who apply for silk are approved by the Lord Chancellor. There is nothing to prevent a barrister from repeating his application should he be unsuccessful on the first occasion that he submits his name. Like the importunate widow, he may eventually succeed. The formal application having been made, he must then await the Lord Chancellor's pleasure. It has been the custom for many years for the list of newly appointed "silks" to be made public on Maundy Thursday. The barristers who have been chosen for this honour are given notice in writing by the Lord Chancellor on the same day.

The new Queen's Counsel must then obtain for himself a set of robes. He will require full levy dress, knee breeches, jabot and frock coat, in addition to two robes—one being his silk robe and the other a cloth robe. On the appointed day, which by custom is the first day of the legal term commencing after the Easter recess, he will, accompanied by his clerk, present himself in full levy dress and medals at the House of Lords where he will be sworn in by the Lord Chancellor and will receive his letters patent.

On the first day of the new term all the new "silks" make their round of all the courts which are sitting in the High Court of Justice. This ceremony takes the following form: all the new "silks" enter the front bench of each court in the order of their seniority of call to the Bar. The first court which they enter is that of the Lord Chief Justice, then that of the Master of the Rolls, followed by that of the President of the Probate Division and then each of the other courts in turn. In each court the presiding judge will call on each of the new "silks" in turn by name—"Do you move Mr. ——?"—when so called on each "silk" will stand up and bow to the judge and then leave the court from the other end of the bench by which he entered.

The purpose for which Queen's Counsel has to have two robes is interesting. When appearing before a judge or judges who are robed in red, a Q.C. has to wear his silk gown. Judges wear their red robes when they are dealing with criminal matters at the

Central Criminal Court or at assize courts when exercising their criminal jurisdiction. On other occasions, in the divisional court or, if appearing before a puisne judge in a civil matter, a "silk" will wear his cloth gown.

ETIQUETTE

The four Inns of Court hold the exclusive right to call persons to the English Bar. Barristers are rightly proud and jealous of the dignity which attaches to the etiquette and conduct of all persons who are admitted to the ranks of their profession. It is therefore incumbent on every person after his call to see that he maintains the dignity and high standing of his chosen profession. Eligibility for appointment to the judicial bench is restricted to barristers who can be of either sex.

The 12 months of pupillage spent in chambers should serve as a training sufficient to instil into a barrister the necessity for him to avoid any breach of professional conduct or etiquette. Indeed, it is the duty of a barrister who takes a pupil to ensure that these vital points on etiquette and professional behaviour are clearly explained to him.

While the benchers of each Inn are endowed with strong disciplinary powers, the Bar Council, which is composed of barristers who are appointed from time to time to serve for certain set periods, has since 1895 taken on responsibility for making rules and delivering rulings in relation to matters of professional etiquette. Since the Bar Council may in an appropriate case pass the complaint on to the benchers of the Inn of the barrister whose conduct is being investigated, the Bar Council may be said to be a tribunal of first instance, whilst the benchers may be regarded as a higher tribunal.

The early years of a practising barrister may turn out to be somewhat frustrating, as well as unproductive from the fee-earning point of view. This often leads young barristers to take on part-time employment. In doing so, however, they have to bear in mind the terms of the Declaration made by them before call. They will find that they are restricted, speaking in broad terms, from carrying on any other profession or business.

There is probably no truer saying that many are called but that comparatively few have the intention of practising as barristers. Of those who start off with high aspirations quite a number are forced through sheer economic necessity to find employment elsewhere. It will be then found that the qualification of barrister-at-law is a useful acquisition when seeking a permanent appointment in either the legal world or in the world of commerce. A practising barrister may at the same time be a Member of Parliament, or a member of a local authority or company director provided that he does not take an active part in the management of the company. It is also possible for him to earn fees for editing and reviewing, or even for coaching pupils for legal examinations.

One of the most important facts for a young barrister to bear in mind is that, apart from dock briefs and legal aid defences at the request of the court in criminal cases, he cannot act without the instructions of a solicitor. This rule also applies to non-contentious legal work done for fees except for certain exempted cases, e.g. patent cases, parliamentary work, and local government work.

It is also of vital importance for a barrister to remember that he must not advertise. He is not allowed to have both his name and qualification as a barrister published other than in connection with articles for legal periodicals and legal textbooks. The writing of a legal textbook, though an arduous occupation, is recognized as a fair means by which a barrister may make himself known as a specialist.

The position of a practising barrister has sometimes been described as akin to that of a London taxi driver: he must not ply for hire, yet he must accept a fare from one who tenders for his services within a given area. In the same way a barrister is bound to accept a brief in any of the courts in which he normally practises provided that he is not already engaged elsewhere on the date he is required, and provided that he is offered a proper professional fee commensurate with his standing and the length and difficulty of the case. Special circumstances such as personal knowledge of the dispute or of the lay opponent, may, however, justify refusal of a particular brief. For this reason, the services of any barrister are available to any firm of solicitors however small.

DISCIPLINE

We have already mentioned that a practising member of the Bar must not advertise. On being called to the Bar and provided that he has completed a minimum period of 6 months in chambers as a pupil, and his master has agreed that there will be a vacancy in the chambers for him after he has been called, he will be entitled to have his name added to the list of barristers who are practising in those chambers. This will render him liable to pay his portion of the chambers rent and expenses, but will bring his name to the attention of solicitors who attend the chambers.

The Bar, as indicated, is very jealous of its standard of honour, and also is very much of a closed shop. It follows, therefore, as we have seen, that a barrister has to observe strict standards of conduct and etiquette from the moment of his call. The young barrister will generally find that he will be given every assistance and consideration both by his fellow members of the Bar and by the magistrates and other occupants of the judicial benches before whom he appears, and that lapses on his part due to his ignorance of procedure and practice will be overlooked in his early days. However, as time goes on, should it appear to the judges and others before whom he practises that his lapses are no longer due to ignorance, he will be liable to find himself coming into conflict with the disciplinary forces of his profession.

A judge may well in the first instance be content to communicate any lapse by a barrister to the head of his chambers, in which case he will expect the head of chambers to take appropriate action to warn the offending barrister so that he will not repeat it. Should, however, the matter be more serious, a report may be sent to the General Council of the Bar and it will then become the subject of consideration by that Council's Disciplinary Committee. In the case of a really serious breach of etiquette or misconduct, it will become a matter for consideration by the benchers of the Inn of which the offending barrister is a member.

When misconduct by a barrister is under consideration by the benchers of an Inn, the barrister will be invited to attend the hearing. He will be able to do so either in person and speak on his own behalf, or he may be represented by another barrister who will conduct his defence for him.

The benchers of an Inn are empowered to inflict heavy punishment on any member of their Inn should they be satisfied that the allegation made against him has been substantiated. They may suspend him from practice for a definite period of time, or they may even, as an extreme measure, disbar him. A barrister has a right of appeal to the High Court from the decision of his benchers.

The Bar Council itself has no power to discipline barristers, but since 1949 the Council has employed a secretary, assistant secretary, and staff, and its influence as the body which represents the profession to the general public has increased considerably. Since 1962 there has also been an executive council of the four Inns which ensures that they act in concert on matters of importance affecting the profession as a whole.

A very recent innovation has been the setting up by the four Inns of Court of a Senate of which Mr. Justice Widgery was elected as the first chairman. One of the purposes of the Senate is to act as a joint body in consultation with the General Council of the Bar, and to take over some of the functions previously exercised separately by each of the Inns.

The Senate is composed of 37 members, consisting of a chairman, 6 representatives from each Inn (4 of whom must be practising barristers), and 6 representatives of the Bar Council. There are in addition 6 *ex-officio* members—the treasurers of the four Inns, the chairman of the Bar Council, and the Attorney-General.

The decisions of the Senate are binding on the four Inns, and cover consideration of conditions for the admission of students including call to the Bar, welfare, legal education, and the exercise of disciplinary powers.

The Senate, while not encroaching on the normal functions of the Council of Legal Education, assures proper control of policy by the appointment of five of its members to the Council.

Another important responsibility of the Senate is the maintaining of "close and friendly" relations with the Law Council. In this aspect, however, the senate in no way assumes any of the functions of the Bar Council.

JUDICIAL APPOINTMENTS

More detailed reference will be made to this matter in Chapter 6 where on p. 132 a table showing the necessary qualifications for some of the major judicial appointments is to be found. Call to the Bar may be regarded as a necessary stepping stone to a large variety of appointments. Many barristers find their way into lucrative business appointments, for example; but here we are concerned only with offices connected with the administration of justice.

One has only to consider the number of courts that are connected with the administration of justice, both in relation to civil and criminal procedure, to realize that there are a host of opportunities for both solicitors and barristers to find employment, apart from acting in the capacity of advocates. Each petty sessional court requires a qualified clerk to the justices, and in the larger courts a similarly qualified deputy. Each county court district throughout the land requires the assistance of at least one qualified registrar. Each Quarter Sessions has to have a qualified clerk of the peace and a deputy clerk of the peace. The High Court of Justice absorbs many qualified persons and the various assize courts in England and Wales all require qualified assize clerks.

Stipendiary magistrates, chairmen of Quarter Sessions, recorders of boroughs, county court judges, masters of the High Court and appointments to the High Court bench are only some of the many higher offices to which a successful barrister may find himself qualified to apply for appointment. In most cases it will be found that a period of seniority in his profession is a requisite factor in establishing his claim to office. A solicitor of 10 years' standing is eligible for appointment as a Master of the Chancery Division of the High Court or as a master of the taxing office, a legal visitor in lunacy or as official solicitor.

CHAPTER 4

Magistrates' Courts Civil Jurisdiction

Domestic courts: Matrimonial; Consent to marriage of an infant; Affiliation; Guardianship of infants — Adult courts: Civil debts; Abatement of nuisance; Ejectment — Juvenile courts: Adoption; Care, protection or control; Education Act cases — School attendances.

IN ADDITION to their jurisdiction in regard to criminal matters, magistrates' courts also have to cope with quite a wide variety of civil work. Before proceeding in Chapters 9 and 10 to deal with the High Court of Justice, it is desirable at this stage to review the principal aspects of civil jurisdiction attaching to magistrates' courts. County courts are courts of first instance whose decisions are subject to appeal to the Court of Appeal, so, similarly, are magistrates' courts which have rights of appeal from their decisions either to Quarter Sessions or to the High Court.

DOMESTIC COURTS

Matrimonial

The civil jurisdiction of magistrates' courts is dealt with by three separate tribunals, namely the adult courts, the domestic courts, and the juvenile courts. It is proposed first to refer to the domestic courts which deal with matrimonial, affiliation, and guardianship of infants cases.

Section 56 of the Magistrates' Courts Act, 1952, enacts that a magistrates' court when hearing domestic proceedings shall be composed of not more than three justices, including so far as practicable both a man and a woman. The business of these courts has to be arranged in such a way as to separate the hearing and determination of these domestic proceedings from other business.

The proceedings thus dealt with include proceedings:

(*a*) under the Guardianship of Infants Acts, 1886 and 1925;
(*b*) under the Matrimonial Proceedings (Magistrates' Courts) Act, 1960;
(*c*) under section 3 or 4 of the Maintenance Orders (Facilities for Enforcement) Act, 1920;
(*d*) under section 4 (3) of the Family Allowances Act, 1945; and
(*e*) under section 3 of the Marriage Act, 1949.

Statutory provisions are laid down by section 57 of the Magistrates' Courts Act, 1952, to the effect that no person shall be present during the proceedings of a domestic court except:

(*a*) officers of the court;
(*b*) parties to the case, their solicitors and counsel, witnesses and other persons directly concerned in the case, and other persons whom either party desires to be present;
(*c*) solicitors and counsel in attendance for other cases;
(*d*) representatives of newspapers or news agencies; and
(*e*) any other person whom it may permit to be present, so that permission shall not be withheld from a person who appears to the court to have adequate grounds for attendance.

Domestic courts have the additional power to exclude persons other than those directly concerned in the case during the taking of any indecent evidence.

Newspaper reports of domestic proceedings are restricted by the provisions of section 58 of the Magistrates' Courts Act, 1952, to:

(*a*) the names, addresses, and occupations of parties and witnesses;
(*b*) the grounds of the application and a concise statement of the charges, defences, and counter-charges in support of which the evidence has been given;

(*c*) submissions on any point of law arising in the course of proceedings and the decision of the court on the submission; and

(*d*) the decision of the court and any observations made by the court in giving it.

This section also lays down penalties for contravention and enacts that no prosecution shall be begun without the consent of the Attorney-General.

A married man or woman may apply by way of complaint to a magistrates' court for an order under the Matrimonial Proceedings (Magistrates' Courts) Act, 1960, against the other party to the marriage on the ground amongst others that the defendant has:

(*a*) deserted the complainant; or

(*b*) been guilty of persistent cruelty to:

 (i) the complainant;

 (ii) an infant child of the complainant; or

 (iii) an infant child of the defendant who, at the time of the cruelty was a child of the family; or

(*c*) been found guilty;-

 (i) on indictment of any offence which involved an assault upon the complainant;

 (ii) by a magistrates' court of certain offences or attempted offences against the complainant under certain sections of the Offences against the Person Act, 1861;

(*d*) has committed adultery; or

(*e*) being the husband wilfully failed to provide reasonable maintenance for the wife or for any child of the family.

Other grounds are to be found set out in section 1 (1) of the Matrimonial Proceedings (Magistrates' Courts) Act, 1960, whilst subsection (2) defines the jurisdiction of magistrates' courts to hear such complaints as being (*a*) if at the date of making the complaint either complainant or defendant ordinarily resides within the petty sessions area, (*b*) except in the case of (*c*) referred to in subsection (1), if the cause of complaint arose wholly or partly within the petty sessions area, and (*c*) in the case of a complaint by virtue of (*c*) in subsection (1) occurring within the petty sessions area.

Application for legal aid in these proceedings has to be made in the prescribed form to the secretary of the appropriate legal aid committee of the Law Society, as magistrates' courts have no power to grant legal aid.

Desertion is a matter of inference, and in order to prove it, a termination of cohabitation which has been brought about by intention of the defendant without consent by the complainant, must be proved. The important question is whether the conduct of the deserting party is such as to prove a clear intention to break off matrimonial relations.

Proof of persistent cruelty, coupled with proof of one spouses' intention to force the other to leave may constitute desertion. Separation by the parties, whether voluntary or by deed of separation does not amount to desertion. Unless an offer by a spouse to resume cohabitation after desertion is bona fide it does not break the desertion; voluntary resumption of cohabitation does, however, put an end to desertion and is a bar to pending proceedings.

There is no precise definition of what amounts to persistent cruelty; it is a question of fact and degree related to the circumstances and the parties.

The following factors are therefore required to be proved:

(*a*) misconduct must be of a grave and weighty nature;
(*b*) there must be real injury to the health of the complainant or a reasonable apprehension of such injury;
(*c*) this injury or apprehension of it must have been caused by the conduct of the defendant;
(*d*) the whole conduct of the defendant can be properly described as cruelty in the ordinary sense of that term.

The conduct must be part of a course of conduct that is

persistent, and the same degree of cruelty has to be proved as is required to substantiate a charge in the divorce court.*

If one or more of the matrimonial offences are proved a magistrates' court may make an order referred to as a "matrimonial order" which may contain one or more of the following provisions:

(*a*) that the complainant be no longer bound to cohabit with the defendant;
(*b*) that the husband shall pay to the wife a weekly sum not exceeding £7 10*s*. 0*d*. according to circumstances;
(*c*) where the husband's earning capacity, through illness or other reason is impaired, that the wife shall pay the husband a weekly sum not exceeding £7 10*s*. 0*d*. according to circumstances;
(*d*) provision for the legal custody of any child of the family who is under 16 years of age;
(*e*) in exceptional circumstances a provision committing the care of a child of the marriage to a specified local authority;
(*f*) also in exceptional circumstances a provision that the child be under the supervision of (i) a probation officer or (ii) of a council of a county or county borough;
(*g*) a provision for access to any child by either party;
(*h*) provisions for the maintenance of any child of the family by either or both parties of a weekly sum not exceeding £2 10*s*. 0*d*., and there is power to extend this in the case of a dependent child, beyond the age of 16 until the child reaches the age of 21.†

The payment of any sum of money directed to be paid by an order made by virtue of the 1960 Act may be enforced in the same manner as the payment of money is enforced under an affiliation order (section 13), that is to say, by an order made on complaint

* Prima facie a husband is under a duty to maintain his wife and the children of the family and if he fails to do so, having the ability without lawful excuse he is guilty of wilful failure to maintain.

† This amount may shortly be increased to £5 by the Maintenance Orders Bill.

not earlier than the fifteenth day after the making of the order.

Appeals from orders made under the Matrimonial Proceedings (Magistrates' Courts) Act, 1960, are regulated by the Matrimonial Causes Rules, 1957 (S.I. 1957, No. 619).

An appeal lies to the divisional court of the Probate, Divorce, and Admiralty Division of the High Court; and by notice of motion it must be stated the grounds of appeal and the extent to which the order is complained of.

Consent to Marriage of an Infant

Before a person who is under 21 years of age can be married (unless that person is a widow or widower), the consent of certain persons are required, and full particulars of these persons can be found set out in the second schedule to the Marriage Act, 1949. In certain circumstances these consents can be dispensed with by the Registrar-General, but normally in the event of any person whose consent is required refusing to give such consent, the court may, on application being made, consent to the marriage.

These proceedings are an example of general jurisdiction, since for the purposes of the Marriage Act, 1949, the court means the High Court, the county court of the district in which any respondent resides, or a court of summary jurisdiction.

The rules regulating the procedure in such applications are contained in the Guardianship of Infants (Summary Jurisdiction) Rules, 1925, and enable applications to be made under section 3 of the Marriage Act, 1949:

(*a*) if made to the High Court, to be heard in chambers;
(*b*) if made to the county court to be heard and determined by the registrar subject to appeal to the judge;
(*c*) if made to a court of summary jurisdiction, to be heard and determined otherwise than in open court.

Provision is also made for the service of notice of the application on the person who has refused consent. The consent of the High

Court must, however, be obtained to the marriage of a ward of court.

Affiliation

The procedure which governs applications in respect of affiliation orders is laid down in the Affiliation Proceedings Act, 1957. Section 1 of this Act provides that a single woman who is with child, or who has been delivered of an illegitimate child, may apply by complaint to a justice of the peace for a summons to be served on the man alleged by her to be the father of the child.

The complaint may be made:

(*a*) at any time within 12 months from the date of the child's birth;
(*b*) at any subsequent time upon proof of payment of money for maintenance of the child by the alleged father;
(*c*) at any subsequent time within 12 months after the man's return to England upon proof that he ceased to reside in England within 12 months next after the birth of the child.

The complaint has to be made to a justice of the peace for the petty sessional area in which the mother resides, and the magistrates' court shall be one for this petty sessional area. Where a summons is issued before birth, it must be made returnable after the day on which the child is expected to be born.

The evidence of the mother is essential, as she must adduce proof to satisfy the court of her claim; and this is so even if the defendant admits paternity. Corroboration of the mothers' evidence in some material particular by other evidence is also essential. The divisional court have expressed the view that corroborative evidence must have some relation to the conduct of the putative father, or some relation to the probability of the person summoned being the father.

Should the court proceed to make an order it will be to the effect:

(*a*) a weekly sum for maintenance and education of the child not exceeding £2 10*s.* 0*d.*;*

(*b*) the expenses incidental to the birth; and

(*c*) if the child has died before the making of the order, the child's funeral expenses.

The court has power to order the payments to be calculated from the date of the birth of the child or within 2 months after that date.

Normally an affiliation order does not remain in force after a child has attained the age of 16 years; the exceptions to this general rule are to be found in section 7 of the Affiliation Proceedings Act, 1957. Before determining the amount of the weekly payment the court must hear evidence in order to ascertain the means of the putative father.

If a child or young person who is the subject of a committal order to a fit person or to an approved school, is illegitimate and there is an affiliation order for his maintenance in force, the court may at the time of making the order direct that the affiliation payments be paid to the person who from time to time is entitled under section 86 of the Children and Young Persons Act, 1933, to receive the contributions.

Any court with summary jurisdiction in the place where the putative father is for the time being residing may subsequently make such an order at any time.

Legal aid in respect of proceedings for or relating to an affiliation order cannot be granted by a magistrates' court; or, in the event of an appeal, by Quarter Sessions. Provision is, however, made by section 1 and the first schedule of the Legal Aid and Advice Act, 1949, for the provision of legal aid in such cases and it empowers regulations to be made with this purpose in view. As a result legal aid can now be obtained by either or both parties to affiliation proceedings on application being made to the Law Society.

* This amount may shortly be increased to £5 by the Maintenance Orders Bill.

An appeal lies to a court of Quarter Sessions from the making of an affiliation order, or from any refusal by a magistrates' court to make such an order, but there is no right of appeal against a refusal to revoke, revive or vary an order.

Guardianship of Infants

The statutory powers of magistrates in relation to the guardianship of infants are contained in the Guardianship of Infants Act, 1886 and 1925. Here again legal aid cannot be given by the magistrates' court, but can be obtained through the medium of the Legal Aid and Advice Act, 1949.

In these proceedings the court decides questions as to the custody and upbringing of infants, including the right of parental access, and maintenance of infants.

The most important factor to be remembered is that the court must regard the welfare of the infant as the first and paramount consideration (section 1, Guardianship of Infants Act, 1925). An order once made may be varied or discharged by a subsequent order. The combined effect of section 5 of the Guardianship of Infants Act, 1886, as amended by the Guardianship of Infants Act, 1925 and section 16 of the Administration of Justice Act, 1928, is to enable the court to make an order whether the application is made by the mother or by the father of an infant.

The effect of section 4 of the Guardianship of Infants Act, 1886, is to bestow on every guardian under the Act such powers over the estate or the person, or both, of an infant as any guardian appointed by will or otherwise. The expression "court" in this connection may mean either the High Court, county court, or magistrates' court. Thus, the Adoption Act, 1958, defines the "court" as meaning the High Court or, at the option of the applicant, but subject to Adoption Rules, any county court or magistrates' court within the jurisdiction of which the applicant or the infant resides at the date of the application. A magistrates' court may, however, refuse to proceed with the application where special circumstances make it more fit to be dealt with by the High Court.

An appeal lies to a single judge of the Chancery Division of the High Court.

ADULT COURTS

Civil Debts

The process of recovering a civil debt takes place in the adult courts which are held in magistrates' courts.

The process is only by way of complaint and section 50 of the Magistrates' Courts Act, 1952, enacts as follows:

> A magistrates' court shall have power to make an order on complaint for the payment of any money recoverable as a civil debt. Any sum, payment of which may be ordered by a magistrates' court, is recoverable summarily as a civil debt except (*a*) a sum recoverable on complaint for an affiliation order or order enforceable as an affiliation order; or (*b*) a sum that may be adjudged to be paid by a summary conviction or by an order enforceable as if it were a summary conviction.

Periodical payments are usually ordered to be made through the justices' clerk, who is by virtue of his office the collecting officer of the court. There is a discretionary power in the magistrates' court to award costs on the hearing of a complaint.

Magistrates' courts are, however, restricted in their powers of committal to prison for default of payment of a civil debt. This action cannot be taken without an order made on complaint, and on proof of means and of refusal or neglect to pay on behalf of the defendant. The jurisdiction of a magistrates' court to commit a debtor to prison can only be exercised by two or more justices sitting at some place appointed for holding petty sessions.

The maximum period of detention for non-payment of a civil debt is 6 weeks (third schedule, Magistrates' Courts Act, 1952). The complaint may be made at any time and the costs incurred by the complainant in the enforcement proceedings are included in the sum to be paid by the defendant before he can be released from custody. Civil debts which are recoverable in this way include overdue electricity or gas bills, and the enforcement of the payment of rates.

Where the claim does not exceed £10, the wages of a servant under a contract to which the jurisdiction of justices extends, are recoverable in the mode directed (Employers and Workmen Act, 1875, section 4), in a court of summary jurisdiction. A similar action in a county court would extend the jurisdiction to £500.

Any charges in respect of gas and any meter rent due to an area board as well as any charges due for the supplying and fixing of any meter or fittings are, provided the amount does not exceed £20, recoverable summarily as a civil debt. If the amount exceeds £20 the sum due is recoverable in any court of competent jurisdiction (Gas Act, 1948, third schedule, para. 22). Twenty-eight days after the demand for payment, the Gas Board is empowered to cut off the supply of gas until payment is made.

A series of statutes have been passed in connection with the supplying of electricity and the recovery of sums due in respect of current consumed and meter rents. Monies due are, therefore, recoverable summarily as a civil debt in a magistrates' court provided that the amount due does not exceed £20 (third schedule, Gas Act, 1948).

The jurisdiction of a magistrates' court in relation to the summary recovery of income tax as a civil debt is subject to a limit of £50, and this includes the recovery of an overdue instalment provided that the sum in question does not exceed that amount. Proceedings may be brought for the recovery of any tax charged under Schedule E in England or Wales at any time within one year from the time that the complaint arose (Income Tax Act, 1952, section 78, as amended by Income Tax Management Act, 1964, schedule 6).

A further example of this debt recovery jurisdiction is to be found in claims made for the recovery of taxi-cab fares.

Abatement of nuisance

Another aspect of the civil jurisdiction of magistrates' courts is in connection with proceedings relating to nuisances under the Public Health Acts. When a local authority is satisfied that a statutory nuisance exists, section 93 of the Public Health Act, 1936, enables the authority to serve what is known as "an abatement notice" on the person by whose act, default, or sufferance the nuisance arises or continues.

In the event of default in complying with an abatement notice, or if the local authority is of the opinion that though abated the nuisance may recur, the local authority can then make a complaint to a justice of the peace, who will issue a summons requiring the person to appear before a court of summary jurisdiction. In the event that the alleged nuisance is proved to exist, or if abated, is likely to recur, then subject to the conditions of section 94 of the Public Health Act, 1936, the court shall make a "nuisance order". The penalty for failing to comply with a nuisance order is a fine not exceeding £5, and a further fine not exceeding £2 for each day on which the offence continues after conviction therefor (section 95, Public Health Act, 1936). Sections 296 and 297 of the Public Health Act, 1936, enable a court to fix a reasonable period from the date of conviction for compliance by the defendant with any directions given by the court; in which event the daily penalty will not be recoverable in respect of any day before that period has expired.

A right of appeal to a court of summary jurisdiction against a requirement, refusal or other decision of the council, is given by virtue of the provisions of section 300 of the Public Health Act, 1936. Notice of appeal must, however, be given within 21 days from the service of the notice by the local authority. Finally, section 301 of the Public Health Act, 1936, gives a right of appeal to Quarter Sessions by a person aggrieved by a decision of a court of summary jurisdiction, subject to the proviso contained therein.

Ejectment

Still another aspect of this jurisdiction relates to ejectment notices in proceedings for the recovery of premises by a landlord where a tenant who has been served with a notice to quit, fails to quit and deliver up the premises to the landlord (Small Tenements Recovery Act, 1838). The landlord must give written notice of his intention to apply at the expiration of 7 clear days to "the justices in petty sessions assembled" to recover possession of the premises. The effect of the above-quoted wording is to restrict the hearing of such proceedings to justices when they are sitting in a petty sessional courthouse as opposed to an occasional courthouse.

Various sections of the Housing Act, 1957, extend the application of the Small Tenements Recovery Act, 1838, to the recovery by the local authority of possession of buildings which are subject to a demolition order or are otherwise required by the local authority. The notice has to be served personally in accordance with the provisions of section 2 of the Small Tenements Recovery Act, 1838. The powers of justices (and there must be two justices), on the necessary matters being proved, are to issue a warrant for giving possession within a named period of not less than 21 nor more than 30 clear days from the date of the warrant.

Before turning to consider juvenile courts it is appropriate to refer to the powers of binding over that can be enforced by magistrates' courts. The Justices of the Peace Act, 1361, gave a general power to justices, which was extended to magistrates' courts by section 124 of the Magistrates' Courts Act, 1952, to order any person to enter into a recognizance with or without sureties to keep the peace or to be of good behaviour, on proof being established that a breach of the peace is likely to occur.

This power is exercised by order on complaint, and failure to comply with such an order may result in the court committing him to custody for a period not exceeding 6 months or until he complies with the order (section 91, Magistrates' Courts Act, 1952). The order, however, must be for a definite period.

The purpose of such a binding over is not to inflict punishment but to prevent an apprehended danger of a breach of the peace. Threats may be either by a person to injure the complainant or to procure others to do so; and they may be by words or gestures and may even be inferred from a course of conduct.

JUVENILE COURTS

We now pass on to consider the third main class of magistrates' courts to deal with civil jurisdiction, namely the juvenile courts. First, it has to be noted that similar restrictions are placed on these courts, both as regards those persons who have a right to attend the proceedings in court, and also as regards newspaper reporting of their proceedings, as have already been referred to under the heading of domestic courts. There are three main sections to be dealt with: adoption, care, protection or control, and Education Act cases.

Adoption

The making of adoption orders constitutes an important part of the jurisdiction of juvenile courts. The power to make such an order is acquired by virtue of section 1 of the Adoption Act, 1958. The applicant must be the mother or father of the infant, or a relative who has attained the age of 21 or another person who has attained the age of 25.

An adoption order may be made in respect of an infant on the joint application of two spouses (*a*) if either is the mother or father of the infant, or (*b*) if one is a relation over 21 years and the other is also over 21. Before an adoption order is made in respect of an infant the court must be satisfied that every person whose consent is necessary has consented, or that such consent may be dispensed with, that the order will be for the welfare of the infant, and that the applicant has not received or agreed to receive any payment other than that sanctioned by the court. The consent of the father of an illegitimate child is not necessary.

An interim order may be made and, where the court makes or refuses to make an order, an appeal lies to a single judge of the Chancery Division of the High Court of Justice.

Upon an adoptive order being made the adoptive parent stands for all effective purposes in the position of a parent of a child born to him or her in lawful wedlock, and where two spouses have adopted an infant, they have the same rights and liabilities relating to custody and maintenance as any other parent.

Care, Protection, or Control

Magistrates' courts as part of their jurisdiction have to adjudicate on cases relating to children and young persons who are in need of care, protection, or control. In order to appreciate what this involves it is necessary to have in mind the following definitions: "child" means a person under the age of 14 years; "young person" means a person who has attained the age of 14 years and is under the age of 17 years; whilst section 2 of the Children and Young Persons Act, 1963, defines "children and young persons in need of care, protection or control" as including a child or young person in respect of whom the court is satisfied that he is (*a*) falling into bad associations or is exposed to moral danger, or (*b*) that lack of care, protection, or guidance is likely to cause the child or young person unnecessary suffering or seriously to affect his health or proper development, or (*c*) that certain offences as set out in the first schedule of the Children and Young Persons Act, 1933, now amended by the third schedule of the Sexual Offences Act, 1956, and section 1 (3) of the Indecency with Children Act, 1960, have been committed in respect of him.

The standard with which a magistrates' court is concerned in these cases is to the effect that the court must be satisfied that the child or young person is not receiving such care, protection, or guidance as a good parent may be reasonably expected to give. Further, the court may exercise these powers if it is satisfied that the child or young person is beyond the control of his parent or guardian.

If a juvenile court is satisfied that the above conditions exist it has power (*a*) to order the child or young person to be sent to an approved school, or (*b*) to commit him to the care of a fit person, or (*c*) to order the parent or guardian to enter into a recognisance to exercise proper care and guardianship, or (*d*) to place him for a specified period not to exceed 3 years under supervision, usually of a probation officer or some other person, e.g. a child care officer.

A local authority has a duty to bring before a juvenile court any child or young person residing or found in the district who appears to be in need of care, protection, or control. Where a local authority satisfies the court that a child or young person who is under its care is refractory, and the court thinks it expedient to do so, the court may order the child to an approved school or commit him to the care of a fit person. The provisions relating to orders made concerning the committal of a child or young person to the guardianship of a fit person are to be found in section 84 of the Children and Young Persons Act, 1933. This section also makes provision for the variation or revocation of any such order.

Section 62 of the Children and Young Persons Act, 1933, as amended by the third schedule of the Children and Young Persons Act, 1963, empowers a juvenile court before which a child or young person is brought (other than a person of or over the age of 16 who is or has been married), to direct that he be brought before a juvenile court acting for the petty sessions area in which he resides. If a court before which a child or young person is brought is satisfied that he is in need of care, protection, or control, the court may make a fit person or a supervision order in respect of him, or commit him to an approved school. Unless such an order is discharged it will remain in force in the case of a fit person or approved school order until the child attains the age of 18. In the case of a supervision order, there must be a fixed period which must not exceed 3 years. A fit person is any person whom the court considers suitable for looking after the child or young person and may include a local authority. Should the conditions as required by section 60 of the Mental Health Act, 1959, also be fulfilled in any case, the court may make a hospital order in respect of the child or young person in question.

The procedure relating to care, protection, or control, where the child or young person's parents have commenced matrimonial proceedings, is governed by rules made by the Lord Chancellor (Magistrates' Courts (Matrimonial Proceedings) Rules, 1960).

Where an order is made by a court committing a child or young person to the care of a fit person, or sending him to an approved school, it shall be the duty of the persons specified in section 24 of the Children Act, 1948, to make contributions in respect of him. Such an order is known as a "contribution order" and may be made at the same time as a court makes a fit person or an approved school order, or subsequently by any court of summary jurisdiction in the place where the person charged is for the time residing.

Education Act Cases—School Attendance

A further important aspect of the work of juvenile courts is in connection with the enforcement of school attendance in relation to proceedings which are brought under the Education Acts. Section 37 of the Education Act, 1944, empowers a local authority if it appears to them that the parent of any child of compulsory school age in their area is failing to cause a child to receive full-time education suitable to his age, ability, and aptitude either by regular attendance at school or otherwise, to serve notice on the parent requiring him to satisfy the authority that the child is receiving full-time education. The time within which a parent on whom such a notice has been served must satisfy the local education authority that the child is receiving the necessary education, has to be not less than 14 days from the service of the notice.

If a parent fails so to notify the authority, then the authority shall serve upon the parent a notice known as a "school attendance order" requiring him to cause the child to become a registered pupil at a school named in the order.

The penalties which can be imposed on any person guilty of an offence against section 37 or section 39 of the Education Act, 1944, are set out in section 40 of the Act, as follows: "a fine not exceeding £1 for a first offender, a fine not exceeding £5 in the case of a second offender, and for a third or subsequent offence, a fine not exceeding £10 or one month's imprisonment or both fine and imprisonment."

When a court before which such a prosecution is brought is satisfied that a child in respect of whom the offence is alleged to have been committed has failed to attend regularly at the school at which he is a registered pupil, then the court may direct that the child be brought before a juvenile court which will make an order, if this is considered to be necessary under section 62 of the Children and Young Persons Act, 1933.

If a local education officer is of the opinion that punishment of the parent would not be sufficient to secure the regular attendance of the child at school, it is his duty to apply to the court for an order directing that the child be brought before the juvenile court.

CHAPTER 5

County Courts

County courts Acts — County court judges — Registrars: Jurisdiction of registrars — Practice and procedure — Jurisdiction of county courts — Trial in county court — Default actions — Pleadings in county court actions — Right of appeal — Transfer: From county court to county court; From county court to High Court — Costs — Execution — Judgment summons.

COUNTY COURTS ACTS

The county courts as administered in England and Wales today are entirely the creation of statute law. Their jurisdiction is laid down through the medium of a series of Acts of Parliament which cover almost the whole field of civil law with the exception of divorce and bastardy.

The procedure of these courts is administered by a code of rules which is under constant review by a standing committee of judges, registrars, and practitioners; the actual composition of which is five county court judges and six other persons (two barristers, two solicitors, and two county court registrars (see section 102 (6) County Courts Act, 1959)). The rules themselves are subject to the approval of the Lord Chancellor.

The forerunners of the modern county courts were known as "Courts of Requests" and operated as small-debt courts. At one time their jurisdiction was limited to £2. It was not until the year 1846 that the first of the County Courts Acts was passed.

The main features of the county court system are convenience of venue, simplicity of procedure, summary determination, and, possibly the most important from a litigant's point of view, moderation of expense.

Between 1846 and 1888 a series of County Courts Acts found their way on to the statute books only to be repealed in due course, until in the latter year the County Courts Act, 1888, was enacted. That Act remained as the principal act and was in fact the main statutory pillar of our present county court procedure until it was successively replaced first by the County Courts Act, 1934, then by the County Courts Act, 1959, each of which amended and consolidated the earlier acts.

Before 1846 a county court, the origin of which is somewhat obscure, was invested with power to deal with disputes between parties provided that the amount in dispute did not exceed the sum of £2. As the value of money lessened this court ceased to serve any realistic purpose. The history of the County Courts Acts has shown a gradual increase in the amount over which a county court can claim to have jurisdiction. Thus, whilst the 1846 Act restricted the sum to not more than £20, the 1888 Act extended it to not more than £50.

In 1903 the amount went up to £100, only to be further extended to £200 by section 16 of the Administration of Justice (Miscellaneous Provisions) Act, 1938, and to £400 by section 39 of the County Courts Act, 1959 and, since 1 January 1966, to £500. Whilst the limits restrict the general jurisdiction of county courts, these amounts can be exceeded under special powers laid down by statute, such as Admiralty Salvage where claims may be entertained on property saved to a value as high as £3,500. Besides the County Courts Acts there are also the County Court Rules which regulate the procedure in these courts and which are themselves the subject of statutory authority. The acts and rules may be found in the *County Court Annual Practice*, commonly known as the "Green Book" from the colour of its cover.

In passing it is worthy of note that originally there were special courts for the workers in the tin mines of Devon and Cornwall which were known as the Courts of the Stannaries. The Stannaries Act, 1836, amalgamated these courts into one, and the Supreme Court of Judicature Act, 1873, transferred the powers formerly held by the Lord Warden to the Court of Appeal. Then, as from 1 January 1897 those courts ceased to exist and the county courts of Cornwall were invested with their jurisdiction.

Before proceeding to point out the method of appointment of county court judges, it will be useful to refer to the way in which the country is divided up into districts for the purpose of county court procedure. The number of county courts to be established was originally determined by the County Courts Act, 1846, which also determined where the courts were to be held and over what district each court should extend its jurisdiction. It has, however, to be borne in mind that though they are called county courts the districts into which these courts are divided bear no relation to the county boundaries.

There are at present in England and Wales sixty-three county court districts, whilst the number of county courts is approximately 400. The present general distribution of these districts is defined by the County Court Districts Order, 1949. The responsibility for providing court-houses and offices rests upon the Minister of Works and Buildings. Days of sitting and times during which the court offices are open vary with the district in which the court is situated, due regard being had as to whether it is in a thickly populated area or a rural one.

Although the Act of 1846 was repealed the above factors were confirmed by the County Courts Act, 1934. The Lord Chancellor has complete authority over county courts as to their number and the boundaries of their jurisdiction, as well as regards the places where they are to be held. In this connection the City of London has the Mayor's and City of London Court which deals with county court matters. This Court is equally subject to the statutes and rules which are applicable to all other county courts.

COUNTY COURT JUDGES

Having dealt briefly with the history relating to the introduction of county courts, we can now consider how county court judges are appointed to or removed from the county court bench. As already indicated, the country is divided into various county court districts and there must be at least one judge for each of these districts. The Lord Chancellor, who has complete control over the appointment of the county court judges, can also direct that two judges, or in some cases three judges, in order to cover the greater London area, shall be appointed to a particular district; and he has complete discretion to transfer judges from one district to another.

The total number of judges must not, however, exceed ninety* (section 4 (1), County Courts Act, 1959, and section 5 (2) of the Administration of Justice Act, 1964); and no person may be appointed a county court judge unless he is a barrister of at least 7years' standing. The appointment is made by personal recommendation of the Lord Chancellor to Her Majesty. It is also incumbent on the Lord Chancellor to satisfy himself as regards the health of a proposed county court judge.

Since, however, a county court judge is by virtue of his office qualified to be appointed a commissioner of assize, a justice of the peace, or an official referee, and may also sit in the High Court as a commissioner to deal with divorce cases, it will be seen that these appointments require knowledge of a wide and diverse nature. Bastardy alone remains a matter for the jurisdiction of magistrates' courts.

Section 5 (1) of the Administration of Justice Act, 1964, enables the Lord Chancellor to appoint any county court judge for a district wholly or partly situated in Greater London to act as deputy chairman of the court or courts of Quarter Sessions for one or more of the London commission areas. The total number of county court judges was increased from 80 to 90 (section 5 (2) of the Administration of Justice Act, 1964) and also empowered the Lord Chancellor to assign up to three county court judges to any district situated wholly or partly in any of those areas. The practice has been, since 1 April 1965, when that Act came into operation, for county court judges to be appointed deputy chairmen

* As this book goes to press a Bill is before Parliament providing for an increase to 97.

for a period of one month or more at a time; and every judge so assigned is by virtue of his office a justice of the peace for each of those areas and therefore does not have to take the statutory oaths relative to a justice of the peace, since he is already one by virtue of his appointment to the county court bench.

A county court judge is entitled to the official designation "His Honour Judge ——" and on retirement can have "His Honour" before his name. Solicitors and barristers who appear before judges at county courts must therefore address them as "Your Honour", save in the Mayor's and City of London Court, where, by tradition, the judge is addressed as "My Lord". The salary of a county court judge is paid out of a parliamentary grant and has recently been fixed at £5775 per annum. The normal retiring age for county court judges is 72, but the Lord Chancellor, if he thinks it desirable, may extend this from time to time up to the age of 75.

County court judges enjoy a graduated pension, but cannot receive the full benefits of such a pension unless they have completed 15 years' service.

A deputy can be appointed by the judge in the event of illness or unavoidable absence, but the Lord Chancellor must be notified immediately. Such an appointment is limited to 14 days except with the Lord Chancellor's approval. The remuneration of a deputy is a matter for the Lord Chancellor with the approval of the Treasury.

Finally, the Lord Chancellor may remove a judge for inability or misbehaviour.

REGISTRARS

In addition to the judge who is allocated to it by the Lord Chancellor, each county court district has a registrar who is also appointed by the Lord Chancellor. The qualification in this case is that of a solicitor of not less than 7 years' standing (section 18, County Courts Act, 1959). A registrar may be appointed for two or more districts, or in the case of a populous district, two persons may be appointed jointly.

The Lord Chancellor, if he thinks it expedient to do so, may, taking into account the amount of business to be performed by the registrar, rule that he shall not directly or indirectly engage in practice as a solicitor or carry on any employment which would prevent him from properly performing his duties as registrar. Such a registrar then becomes "a whole-time registrar", or in the case of an assistant registrar "a whole-time assistant registrar".

A registrar may with the approval of the judge appoint a deputy to act for him in case of illness or unavoidable absence. The qualification of 7 years' standing as a solicitor is also applicable to any such appointment. The power to appoint as many assistant registrars as he considers necessary is given to the Lord Chancellor by virtue of the provisions of section 19 of the Act of 1959. All such appointments are, however, subject to the concurrence of the Treasury.

The conditions of employment of registrars are similar to those which apply to county court judges, and the Lord Chancellor has power to remove them from office. The normal retirement age for registrars is 72, but here again the Lord Chancellor has the power to extend this from time to time up to 75 years.

Jurisdiction of Registrars

Before turning to consider the much wider question of practice and procedure in county courts, it is well to point out that whilst the judge is the main dispenser of cases dealt with in these courts, the registrar is endowed under the county court rules with a restricted right of dealing with disputed claims in connection with matters that do not exceed £30.

Since, however, the greater portion of a registrar's duties are carried out as a preliminary to or consequent upon court decisions, it will be helpful to refer briefly to some of these duties. It has to be remembered that all such duties are imposed under the county court rules which have statutory authority. Certain of these duties a registrar performs personally but others are carried out by clerks, bailiffs, and other officers who are appointed for this specific purpose.

First of all a registrar has to keep records of court proceedings in a manner as prescribed by the Lord Chancellor. In order to give the exact nature and details of all these administrative and executive duties it would be necessary to refer at length to the county court rules. Since, however, it is not the purpose of this book to go into such details, it is only necessary to make a passing reference to them. They include the issue and service of summonses, the preparation and service of every judgment of the court, the execution of warrants, and orders of commitment.

While a registrar has a limited jurisdiction, as already referred to, there is a right of appeal to the judge with regard to any judgment or order given by a registrar. The registrar is the taxing officer of a county court, and here again the judge may review his taxation. A registrar also has to account for all fees, penalties, forfeitures, and fines which have to be paid to him, together with any monies ordered to be paid into court.

The appointment of such additional officers as clerks, bailiffs, ushers, and messengers is a matter for the Lord Chancellor to determine, and he may direct what duties they are to perform; but the numbers of persons appointed and their salaries are subject to the concurrence of the Treasury.

Having thus briefly referred to the appointments of county court judges, registrars, and other members of the staff who are required in order to carry out the work of a county court, we now consider the practice and procedure of these courts.

PRACTICE AND PROCEDURE

The most modern of the statutes dealing with county court procedure and practice are the County Courts Act, 1959, and the County Courts (Jurisdiction) Act, 1963, which increased the jurisdiction of county courts in claims relating to land.

As it has already been seen, the jurisdiction of a county court has certain territorial limits. The requirements are that the cause of action should have arisen wholly or in part within the district of the court, or that the defendant should reside or carry on business within the district. Equally, being of statutory creation, its jurisdiction is limited by the statutes which lay down the scope of its powers, both for the types of action and the financial limits of the claims that it may hear.

In the course of time many matters have been expressly assigned by statute to the county court which do not fall within its general jurisdiction, and these form an important part of its business. It is, however, outside the scope of this book to describe these matters in detail. The importance of this aspect of county court jurisdiction can be illustrated by mentioning some of the concerns which fall within the special jurisdiction of county courts—the adoption of children; legitimacy; guardianship of infants; leases of business premises under the Landlord and Tenant Act, 1954; the Rent Restrictions Acts; housing; hire purchase; winding up of small companies and disputes between husband and wife under the Married Women's Property Act, 1882. This list will give some idea of the diversity and complexity of the work of the county courts and the very important part they play today in the administration of civil justice.

JURISDICTION OF COUNTY COURTS

The general jurisdiction of the county courts follows broadly that of the Queen's Bench and Chancery Divisions of the High Court, except that actions for libel, slander, seduction, and breach of promise of marriage are excluded, and a limit is set to the sum which may be recovered in these courts. In actions in contract and tort the limit is now £500. If, however, the parties agree in writing that action for a greater amount should be brought in the county court, then there is no restriction on the amount which may be claimed or awarded.

Where the cause of action exceeds the limit above which an action cannot be tried in a county court, a plaintiff may abandon his claim to any amount in excess of that limit, and the county court will then have jurisdiction to hear and determine the action. Once abandoned, however, he cannot revive the abandoned portion of his claim, nor can he recover costs other than those attached to the residue of his claim which is dealt with by the county court.

In actions concerning land, which mainly comprise "possession actions", i.e. actions by landlords to recover possession of houses, the limit of jurisdiction is that the net annual value for rating should not exceed £400; and in equitable matters such as proceedings in relation to trusts, mortgages, partnerships, and maintenance of infants, county courts have the equitable powers of the High Court but jurisdiction is limited to those cases where the amount involved does not exceed £500.

In contentious probate matters the county court of the district in which the testator had his last place of residence has jurisdiction where the estate at the time of the testator's death was worth less than £1000 after deducting funeral expenses, debts, and encumbrances. Some county courts outside London also have jurisdiction in bankruptcy and over the winding up of small companies.

Some county courts have Admiralty jurisdiction to a limited extent. The limitation in salvage claims is restricted to the value of the property salvaged which must not exceed £3500, and in all other claims £1000. Finally, county courts have no jurisdiction to try any action in which the title to any toll, fair, market, or franchise is in question.

The jurisdiction of the county court over transferred actions is dealt with later.

The Matrimonial Causes Act, 1967, empowers county court judges to try undefended matrimonial causes and also gives jurisdiction for ancillary relief for protection of children.

TRIAL IN COUNTY COURT

There is one further matter relating to the jurisdiction of county courts to be referred to—the right of trial by jury. Of recent years this practice has tended to become extremely rare. A jury in a county court consists of eight persons.

In all proceedings in a county court, trial must be without a jury unless the court orders otherwise on an application by any party to the proceedings. The application must be made in the manner and time prescribed as laid down in the County Court Rules, 1936, order 21, rule 1, that is by notice of application, which must be given not less than 10 clear days before the return day (the day appointed for the appearance of the defendant or for the hearing of the proceedings); but if it is not so given the judge or registrar may postpone the trial in order to allow a jury to be summoned.

In any event a trial in a county court shall be without a jury in the following cases:

(*a*) Admiralty proceedings;
(*b*) proceedings under the Rent and Mortgage Interest Restrictions Acts, 1920–39; the Rent Act, 1957; or the Rent Act, 1965; and
(*c*) any appeal to the county court under the Housing Act, 1957.

Where, however, the court is satisfied on an application for trial by jury, either that a charge of fraud against the party making the application is in issue, or a claim in respect of libel, slander, malicious prosecution, false imprisonment, seduction, or breach of promise, the court shall order trial by jury; unless it is of the opinion that the trial requires prolonged examination of documents which cannot be conveniently done with a jury.

It is the registrar's duty to summon a jury, the number to be summoned being sixteen, of whom eight will be empanelled for the purpose of a trial (section 96, County Courts Act, 1959). Any party to the proceedings has a right of challenge to a juror similar to that pertaining to a trial in the High Court. Finally, the verdict of the jury must be unanimous.

As already stated, the county court is intended to provide a relatively inexpensive forum for the trial of actions, and therefore its rules are drafted with this always in mind. That does not mean to say that the most fundamental rules have been dispensed with. For example, it is still necessary for the parties to make known to each other the nature of their respective cases by pleadings, albeit very often in a simpler form than that used in the High Court.

DEFAULT ACTIONS

The commencement of proceedings will differ according to whether the action is an ordinary action or what is termed "a default action", that is, an action for a liquidated sum in which the plaintiff believes that the defendant is unlikely to dispute his claim.

As the latter type of case forms a high proportion of county court actions, it is clearly desirable to have a special form with which to commence the action in order to avoid unnecessary expense. Frequently all that the defendant wishes to do is to admit his debt and to be allowed to pay it off by instalments, and this the court has power to order if the parties cannot agree. Consequently, the intended plaintiff can obtain from the court a special printed form of praecipe (this being the document which initiates the proceedings), which he completes by giving particulars of the parties and the nature and amount of his claim and costs. Following upon this the court will issue a default summons and serve it on the defendant. The summons will call on the defendant within 8 days either to pay the sum claimed and the costs or to file a defence admission or counterclaim, and warn him that if he does not do any of these things judgment may be obtained and enforced against him.

If the defendant fails to take any of these steps within the 8 days the plaintiff may obtain another form of praecipe from the court and enter his judgment. It frequently happens, however, that the defendant will admit the claim and ask for time to pay by instalments. The plaintiff may accept the defendant's proposal as to mode of payment, whereupon the registrar enters judgment accordingly. If the plaintiff does not do this, the registrar fixes a day when he decides upon the date of payment or the instalments by which payment is to be made, and enters judgment accordingly. On failure to comply with a money judgment, the defendant may be brought before the court for his financial means to be examined if the plaintiff so desires, under a judgment summons, and this form of procedure is commonly used against reluctant debtors. Where a debtor persistently defaults in paying his instalments under a judgment the court may make a "Committal order" which orders that unless the debtor pays the instalments he will be committed to prison. It is not unusual to find in a county court a list of fifty or more judgment summonses to be heard in one day, many of them for hire purchase debts. The procedure is referred to later under the heading "Execution".

PLEADINGS IN COUNTY COURT ACTIONS

In the case of ordinary actions the procedure closely resembles that in the High Court described in a later chapter.

Where the parties are legally represented, the pleadings may be as fully comprehensive as High Court pleadings. The plaintiff will deliver to the defendant a statement of his case entitled "particulars of claim", and the defendant will similarly deliver his written defence (and counterclaim, if any). There is provision in the rules whereby interlocutory steps may be ordered or permitted to be taken. These may include payment of monies into court, discovery, orders for further and better particulars of the pleadings, and third-party proceedings in order to bring in further parties.

Not infrequently, however, the parties are not legally represented, and in these cases the issues will often be set out in the printed forms supplied by the court. These are, firstly, the praecipe, of which there are several types to suit the kind of action which is being brought. The plaintiff, as already mentioned, completes this form by giving particulars of the parties and of his claim; he then takes or posts it to the court office, with two copies of his particulars of claim, i.e. a document specifying his cause of action and the pecuniary or other claim which he seeks to establish, together with the appropriate fee. The court will then issue to the plaintiff a plaint note which is his authorization to proceed with the action, and which gives him instructions as to his rights. At the same time the court will issue a summons fixing the date, time, and place of the hearing, also annexing one of the copies of the particulars of claim. Although service may be effected otherwise, it is the usual practice for the bailiff of the court to serve the summons on the defendant personally. If there is reason to believe that he is avoiding service, the court may order service by other means. The leave of the court must be obtained if service is to be made abroad.

On receipt of service the defendant should within 8 days complete and return to the court the form delivered to him with the summons stating whether he contests or admits the claim. If he is contesting it, it will generally be in his interest for him to file a proper defence. He may also make a payment into court which may have the effect of saving him costs in the event that judgment is given against him. The rules do not oblige him to deliver a defence before the hearing, but he may be ordered to pay any costs caused by his failure to do so.

Application may be made by either party in the course of the proceedings either *ex parte* or on one day's notice, and such applications are heard by the registrar, subject to an appeal to the judge.

The conduct of the trial regarding procedure and evidence are essentially the same as in a case heard in the High Court. The judge is responsible for the arrangement of the business of the court. Parties may appear in person or be represented either by a solicitor or counsel.

RIGHT OF APPEAL

An unsuccessful party has a right of appeal in all cases decided by the registrar, to the judge; and from a decision of the judge, his appeal lies to the Court of Appeal which has power to (*a*) order a retrial, (*b*) order judgment to be entered for either party, or (*c*) to make a final order to ensure the determination of the matter on the merits of the real question between the parties.

Any party to any proceedings in the county court who is dissatisfied with the judge's direction or determination on a point of law or equity, may appeal to the Court of Appeal without leave in the majority of cases.

However, in all cases where the claim is founded in contract or tort (excepting where the claim is for the recovery of land or where the title to a hereditament is in issue), and the amount of the claim at the time of the issue of the plaint did not exceed £20, leave to appeal is necessary. Any party to county court proceedings also has a right of appeal to the Court of Appeal on questions of fact where the claim is for the recovery of land of net annual value for rating in excess of £60, or for relief which includes a claim in tort or contract for an amount over £200. There are other cases where an appeal lies without leave on a question of fact. These are set out in the County Courts Act, 1959, but for these exceptions, and those set out above, leave to appeal on questions of fact has to be obtained.

It is incumbent on a county court judge when requested to do so by either party in an action which is being tried by him, to take a written note during the course of the hearing; and he is bound to furnish a note of any question of law raised at the hearing of the facts given in the course of the evidence, and of his decision and determination in the matter.

TRANSFER

From County Court to County Court

Transfer may be made from one county court to another—from a county court to the High Court, and from the High Court to a county court. Each transfer requires separate consideration, as the choice of venue is one which may affect costs and a wrong decision may penalize the litigant. This point is explained more fully under the heading "Costs".

Transfer from a county court may be made where the action has been commenced in a court which has no jurisdiction to try it, to a court having such jurisdiction; or, exceptionally it may be retained. Transfer may also be ordered where the judge has any interest in the subject matter of the action or where the judge or an official of the court is a party.

Apart from this, an action may be transferred where the circumstances justify or require it. This involves an important exercise of judicial discretion as the parties may have widely divergent views as to where the action should be tried and each may choose his "home ground". In such cases the court will have to decide where the balance of convenience and hardship lies.

From County Court to High Court

Under certain circumstances a plaintiff in an action in contract or tort has a right to have his action transferred from a county court to the High Court. This right can only be exercised provided that the judge is satisfied that there is reasonable ground for doing so. Frequently the grounds are that the amount recoverable may exceed the county court limit.

Likewise, a defendant has a right to have an action which is founded on contract or tort in which the plaintiff claims no more than £40 transferred to the High Court provided that he (*a*) gives security for the amount claimed and costs up to £450, the amount of which has to be approved by the registrar, and (*b*) that the judge certifies that in his opinion some important question of law or fact is likely to arise.

A county court has, however, jurisdiction to try counterclaims without any restriction as to the amount involved, or involving a claim otherwise outside its jurisdiction (e.g. libel or slander), unless application is made by any party to have either the whole proceedings or the counterclaim transferred to the High Court. If transfer is effected to the High Court on the counterclaim only, and judgment has already been given for the plaintiff in the county court, execution must then be stayed pending the hearing of the counterclaim.

Similar rights apply to the transfer of actions of contract and tort from the High Court to the county court. Further, in an action founded on tort a defendant may, if he can show by means of an affidavit sworn by himself or by some other person on his behalf, that the plaintiff has no visible means to pay the costs of the action in the event that judgment is not given in his favour, the defendant can apply to have the action transferred to a county court unless the defendant furnishes security for costs. The county court is not limited in these circumstances by the amount it may award.

COSTS

Perhaps one of the most difficult points that the practitioner has to decide in advising a plaintiff in actions in tort and contract where the claim is in the region of £400 is whether he should commence his action in the High Court or in the county court. Where the value of the claim is clearly below £75 the choice is comparatively simple because the rules provide that the successful plaintiff who recovers less than £75 in the High Court, unless his case has been transferred to an official referee, will be awarded no costs. If he recovers more than £75 but less than £400 he will be awarded only such costs as he would have been awarded had he brought his action in the county court, but as the amount at stake is not always the only criterion for judging the importance of the case, the trial judge has discretion as to whether he should be awarded costs on the High Court scale. Hence, the decision is of considerable importance financially, and has to be considered and reviewed as the action proceeds with a view to transfer from the High Court to the county court or vice versa should it appear necessary (see County Courts Jurisdiction Order, 1965).

In certain circumstances where the claim is for a liquidated amount of more than £40 but less than the county court limit a plaintiff may recover High Court costs. The usual circumstances are where the plaintiff obtains judgment under Order 14 before a master of the High Court or where he obtains judgment in default of appearance or defence by the defendant, or the defendant pays the amount claimed or not less than £40 within the time limit stated by the court. These are not the only matters which affect costs, but they deserve mention as they clearly have an important bearing on the matter.

The successful party then has to take steps in order to recover his costs, and within 14 days of the delivery of the judgment in his favour, he should lodge his bill of costs together with vouchers. The processes by which the amount can be recovered are then set in motion, and these will be referred to under the sub-title of "Execution".

There are four scales of costs which are applicable to actions dealt with by the county courts. It is not necessary to set out the details of each scale; it is sufficient only to refer broadly to the classification of these scales. Thus scale 1 is applicable to actions which involve amounts of over £2 but not exceeding £10; scale 2 covers amounts which exceed £10 but do not exceed £30; scale 3 applies to amounts that exceed £30 and do not exceed £100; and scale 4 covers amounts that exceed £100. In proceedings where no scale is prescribed the judge has a complete discretion. As already indicated, the registrar is the taxing master for county courts, but an aggrieved party has the right to claim to have his taxation reviewed by the judge.

EXECUTION

There are various means open to a judgment creditor by which he can enforce a judgment in his favour. He may do so by execution against the debtor's goods, in which event the registrar will issue a warrant of execution.

In the event that payment has been ordered by instalments, execution cannot be issued until after the default in payment of some instalment according to the order. The warrant must be endorsed with the total amount to be levied. If the amount due together with the fees thereon is paid before the actual sale of the goods and chattels, such goods and chattels shall be discharged and set at liberty.

Goods which may not be seized are wearing apparel, bedding, and the tools and implements of the debtor's trade to the prescribed value, namely £50 (see section 37 (2) Administration of Justice Act, 1956). The warrant of execution authorizes the seizure of any money, banknotes, bills of exchange, promissory notes, bonds, specialities or securities for money belonging to the debtor (see Protection from Execution (Prescribed Value) Order, 1963). Until the sale, goods seized in execution shall be left in a safe place.

Penalties for persons rescuing or attempting to rescue goods seized are laid down in section 127 of the County Courts Act, 1959, and these include power of a county court judge to commit to prison for a period not exceeding one month.

Goods seized must not be sold for a period of at least 5 days following the day of seizure unless they are of a perishable nature or the person whose goods are seized so requests in writing. The sale can be effected only by brokers or appraisers appointed under the Act, who are appointed from time to time by the registrar. Unless otherwise ordered by the court, sales under execution must be public.

When a writ from the High Court and a warrant are issued from a county court in relation to goods of the same person, the right to seizure is determined by the priority of the time of delivery of the writ or of the application to the registrar. A warrant of execution issued by a county court in one district may be sent to the registrar of any other county court within the jurisdiction of which the goods and chattels are believed to be.

A sum standing to the credit of a person in a deposit account in a bank shall be attachable, but this does not apply to Post Office Savings Bank accounts, Trustee Savings Bank accounts, or Savings Bank accounts. An alternative step to the above is for the creditor to enforce his judgment by means of a judgment summons with a view to committal under the Debtors Act, 1869.

JUDGMENT SUMMONS

If a debtor fails to appear on a county court judgment summons on the day and time fixed for hearing, the judge may adjourn the judgment summons to another specified time and date and order the debtor to attend then. If a debtor so ordered to attend fails to do so, the judge may make an order committing him to prison for a period not exceeding 14 days.

Other possible means of execution are by warrant of attachment for breach of injunction or undertaking; or by garnishee proceedings which, in effect, means a creditor taking proceedings to obtain payment to him of the amount owed to the judgment debtor from any other person.

CHAPTER 6

The High Court of Justice

Effects of the Judicature Acts — Rules of the Supreme Court — Divisions of the High Court — Divisional courts — The judges — Official referees — Officials of the court: Masters; Registrars — Mental Health Act. 1959 — Restrictive practices court — Organization: The judges; The masters and registrars — Jurisdiction — Types of civil action — Contract — Tort — Law of property — Allocation of business — Table showing qualifications for offices in the High Court.

EFFECTS OF THE JUDICATURE ACTS

In Chapter 1 a description has been given of the superior courts existing prior to 1873, but it is well to review at this stage the position as it was then.

There were far too many courts of first instance—no fewer than seven, excluding the assize courts. These were the three common law courts, the Queen's Bench, the Common Pleas, Exchequer, the Chancery Court and the Admiralty, Probate, Divorce and Matrimonial Causes courts. The conflict between law as administered in the common law courts and equity in the chancery court still existed, although not to its former extent, and the limits of the jurisdiction of the courts was difficult to find. Further, the system was unnecessarily complex and unwieldy.

The same could be said of the appellate courts, the principal of which were the Court of Exchequer Chamber to hear common law appeals and the Court of Appeal in Chancery to hear chancery appeals. In addition to these, appeals from the Admiralty Court and in lunacy lay to the Judicial Committee of the Privy Council, and there were also other chancery appeal courts of limited jurisdiction.

The Supreme Court of Judicature Act, 1873, made the first step in the reorganization of the courts into the system which exists today. It abolished the courts referred to above and established a Supreme Court of Judicature consisting of the Court of Appeal and the High Court of Justice, vesting in the Court of Appeal most of the appellate jurisdiction of the appeal courts referred to above. It also divided the High Court into five divisions, namely the Chancery, Queen's Bench, Common Pleas, Exchequer, and Probate, Divorce, and Admiralty divisions.

Moreover, the Act provided that the rules of equity should prevail over the common law rules in the event of conflict between the two, and that in future the judges of all divisions should give effect to both sets of rules where applicable. In this way both sets of rules were preserved, but the litigant no longer had to choose between exercising his rights at common law or seeking the discretionary relief of chancery; or perhaps having to pursue each in separate courts. Henceforth he could obtain all the remedies of the old common law courts and the old chancery court in the one court.

Furthermore, it was often fatal to a litigant before 1873–75 if he commenced his action in the wrong court. After the Judicature Acts, 1873–75, if he started in the wrong division his case would be transferred to the right one.

As we shall see later, although all divisions have jurisdiction to try any matter within the jurisdiction of the High Court, for practical reasons some matters are specifically allocated to a particular division because its judges and officials are well versed in that matter and the procedure and machinery are geared to deal with it.

In 1881 the Queen's Bench, Common Pleas, and Exchequer divisions were consolidated into the Queen's Bench Division, and the basis of the High Court was then almost complete.

The effects of the earlier statutes were re-enacted and consolidated in the Supreme Court of Judicature (Consolidation) Act, 1925; and although some amendments have been made since, it is mainly by virtue of the provisions of this Act that the administration of justice in the Supreme Court as it is administered today is regulated.

RULES OF THE SUPREME COURT

As we have already observed, rules play a vitally important part in any common law system, and our system is no exception. The Rules of the Supreme Court, revised and brought up to date in 1965, embody the code of practice and procedure which guides and governs the course of proceedings in the Supreme Court. They are practical rules for the guidance of practitioners and are born of centuries of experience. They were formulated first in the Common Law Procedure Acts of 1852 to 1860 and the Chancery Amendment Act of 1858; and later reformed by the Judicature Acts of 1873 and 1875. The former Act, authorizing the making of the rules, has since been amended by the Administration of Justice Act, 1925.

The rules therefore carry statutory authority and are amended from time to time to meet the changing circumstances since the first set of rules were laid down in 1883—"the 1883 rules". The rules are not a fully comprehensive code like the Code Napoléon is in France; and, indeed, section 103 of the Judicature (Consolidation) Act of 1925 expressly provides that:

> Save as is otherwise provided by this Act or by Rules of Court, forms and methods of procedure which, under or by virtue of any law, custom, general order or rules whatsoever were formally enforced in any of the courts the jurisdiction of which is vested in the High Court or the Court of Appeal respectively and which are not inconsistent with this Act or with Rules of Court, may continue to be used in the High Court and the Court of Appeal respectively.

It will thus be seen that an understanding of the rules is fundamental for every practitioner engaged in litigious work. The rules are divided and subdivided into orders and rules respectively, and an idea of the complexity of the subject can be given by the fact that there are no less than 109 orders alone and that the *Annual Practice* (White Book) in which they are at present contained, together with annotations, decided cases and statutes relevant to procedure, covers approximately 4000 pages. It is usual when referring to an order and rule of the Rules of Supreme Court to designate it thus: "O. 14, r. 1 R.S.C.". They will be described in this way thereafter.

DIVISIONS OF THE HIGH COURT

The Judicature Acts of 1925 and 1944 laid down that the High Court should be constituted of the Lord Chancellor, the Lord Chief Justice, the President of the Probate Division, and the puisne judges, the latter being styled "Justices of the High Court".

Resulting from the reforms laid down in the various Acts referred to above the High Court itself now consists of three divisions: the Chancery Division, composed of the Lord Chancellor and not less than five puisne judges; the Queen's Bench Division, consisting of the Lord Chief Justice and not less than seventeen puisne judges; and the Probate, Divorce, and Admiralty Division, consisting of a president and not less than three puisne judges.

From the ranks of the Queen's Bench judges there is drawn one judge to hear commercial cases, such as disputes about shipping transactions and insurance. This court, which is known as the Commercial Court, has in fact no greater jurisdiction than any other court of the Queen's Bench Division, but its judge is customarily a former barrister versed in commercial law, and its procedure has been adapted to meet commercial requirements to some extent.

Again, while not a separate division of the High Court, there was created in 1956 by the Restrictive Trade Practices Act, a new court to deal with agreements containing restrictions as to prices, or quantities, or qualities of goods or methods of distribution, and to determine whether they are in the public interest or not. This court consists of five judges, three being puisne judges of the High Court, one from the Court of Sessions of Scotland, and one from the Supreme Court of Northern Ireland. One of these judges is selected by the Lord Chancellor as President. In addition, the Crown may, on the recommendation of the Lord Chancellor, appoint not more than ten suitably qualified lay persons to sit with the presiding judge as part of the tribunal.

DIVISIONAL COURTS

The Chancery, Queen's Bench, and the Probate, Divorce, and Admiralty Divisions each has its own appellate courts to hear appeals from the decisions of inferior courts in matters which are the particular province of the division. These are known as divisional courts and are presided over by at least two judges. The Queen's Bench Divisional Court usually sits with three judges and has original jurisdiction over the prerogative orders of mandamus, certiorari, and prohibition and over the grant of *habeas corpus* apart from its appellate jurisdiction.

The Chancery Divisional Court deals with bankruptcy appeals from county courts while the Divorce Divisional Court deals with appeals from magistrates in matrimonial disputes.

THE JUDGES

The judges of the High Court are the Lord Chancellor, the Lord Chief Justice, the President of the Probate, Divorce, and Admiralty Division, and the puisne judges. The Judicature Act of 1925 enacted that there must be at least 25 and not more than 32 puisne judges. The Lord Chancellor is empowered to attach these puisne judges to any one of the three divisions, although they may be required to sit in any other division or in the Court of Appeal.

It is interesting to note that between the years 1944 and 1964, the maximum number of puisne judges who could be appointed was raised by various stages from the above-mentioned figure of 32 to that of 56. Whereas the Judicature (Amendment) Act, 1944, retained the minimum and maximum numbers as laid down in the 1925 Act, the latter Act also contained a proviso which had the effect of simplifying the procedure under which these minima and maxima were to be determined by the Lord Chancellor with the concurrence of the Treasury. The principle laid down was that the minimum number should not be exceeded unless the state of business of the High Court as a whole required it.

The increases to the maximum number of such appointments that became statutorily permissible during the following two decades clearly illustrate the enormous increase in the business of the High Court throughout that period. This increase covers both civil and criminal jurisdiction.

Thus the first increase to the statutory maximum was enacted by section 49 of the Patents and Designs Act, 1949, which made provision for the appointment of one additional puisne judge, raising the maximum number to 33. In the year 1950 section 1 of the High Court and County Court Judges Act of that year further increased the maximum to 39 by allowing for the appointment of an additional 6 puisne judges. The next increase was by virtue of the provisions of section 32 of the Restrictive Trade Practices Act, 1956, which authorized a further addition of 3 puisne judges, as already mentioned, increasing the maximum number to 42. In 1960 section 6 (1) and the second schedule of the Administration of Justice (Judges and Pensions) Act, 1960, further increased the maximum number to 48 by providing for yet a further 6 additional puisne judges. The Criminal Justice Administration Act, 1962, again raised the maximum number to 53, and, finally, section 9 of the Resale Prices Act, 1964, enacted a maximum figure of 56*.

Whilst the High Court was kept busy with its civil jurisdiction, the main reason for these continued increases was the general increase in crime throughout the country which resulted in bigger calendars of crime which had to be dealt with at the assize courts. Two factors emerged from this increase in criminal work. Since the time which was available for assize court work was necessarily limited, it was found that in order to deal with the urgent criminal

* As this book goes to press a Bill is before Parliament providing for an increase to 70.

work, no time remained in which to dispose of the civil work. It also became necessary for more than one judge to be sent to the various assizes. This resulted in a hold up of the work in the Supreme Court in London.

Puisne judges are appointed by the Crown by letters patent, and it is now invariable practice for the sovereign to bestow the accolade of knighthood on each puisne judge on his appointment to the bench. The necessary qualification for such an appointment is that of a barrister of not less than 10 years' standing, and for appointment as a Lord Justice of Appeal, or a Justice of the Court of Appeal, a puisne judge or a barrister of not less than 15 years' standing. Any person qualified for appointment as a Lord Justice of Appeal, or a Justice of the Court of Appeal qualifies for appointment as Lord Chief Justice, Master of the Rolls, or President of the Probate, Divorce, and Admiralty Division.

All judges of the High Court, whatever their rank, are addressed in court as "My Lord" and the official prefix to their title is as follows: For a puisne judge, "the Honourable Mr. Justice"; and for the Lord Chancellor, the Lord Chief Justice, the Master of the Rolls, the President of the Probate, Divorce, and Admiralty Division, the Lords of Appeal in Ordinary and Lords Justices of the Court of Appeal, "the Right Honourable".

OFFICIAL REFEREES

There is one further class of judicial appointment to the Supreme Court to which reference should be made at this point, namely the official referees. Section 9 of the Administration of Justice Act, 1956, empowers Her Majesty to appoint persons to be official referees, and there are three such persons appointed at the present time. Official referees are persons by whom, on the application of any party interested in a cause or matter in the Chancery or Queen's Bench divisions, other than a criminal proceeding by the Crown, the court or a judge may order that the matter be tried with or without assessors. Official referees bear the title "judge" and their particular function is to deal with complicated and prolonged matters such as building contract disputes.

OFFICIALS OF THE COURT

We have dealt with the highest judicial appointments of the Supreme Court under the sub-heading of "The Judges", and will now refer to the various other officials and officers who are required in order to carry out the administration of justice in the three divisions of the High Court.

Masters

The first important group that it is proposed to deal with are the masters. It is important to point out that these masters are distinct from the masters of the bench or "benchers" of the four Inns of Court, who are elected within their Inns. There are eight masters of the Queen's Bench Division of the High Court, the senior of whom holds the additional appointment of Queen's Remembrancer. These masters are appointed by the Lord Chancellor, the Lord Chief Justice, and the Master of the Rolls by agreement among themselves. The main duties of the Queen's Bench masters are to control and superintend the Central Office of the Supreme Court, to carry on judicial work in chambers, and to issue directions on points of practice. Three masters sit daily in chambers and their decisions are subject to an appeal to a judge. There is also the Queen's Coroner and Attorney and Master of the Crown Office together with an Assistant Master who are attached to the Queen's Bench Division. There is also an additional appointment as Secretary to the Masters.

To become a master of the Queen's Bench Division one must be a barrister of not less than 10 years' standing, an official referee, or a master in lunacy.

There are also eight masters of the Chancery Division of the High Court who exercise similar jurisdiction to that of the Queen's Bench masters. In their case the qualification is to be a practising solicitor of not less than 10 years' standing, or a taxing master or the official solicitor to the Supreme Court.

In addition to the above-mentioned masters there are eleven masters of the Supreme Court (Taxing Office), one of whom sits daily to deal with short and urgent taxations of costs, while the remainder deal with cases as they are referred to them. The appointment of a taxing master is made bv the Lord Chancellor with the concurrence of the Treasury. The qualification for such an appointment is that of a practising solicitor of not less than 10 years' standing or a solicitor who has held one of certain appointments for the requisite period of time. All taxations of bills of costs, whether in the Chancery or Queen's Bench Division, are now dealt with in the department of the Central Office known as the Supreme Court Taxing Office.

In the Queen's Bench Division there is also the Crown Office and Associates Department which consists of a master holding the offices of Queen's Coroner and Attorney and Master of the Crown Office, one assistant master, a clerk of the lists (Queen's Bench Division), a head clerk, chief associate, and sixteen associates. The duties of the associates are to sit in court in this division under the judges and be responsible for keeping the court records and drawing up the orders of the court.

Registrars

In the Probate, Divorce, and Admiralty Division there are, as its title implies, three different species of cause or action to be dealt with.

The first two, Divorce and Probate, are grouped together in one department. In London this is the Principal Probate Registry and Divorce Registry. At the present time there is one chief registrar and other registrars carrying out the dual functions of Probate and Divorce Registrars. The qualifications required are that they must be either a practising barrister or solicitor of not less than 10 years' standing or a district probate registrar of not less than 5 years' standing, or have served for not less than 10 years as a clerk in the Principal Registry.

The Admiralty section of the Division is quite distinct from the others. As the name of the Court—Admiralty and Prize Court—suggests, it is concerned solely with maritime matters and its affairs are looked after by a department known as the Admiralty Registry and Marshal's Office and Registry of the Prize Court. The principal officials under the president are the registrar, marshal, and the chief clerk; the qualification for the former is that he must be a barrister or solicitor of 10 years' standing. There are also four nautical assessors whose function is to sit with the president and advise him on technical matters.

In addition to the masters and registrars who have been mentioned already, there are other officials not perhaps well known to the public to whom reference should be made. For instance, the Companies Courts and the Bankruptcy Court have each three chancery judges who preside, and to them are assigned such matters as the winding-up of limited companies and bankruptcy. The former court has one registrar, the latter three. In either case the qualification is that of a barrister or a solicitor of not less than 10 years' standing. Moreover, the Chancery Division has its own Registrar's Office which is staffed by a chief registrar and four other registrars.

Below all these are a number of principal clerks, secretaries, and clerks, who are seldom recognized, but whose important part in the administration of civil justice should not be overlooked. There are, for example, examiners of the court who are empowered to examine witnesses on oath in all divisions; conveyancing counsel, and last but vitally important, are the ushers of the courts, recognizable by their stuff robes, who help to keep "order in court". They also administer the oath to witnesses and keep an eye on members of the general public who visit the High Court.

As the jurisdiction of the High Court extends over the whole of England and Wales, there are also a number of district registries in the major centres of population which deal with interlocutory matters in a similar way to the masters and registrars of the High Court. The principal officer of the District Registry is the district registrar and his qualification requires that he must either be a registrar of a county court or a solicitor of not less than 7 years' standing. In practice he will often be found to be the county court registrar acting in both capacities.

The picture would not be complete without making reference to some of the less well-known aspects of the work of the High Court which, although not strictly High Court work, are carried on under the judges.

Although the purpose of the present study is to deal primarily with the administration of civil justice, it is necessary to refer very briefly to the Registrar of Criminal Appeals Office of the Supreme Court in order to complete the picture with regard to High Court appointments. This office which, as its name implies, deals with appeals in criminal proceedings, consists of a registrar, an assistant registrar, and three deputy assistant registrars—who must all be barristers of not less than 5 years' standing, and are appointed by the Lord Chief Justice.

There is the Courts Martial Appeal Office which also deals with criminal matters. The judges who hear these matters now are the "*ex-officio* and ordinary judges of the Court of Appeal and such of the judges of the Queen's Bench Division of the High Court as the Lord Chief Justice may, after consultation with the Master of the Rolls, from time to time nominate for the purpose" (section 1 (1) of the Courts Martial (Appeals) Act, 1951, as amended by the first schedule to the Criminal Appeal Act, 1966). The staff here consists of a registrar, an assistant registrar, and a chief clerk.

A superintendent is appointed to the Scrivener's Department.

We come now to the two chief legal advisory departments of the High Court, namely the Official Solicitor's Department and the Law Officers' Department. The former consists of the official solicitor, an assistant solicitor, four senior legal assistants, two legal assistants and a staff of chief, senior principal, and principal clerks; whilst the latter consists of the Attorney-General, his parliamentary private secretary, the Solicitor-General, his parliamentary private secretary, a senior legal secretary and a legal secretary. In addition, junior counsel are appointed to the

Treasury and these appointments customarily lead to the High Court Bench.

MENTAL HEALTH ACT, 1959

There are two classes of work which arise out of the Mental Health Act, 1959. Sections 100–107 of that Act empower the Lord Chancellor from time to time to nominate one or more judges of the Supreme Court to act under the Court of Protection for the management of the property and affairs of a person if he is satisfied that such a person, by reason of mental disorder, is incapable of managing and administering his property and affairs.

The office of the High Court which deals with these matters is known as the Court of Protection, and the Lord Chancellor has appointed a master, a deputy master, and four assistant masters to carry out its procedure. The principle underlying the administration of this court is that regard shall be had first of all to the requirements of the patient, and the judge has power to make such orders and to give such directions as he thinks fit.

The other office which was created in order to deal with cases arising under the Mental Health Act, 1959, was that of the office of the Lord Chancellor's Visitors. Section 108 of the Act lays down that the Lord Chancellor should appoint medical and legal visitors to be known as the Lord Chancellor's Visitors. The appointments are subject to the concurrence of the Treasury and special knowledge and experience of cases of mental disorder is a requisite qualification for appointment as a medical visitor. The duties of these visitors are to visit patients in accordance with the directions of the judge and to make such reports on their visits as the judge may direct. The Lord Chancellor has in fact appointed one legal and three medical visitors together with the master or deputy master of the Court of Protection.

RESTRICTIVE PRACTICES COURT

Mention has already been made of the Restrictive Practices Court. Its work is of paramount importance and is likely to become even more so in an age in which monopolies and restrictive practices are under constant attack.

Because of the nature of the inquiry one might have expected a special body on the lines of the Transport Tribunal or the Lands Tribunal to have been created; but that was not done. Instead, the Restrictive Practices Act established a superior court of record just like the High Court; and therefore although the Restrictive Practices Court is not part of the High Court it has an equivalent status and is partly staffed by judges of the High Court and other superior courts of Scotland and Northern Ireland.

Apart from the Court itself, the Act also created the office of Registrar of Restrictive Trade Agreements. The Act requires the registration of most restrictive trading agreements with the registrar, and it is his function as an entirely independent person to decide whether the agreement should be registered or not. In the case of any dispute as to the registration of any agreement, the matter is referred to the Court to decide whether or not registration should be allowed. Hence, we have a court in the full sense of the word dealing with matters which are usually the concern of the individual alone; that is, the protection of trade interests, unless Parliament chooses to control such matters itself.

ORGANIZATION

The Judges

The work of the High Court is mainly carried out by the puisne judges who sit alone, unless a jury is called for, or they may sit in one of the divisional or appeal courts. In these days juries in civil actions or causes are rarely seen, unless the matter is one of those which fall within section 6 (1) of the Administration of Justice Act, 1933, which gives a right to either party to have a jury in any case where a claim in respect of libel, slander, malicious prosecution, false imprisonment, seduction, or breach of promise of marriage is in issue. It is left to the discretion of the court or judge to allow a trial by jury in other cases.

Judges also sit in chambers to hear appeals in the Queen's

Bench and Chancery divisions from masters and district registrars and in the Probate, Divorce, and Admiralty Division from registrars and district registrars, as well as some original claims such as for interim injunctions. Judges are also available to hear urgent applications *ex parte* and to sit in the Court of Appeal when required. The Queen's Bench judges go out on circuit regularly to try civil and criminal cases throughout the country, and it is not unheard of for the judges of the Probate, Divorce, and Admiralty Division to perform a similar function in respect of matrimonial cases. After a short and unsuccessful experiment, Chancery judges now no longer go on circuit.

The Masters and Registrars

Before an action or cause arrives at the day of trial there are often many matters which have to be thrashed out, many steps which have to be taken, and many major battles or minor skirmishes which have to be fought. These are called interlocutory proceedings and many an action or cause has been virtually won or lost in the course of these as the issues become clearer and the strengths and weaknesses of the respective cases are exposed.

The masters and registrars are, subject to the right of appeal to a judge in chambers, in control of this stage of the action—the Master of the Queen's Bench Division is even more so than is the Chancery Master or the Divorce Registrar. The Queen's Bench master has extremely wide powers; he gives directions as to every aspect of the conduct of the case up to trial, decides where it shall be tried, and, with the agreement of the parties, may even try the case himself. He is a very important officer in the administration of justice.

Indeed, such is the importance that attaches to these preliminary or interlocutory stages leading up to an eventual trial in the High Court, that it has been considered worth while to devote a whole chapter to this phase of litigation. The reader will therefore find that Chapter 9 covers this stage of an action.

JURISDICTION

The civil jurisdiction of the High Court is unlimited as to amount, and extends to the declaration of rights between parties where no other claim is involved. It has full jurisdiction over all the old common law actions in tort, contract, and the law of property, with their modern variations, except where Parliament has decreed that jurisdiction should be vested elsewhere, as for example, in one of the special tribunals, a branch of the administration or the county court. Subject to these exceptions the jurisdiction of the High Court is only limited by considerations of private international law as set out in the R.S.C.

Putting it broadly, one can start an action in the High Court against any person who is actually in England or Wales upon whom personal service of a writ of summons can be effected, whatever his or her nationality, unless either the person can claim diplomatic or other immunity, or he falls within the class of persons known as "persons under disability" to which reference will be made later in this chapter. In the latter event the person may be sued but the writ will have to be served on his representative.

Furthermore, also broadly speaking, any person outside England and Wales may be sued where the R.S.C. provide that service may be effected upon him outside the jurisdiction. The principal cases in which service out of the jurisdiction is permitted are set out in O. 11, R.S.C. Reference to the order itself should be made for the full list, but those most usually encountered are actions where the whole subject matter of the action is land situated within the jurisdiction; actions to recover damages or obtain other relief in respect of breach of a contract which was made either within the jurisdiction or made by or through an agent trading within the jurisdiction or which is by its express terms or by implication governed by English law; and actions founded on torts, such as negligence, trespass, or nuisance, committed within the jurisdiction.

Leave both to issue the writ and to serve it has to be obtained from a master, and the master may refuse leave even in a case within those set out in O. 11, as for instance, where the plaintiff has a more suitable remedy elsewhere.

Unless service is to be effected in Scotland, Northern Ireland, or the Isle of Man, the writ itself will not be served; instead a special form known as notice of the writ will be served.

TYPES OF CIVIL ACTION

It is not possible to describe within the limits of a book of this nature every type of action which may find its way into the High Court. They may arise at common law or in chancery or from the many statutes and statutory regulations with which Parliament has regulated the words and actions of citizens, and they are far too numerous to deal with individually. It is sometimes said that "knowing the law" is not so much a question of knowing the law, but one of knowing where to look for it; and this is perhaps a useful thing for the student and aspiring lawyer to bear in mind. Remember that the law is not divided into neat compartments. There may be a number of routes by which a litigant might reach his goal; the duty of his legal advisers is to try to find the one which will.

CONTRACT

The common law actions divide themselves naturally into two streams. Firstly, actions regarding contracts—a contract in its most simple form being an agreement between two or more persons for money or other valuable consideration (such as mutual promises) whereby the parties to the agreement bind, and intend to bind themselves in law, either expressly or by implication, to carry out their respective parts of the agreement.

There must be some consideration for the agreement, otherwise it cannot be sued upon at law, although it may be morally binding. Further it must be a contract which is not contrary to public policy for the courts to recognize, such as, for example, a contract to evade the criminal law. The law of contract includes such matters as actions for debt, hire-purchase, and the sale of goods. A good example of the way in which Parliament has encroached upon the common law is provided by the Sale of Goods Act, 1893, where the law relating to this aspect of trade is largely re-stated and codified.

A simple example of overlapping is the relationship of a master and his servant, although there are many others such as doctor and patient, and solicitor and client. The master agrees to employ and the servant agrees to serve, and the law implies certain things into their agreement, viz. the master to pay and the servant to do his job. However, the law also implies, among other things, that it is a term of the agreement that the employer will take reasonable care for the safety of his servant. This is an implied term of the contract of service, but it is also the common law duty of the employer in tort, as we shall see presently. Hence, in the event of breach the servant's remedy may lie both in contract and in tort, or either.

TORT

A tort is a civil wrong actionable at law. Broadly, it is based upon the "good neighbour" principle and upon a duty implied by the common law that you must take reasonable care not to injure your neighbour or his lawful rights. Your neighbour for this purpose is any person you should reasonably contemplate might be affected by your actions. The range is obviously enormous and includes the whole of the law of trespass and its derivatives, such as actions for conversion and detention of goods, trespass to land and to the person, libel and slander, nuisance, and, most important of all, negligence.

An action in negligence is an action for damages for the injury suffered, the measure of damages being that which will put the injured party back in the position in which he was before—so far as money can do this.

A very high proportion of the time of the Queen's Bench judges is spent in trying a class of action, frequently known as "running down" actions. They are so called because many of them arise out of highway accidents. The duty owed by a driver to other drivers and to pedestrians is to take reasonable care to avoid injuring them, and if he fails, he (or his insurance company) is liable in law to compensate them. Likewise, an employer who fails to take reasonable care to provide his servant with a safe place in which to work, or safe plant and machinery, or a safe system of work, will have to compensate his servant if his failure results in injury to the servant. This branch of the law is one where Parliament has intervened to protect the servant. In the Factories Acts and the regulations which have been made pursuant to the Acts there will be found a multitude of provisions imposing stringent and often absolute duties on the master, which bear no relation to the common law.

LAW OF PROPERTY

This is perhaps the most difficult subject of all to explain. In common parlance, when one speaks of property one is talking of everything which can be owned. In English law, however, a distinction is drawn between "real property" and "personal property". To the lawyer real property means the freehold interest in land and interests in land such as leaseholds and rights over land in the nature of easements; whereas personal property relates to the rights a person possesses over lesser interests in land, and over other possessions of a moveable nature, which are called chattels, such as furniture, motor-cars, jewellery, etc.

ALLOCATION OF BUSINESS

The allocation of different species of action to the various divisions of the High Court is still determined largely by their historical descent from the older courts, and this has led to some obvious anomalies. Hence an executor who has a difficult will to administer and warring heirs to contend with will find that he has to go to the Chancery Division to have the will construed but to the Probate Division to decide the dispute between the heirs.

Likewise one might expect the work of the Admiralty Court and the Commercial Court to be assimilated as a matter of common sense, but it is not. The work of the Divorce Court is annexed to that of Probate and Admiralty, although it has no logical connection, for its concern is with matrimonial affairs; but here again one finds that the Divorce Court has an overlapping jurisdiction with the Chancery Division over children, and with the Queen's Bench Division over married women's property.

Subject to the more obvious allocation of work to the Probate, Divorce, and Admiralty Division and the other specialized courts referred to already, the remainder of the work in the High Court is divided between the Queen's Bench and Chancery divisions.

By virtue of section 56 of the Judicature (Consolidation) Act, 1925, all actions which were within the exclusive jurisdiction of the old common law courts, viz. Queen's Bench in its original jurisdiction, Common Pleas, and Exchequer before the Act of 1873, were assigned to the Queen's Bench Division, and the Division now has jurisdiction over all the old common law actions, e.g. contract and tort, together with any other causes of action assigned to it by statute.

By virtue of the same section there is assigned to the Chancery Division all causes and matters in respect of which exclusive jurisdiction was given to the Court of Chancery under any Act of Parliament. It also deals with all other causes and matters which are assigned to it by statute, together with a number of causes which are particularly suited to the rules and procedure of equity, such as trusts, partnerships, wardship of infants, and the specific performance of contracts.

A reasonably safe rule to follow is that an action should be commenced in the Queen's Bench Division unless it is one which is specifically assigned to the Chancery Division by section 56 or by the R.S.C. or by statute or if it is a probate, divorce, or Admiralty matter. In any event, if the wrong division is selected inadvertently the court in the division in which the action is proceeding has power under O. 4, r. 3 R.S.C. to transfer it to the correct one. The only penalty which is likely to be incurred in such an event is that the plaintiff will be ordered to pay the costs thrown away by the error.

TABLE SHOWING QUALIFICATIONS FOR OFFICES IN THE HIGH COURT

Office	Qualification
Lord Chancellor Lord Chief Justice Master of the Rolls President of Probate, Divorce, and Admiralty Division	Any person qualified for appointment as Lord Justice of Appeal or a Justice of Court of Appeal.
Lord Justice of Appeal	Practising barrister 15 years
Puisne Judge—High Court	Practising barrister 10 years
Permanent Secretary to the Lord Chancellor and Clerk of the Crown	Practising barrister of not less than 10 years' standing
Master of the Queen's Bench Division	Practising barrister of not less than 10 years' standing
Master of the Crown Office	An official referee A master in lunacy
Official referee	A practising barrister of not less than 10 years' standing A master of the Queen's Bench Division A master in lunacy
Master in lunacy	A practising barrister of not less than 10 years' standing A master of the Queen's Bench Division An official referee
Registrar in Bankruptcy High Court	A practising barrister or solicitor of not less than 10 years' standing
Master of the Chancery Division	A practising solicitor of not less than 10 years' standing A master of the Taxing Office The official solicitor of the Supreme Court
Master of the Taxing Office	A practising solicitor of not less than 10 years' standing An admitted solicitor of not less than 10 years' standing who has held one of certain offices in the High Court A master of the Chancery Division The official solicitor of the High Court

Legal visitor in lunacy	A practising barrister or solicitor of not less than 10 years' standing
Official solicitor	A practising solicitor of not less than 10 years. A solicitor who has held office with 10 years' admission
	A master of the Chancery Division
	A master of the Taxing Office

CHAPTER 7

Appellate Jurisdiction of the Supreme Court

The Supreme Court—Appeals from masters and registrars (O.58, R.S.C.) — Appeals from official referees—Appeals from the Judge in Chambers (O.58 R.S.C.): Queen's Bench Division; Chancery and Probate, Divorce, and Admiralty Divisions — Appeals to divisional courts: Queen's Bench Divisional Court — Appeals from divisional courts — Appeals to the Court of Appeal (O.59, R.S.C.): Constitution — Civil jurisdiction, powers and procedure of the Court of Appeal — House of Lords: Hearing of appeals; Method of giving judgment; Security for costs — Judicial Committee of the Privy Council — Jurisdiction — Law reports — Shorthand notes.

THE SUPREME COURT

The constitution of the Supreme Court of Judicature is laid down by the Supreme Court of Judicature (Consolidation) Act, 1925. The Court consists of the High Court and the Court of Appeal.

Broadly speaking, the appellate jurisdiction of the Supreme Court is administered by means of a three-tier system, with the House of Lords acting as a final court of appeal in cases in which a right of appeal to this ultimate tribunal is permitted. The lowest of the three tiers consists in the right of appeal that lies from the decision of a master or registrar to a judge in chambers; the next step up the scale is represented by the divisional court, and the top layer is the Court of Appeal. It is proposed now to examine these three tiers more closely.

APPEALS FROM MASTERS AND REGISTRARS (O. 58, R.S.C.)

The jurisdiction of the Queen's Bench and chancery masters, registrars of the Probate, Divorce, and Admiralty Division, and district registrars has been referred to in the previous chapter. A Queen's Bench master and a registrar of the Probate, Divorce, and Admiralty Division are in the fullest sense the deputies of the judge in chambers and exercise nearly all his jurisdiction. The principal exceptions are those matters which relate to crime, the liberty of the subject, divisional court business, the grant of injunctions when in dispute and appeals from district registrars. The chancery master's powers are more restricted. Any party to an application to a chancery master may as of right have the application adjourned to the judge and any order made is in fact the judge's order. Hence, the appeals from chancery masters are in a different category.

The jurisdiction of a district registrar is equated to that of the particular division of the High Court with whose business he is concerned at the time. As a general rule appeals from Queen's Bench masters and the registrars on questions of law and fact lie to a single judge in chambers and leave to appeal is not required. This rule governs all appeals in matters of practice and procedure, which include the interlocutory stages of an action which are dealt with in Chapter 9.

The appeal is a complete rehearing of the dispute by the judge and it is brought by notice in writing which must be issued within 5 days after the order appealed against, or 7 days in the case of district registrars, and served on the other side not less than two clear days before the date fixed for hearing. By way of exception to the general rule, appeals from certain final, as distinct from interlocutory, orders of a Queen's Bench master and a registrar lie direct to the Court of Appeal.

The principal matters covered by this exception, are any judgment, order or decision given or made by a Queen's Bench master or registrar: (*a*) on any question or issue tried before or referred to him, or (*b*) on any assessment of damages after interlocutory judgment has been entered, or (*c*) in interpleader or garnishee proceedings, or (*d*) on an application for leave to sign final judgment in default of appearance or defence in actions arising out of hire purchase or conditional sale agreements.

APPEALS FROM OFFICIAL REFEREES

Appeals from official referees lie to the Court of Appeal, but only on a point of law or on questions of fact relevant to a charge of fraud or a breach of professional duty or in cases of contempt of court.

APPEALS FROM THE JUDGE IN CHAMBERS (O. 58, R.S.C.)

Queen's Bench Division

In the Queen's Bench Division appeals from the judge in chambers lie direct to the Court of Appeal with the exception of applications to set aside or discharge any of the prerogative orders of prohibition, certiorari, or mandamus or an order made in respect of *habeas corpus*. As a general rule there is no right of appeal against an interlocutory judgment or order of the judge without the leave of the judge or the Court of Appeal. The principal exceptions to this rule are where the liberty of the subject or the custody of infants is concerned, or an injunction is granted or refused or an order refusing a defendant unconditional leave to defend has been made by the judge.

There is generally a right of appeal to the Court of Appeal from any final judgment or order of the judge. There is, however, no appeal from any judgment in a criminal cause or matter or from an order allowing an extension of time for appealing, or from an order giving unconditional leave to defend, or where any statute provides that the decision is to be a final one.

There is no right of appeal without the leave of the judge or the Court of Appeal from a consent order or an award of costs where costs are left to the judge's discretion. Notice of appeal against an interlocutory order has to be served within 14 days.

Chancery and Probate, Divorce, and Admiralty Divisions

In these divisions the unsuccessful party has two choices. He may either, with the leave of the judge or of the Court of Appeal,

appeal from the judge in chambers to the Court of Appeal, or apply to the judge in open court to set aside or discharge the order and, if this is refused, he may appeal to the Court of Appeal without leave. These rights are in addition to the right of either party to a hearing before the chancery judge in chambers to ask for an adjournment into open court.

Apart from the distinctions which are noted above, the restrictions and limitations on the right of appeal are the same as in the Queen's Bench Division, where these are applicable to matters within the jurisdiction of either division.

APPEALS TO DIVISIONAL COURTS

The composition and jurisdiction of the divisional courts have been dealt with briefly in Chapter 6. These courts are now considered in rather more detail. Each division of the High Court has a divisional court which is constituted by two or sometimes three judges of that division. A Queen's Bench divisional court is frequently presided over by the Lord Chief Justice, and a Probate, Divorce, and Admiralty divisional court by the President of that Division. As a general rule, appeals are heard by a divisional court of the appropriate division in all cases where there is a right of appeal from any lesser court, tribunal or person and not to the Court of Appeal nor to a single judge. Such appeals are brought by originating notice of motion. Thus, an appeal from a magistrates' court in matrimonial causes lies to a Probate, Divorce, and Admiralty divisional court, and appeals from county courts in bankruptcy and land registration are heard by a Chancery divisional court. A Queen's Bench divisional court has a wider appellate jurisdiction than either of the other divisional courts and this will be considered presently.

First, however, it should be mentioned that a number of statutes expressly provide that there shall be a right of appeal to the High Court and, where the subject matter is suitable for the Chancery Division, the appeal is heard by a single judge of that division. Appeals from some decisions in relation to industrial insurance, trade unions, friendly societies, and copyright, to name but a few, are decided by a single judge of that Division.

Queen's Bench Divisional Court

A divisional court of this division hears all appeals to the High Court which are not required by a statute or the rules of the Supreme Court to be heard by a divisional court of one of the other divisions or by a single judge. It deals with all appeals by way of case stated for the opinion of the High Court from magistrates' courts and Quarter Sessions. In the exercise of its criminal jurisdiction it deals also with applications for a writ of *habeas corpus* and applications for the prerogative orders of mandamus, prohibition, and certiorari. However, these orders may also be made by this court in civil suits in order to review and control the proceedings of inferior courts of civil jurisdiction, tribunals, and persons. While strictly not modes of appeal they have a similar purpose in that they bring proceedings under the scrutiny of the High Court. This particular aspect of High Court jurisdiction is considered more fully in Chapter 11. Applications to set aside or discharge any of the prerogative orders made by a judge in chambers have to be made to a Queen's Bench divisional court.

In addition to the powers of review which are referred to above a Queen's Bench divisional court also has jurisdiction to hear appeals from courts, tribunals, and persons specified in the Tribunals and Inquiries Act, 1958, and other enactments. Such appeals may be brought either by originating motion requiring the court to re-hear the dispute or by application for an order requiring the inferior court or tribunal to state a case for the opinion of the High Court. These appeals are also dealt with in Chapter 11.

APPEALS FROM DIVISIONAL COURTS

Where a divisional court is exercising an original jurisdiction at common law or under a statute there is a right of appeal to the

Court of Appeal and leave is not required. Where, however, a divisional court has exercised its appellate jurisdiction, an appeal to the Court of Appeal from its decision lies only with leave from the court itself or the Court of Appeal.

Appeals from a Queen's Bench divisional court in criminal causes and matters and in proceedings for contempt of court lie direct to the House of Lords subject to leave to appeal being granted either by the divisional court or the Lords.

APPEALS TO THE COURT OF APPEAL (O. 59, R.S.C.)

Constitution

The Court of Appeal was created by the Supreme Court of Judicature Act, 1873. Its constitution is laid down by the Supreme Court of Judicature (Consolidation) Act, 1925, as amended and the Criminal Appeal Act, 1966. The judges who are appointed to the Court of Appeal are entitled Lord Justices of Appeal. In addition to the regular Lord Justices, the Lord Chancellor, the Lords of Appeal in Ordinary, the Lord Chief Justice, the Master of the Rolls, the President of the Probate, Divorce, and Admiralty Division and former Lord Chancellors are entitled to sit as members of the Court. The Lord Chancellor may also require any High Court judge to sit as an additional member of the Court.

Until 1966 the Court of Appeal was concerned only with appeals in civil cases, but on 1 October 1966 the Criminal Appeal Act, 1966, came into force. This Act abolished the Court of Criminal Appeal and created two divisions of the Court of Appeal, one criminal and the other civil. The Civil Division now exercises the whole jurisdiction of the Court other than that exercised by the Criminal Division. There are generally three or even four courts sitting at a time to hear civil appeals. Two judges constitute a Court of Appeal in interlocutory civil matters, but three are required to hear appeals from final judgments and orders in civil cases. A full Court of Appeal consists of five judges.

A judge cannot sit as a member of the Court of Appeal when the hearing relates to an order or judgment delivered by himself or from a judgment of a divisional court of which he was a member.

CIVIL JURISDICTION, POWERS, AND PROCEDURE OF THE COURT OF APPEAL

As a first general rule, the Court of Appeal has no original jurisdiction. It can, however, make orders to preserve the *status quo*, e.g. injunctions, pending an appeal from its decision to the House of Lords, and there are a few statutory exceptions to the rule, e.g. the Fugitive Offenders Act, 1967.

It is important to bear in mind that the Court was created by statute and its jurisdiction is limited and defined by statute. The principal enactment is the Supreme Court of Judicature (Consolidation) Act, 1925, sections 26–32 inclusive, and Rules of the Supreme Court also govern the practice and procedure of the Court. As a second general rule, there is a right of appeal on law and fact in civil matters from any judicial order or decision to the Court of Appeal. There are important exceptions to this rule and most of these have been referred to in the earlier sections of this chapter.

As we have seen, the Court of Appeal has jurisdiction to hear appeals from certain orders and decisions of masters and registrars, official referees, judges in chambers, and divisional courts. In addition to the tribunals mentioned above, the Court hears appeals from the Restrictive Practices Court, the Patents Appeals Tribunal, and from the Lands Tribunal and the Transport Tribunal on questions of law by way of case stated. Finally, and probably most important, it hears appeals from the decisions of the High Court by judge or judge and jury and from the judges of the county courts.

There is no right of appeal to the civil side of the Court of Appeal against a judgment of the High Court in criminal matters, with few exceptions; nor from an order allowing an extension of time for appealing; nor from a judge's order giving unconditional leave to defend; nor from a decision of the High Court or a judge thereof which is stated by a statute to be final; nor from an order absolute for dissolution or nullity of marriage, nor from a prize court; nor from an order made by a judge in chambers on an application for leave to apply for an order of mandamus, prohibition, or certiorari. In other cases leave to appeal may have to be obtained from the trial court or the Court of Appeal.

An appeal to the Court of Appeal is stated to be "by way of rehearing", but this is misleading. In practice the majority of appeals take the form of a review of the evidence given in the lower court either contained in the transcript taken from the shorthand note or in the judge's note. Oral evidence is not usually given, although the Court has power in some circumstances to hear or receive additional evidence, either oral or by affidavit or deposition.

The Court of Appeal has all the powers of the High Court and may draw inferences of fact and make any order which the trial court could have made. It may uphold the decision of the trial court or reverse it or it may substitute its own judgment for that of the trial court. It may also, in exceptional cases, e.g. misdirection of a jury by a judge, order a new trial, but this is only ordered where the Court is satisfied that some substantial wrong or miscarriage of justice has occurred.

Any appeal must be brought by motion to the Court and notice in writing of the motion, specifying the grounds of appeal and the form of the order which is asked for, must be served on the other party. An appellant is limited to the case he relied on in the lower court. He is also limited to the grounds set out in his notice, subject to the Court's power to allow amendment. The time limited for appealing in the case of interlocutory orders is 14 days, in company winding-up or bankruptcy 21 days, and in any other case 6 weeks. A respondent who wishes to cross-appeal, as distinct from merely resisting the appeal, must give to the appellant notice in writing of the grounds of his cross-appeal and the order he is asking the Court to make. His notice must be served, in the case of an appeal against an interlocutory order, within 4 days after the service of the notice of appeal, and in any other case, within 21 days. These times may be enlarged by the Court. The appellant must, within 7 days after service of his notice, set the appeal down for hearing by lodging with the Court a copy of the judgment or order appealed against, two copies of the notice of motion, and list of exhibits, if any. Where leave to appeal is necessary, the application for leave should first be made to the trial court. If leave is refused by the trial court, leave may be sought by motion to the Court of Appeal.

It is important to bear in mind that an appeal does not automatically operate as a stay of execution of the judgment of the lower court. The trial judge must be asked expressly for an order to that effect.

In special circumstances the Court of Appeal may order security to be given for the costs of an appeal. This is usually done when the respondent is able to show that the appellant, if unsuccessful, will be unable to pay the costs of the appeal. The general rule with regard to costs in a hearing before the Court of Appeal is that a successful appellant or respondent gets his costs. He may, however, be deprived of them in certain circumstances. Further, the general rule empowers the Court of Appeal to allow the costs of a successful appellant or respondent in the court below as well as in the Court of Appeal.

Although an appeal to the Court of Appeal is a rehearing, appeals on questions of fact from the decisions of judges sitting alone raise questions of principle. The burden is on the appellant to show that the trial judge was wrong in his decision as to the facts, and the burden is a heavy one. Unless the Court of Appeal is satisfied that he was wrong, the appeal will fail. The reason is that the judge has seen the witnesses and he has not only heard their evidence but has seen how they gave it. He has, therefore, had the advantage of being able to assess their credibility and reliability, which the Court of Appeal has not had. Likewise the Court of Appeal will not substitute its own discretion for that of a trial judge unless it is satisfied that he has erred in principle in exercising his discretion.

Appeals from county courts to the Court of Appeal have been dealt with in Chapter 5 at pp.106 and 107, and reference should therefore be made to these pages to complete this chapter on appeals.

HOUSE OF LORDS

Although not a part of the Supreme Court, the House of Lords is the highest court of appeal and hears appeals from the Court of Appeal and the Queen's Bench Divisional Court in England and the highest courts in Scotland and Northern Ireland.

The persons who are entitled to sit as members of this tribunal are designated as Lords of Appeal and they consist of the following holders of judicial offices: the Lord Chancellor, the Lords of Appeal in Ordinary, together with any peer of Parliament who either holds or has held office as Lord Chancellor, a member of the Judicial Committee of the Privy Council, Lord of Appeal in Ordinary or a judge of the Supreme Court of England or Northern Ireland or of the Court of Session in Scotland.

The qualification for appointment as a Lord of Appeal in Ordinary has already been referred to under the sub-heading "The Judges" in Chapter 6 (see p. 119), and this office entitles the holder to sit and vote for all business as a member of the House of Lords during his lifetimc.

The chief officials of the House of Lords are the Clerk of the Parliaments, the Gentleman Usher of the Black Rod, the Clerk Assistant, the Reading Clerk, the Fourth Clerk at the Table (Judicial), and the Serjeant at Arms. These officials are all appointed by the Crown under letters patent, except the Clerk Assistant, the Reading Clerk, and the Fourth Clerk at the Table (Judicial) who are appointed by the Lord Chancellor subject to the approbation of the House.

Hearing of Appeals

The House of Lords sits for the hearing of appeals on Mondays, Tuesdays, Wednesdays, and Thursdays, from 10.30 a.m. to

4 p.m. except on Mondays when the sitting commences at 11 a.m. For this purpose a quorum of three is required.

The Lord Chancellor, or in his absence the next senior Lord of Appeal in Ordinary, presides. Since 1948, in order to secure sufficient time in which to deal with the hearing of appeals, the House of Lords has set up a Sessional Committee—the Appellate Committee, which consists of all lords who are qualified by statute to hear appeals. It is this Committee nowadays which in practice hears appeals to the House of Lords; but the actual judgment is delivered by the House of Lords itself from the report of the Appellate Committee. In practice this will generally mean that the Lords of Appeal who heard the appeal will also deliver the judgment but they will do so in the House of Lords and as members of that House.

The House of Lords has statutory power to regulate its own procedure regarding the hearing of appeals (section II, Appellate Jurisdiction Act, 1876, and the Administration of Justice (Appeals) Act, 1934) and these are now laid down by the Standing Orders and Directions of the House which regulate the judicial business.

The Appellate Committee is appointed by the House of Lords at the beginning of each session of Parliament to "consider of petitions in matters relating to causes . . . and of other matters relating thereto." In practice the Committee is attended only by Lords of Appeal, and parties may appear before it either in person or by agents. In order to be represented by counsel, application has to be made to the Clerk of the Parliaments.

An application for leave to appeal to the House of Lords has to be made in the first instance to the Court of Appeal, and if refused it must be made to the House of Lords within one month from the date on which the order is pronounced. Such an application is made to the House of Lords by means of a petition which is referred to the Appellate Committee; and either the Court of Appeal or the House of Lords may impose conditions when granting leave to appeal.

Method of giving Judgment

The method by which a judgment of the House of Lords is given requires that one hour before the sitting is due to commence, written copies of the opinions of the members who have adjudicated are handed to the parties. Although it can still be done, the opinions are not read out, and the actual delivery of the decision has become a purely formal matter. The decision of the House of Lords is based in accordance with the opinion of the majority. The House of Lords has power to remit a case to the lower court in order that that court may try or report on a specified question of fact or law before it delivers its own final judgment.

Security for Costs

The normal time limit within which an appeal to the House of Lords has to be lodged, unless this period is further limited either by statute or by order of the House of Lords, is 3 months from the date of the order which is the subject of the appeal.

The normal practice is that no party to an appeal will be heard unless he has lodged a case which sets out a statement of his argument. This entitles the party to the right to be heard by two counsel, and he will need to have his case signed by at least one counsel who either appeared for him in the lower court or who has been briefed in order to do so on the hearing of the appeal. All the requisite documents for the hearing of the appeal have to be prepared by the appellant and be lodged in the form of an appendix to his case. This has to be done within a period of 6 weeks from the date of the presentation of the appeal.

The appeal has then to be set down for hearing and although there is no time limit in which the respondent has to lodge his case, he will only be allowed to do so on petition, once a date for the hearing of the appeal has been fixed.

Unless the House of Lords absolves him from so doing, an appellant has to give security for costs to the amount of £1000.

JUDICIAL COMMITTEE OF THE PRIVY COUNCIL

The Privy Council itself is of very ancient origin, King Alfred the Great instituted it in the year 895, but by the year 1679 when it was reconstituted it had become unwieldy. It was not, however, until the year 1833 that the old practice of hearing appeals before a committee which in fact consisted of the whole Privy Council, was modernized. The Judicial Committee Act, 1833, enacted that appeals were to be heard by a committee entitled the Judicial Committee of the Privy Council. The statute laid down that this Committee was to consist of the Lord President of the Council (who has in fact remained as one of the great officers of state and in modern times is a member of the Cabinet), the Lord Chancellor, ex Lord Presidents, the Lords of Appeal in Ordinary, and such other members of the Privy Council who have held "high judicial office", together with two other privy counsellors to be appointed by the Sovereign by sign manual.

The membership of this Committee was extended in 1962 by the inclusion of holders of high judicial office in the Commonwealth, and there is now no limit as to the number of such additional members.

JURISDICTION

The year 1833 was a revolutionary one as far as jurisdiction of this final appeal tribunal in the land was concerned. Up to that time the Sovereign used to sit with his Council to hear appeals within the kingdom. Resulting from the Judicial Committee Act of that year, however, all appeals, including appeals from the dominions and colonies came to be heard by the Judicial Committee, whose province it became to advise the Crown upon the action to be taken.

This jurisdiction was extended even further by the Judicial Committee Act, 1844. Originally a special order was required in order to refer a petition or appeal to the Judicial Committee. An Order in Council dated 18 October 1909, however, referred all petitions and appeals to the Judicial Committee. It is by virtue of that order that all petitions and appeals are now so referred.

There are two main classes of appeals which are dealt with by the Privy Council, namely appeals as of right and appeals by special leave. In modern times, the Judicial Committee has a limited sphere of operation. With the changes in the Commonwealth and the grant of independence to most of the colonies, it has lost the greater part of its appellate jurisdiction.

At the present time it is still the final court of appeal from the colonies, protectorates and trust territories, and the Channel Islands and Isle of Man, and from the ecclesiastical courts and Admiralty prize courts, but its jurisdiction is shrinking.

LAW REPORTS

It will readily be appreciated what an important part the provision of accurately reported records plays in the administration of civil justice. While Parliament enacts the statutes that regulate the conduct of our many civil transactions in business and otherwise, it is the interpretation by the courts which finally determines the outcome of civil actions.

The only authentic reports of court proceedings available in earlier times were the written judgments of the judges. Originally the proceedings were conducted in a strange mixture of English and French, and it was not until the year 1362 that it was enacted that all pleadings and judgments in the courts at Westminster should be in English.

At first the reporting of cases was done by barristers, and, as the number of barristers so occupied ran into three figures, it can easily be imagined what a multiplicity of reports emerged from their labours. Some of these reports were undoubtedly accurate, but others could not fairly be so described. A further disadvantage was that the reports were more often than not subject to considerable delay before publication.

This state of affairs continued up to the middle of the nineteenth century when it was pointed out, with some force, that there were no less than sixteen sets of authorized reports in publication in addition to some further five sets of irregular reports. It was about this time that a Council of Reporting was first mooted. It was urged that reports should be produced that were both accurate and capable of speedy publication; and to ensure accuracy it was suggested that they should be submitted to the judges for revision.

Resulting from this protest the first Council of Law Reporting was set up in 1865. The Council at that time consisted of twenty-two barristers including both the Attorney-General and the Solicitor-General. It was guaranteed funds by the four Inns of Court and the Law Society, and in the year 1865 reporters duly appointed by the Council began work in Westminster Hall. In 1866 the first volumes of the Queen's Bench and Common Pleas Reports were issued, and were followed in 1869 by the Law Reports for the Probate and Divorce Division.

The Council of Law Reporting was incorporated under the Companies Acts, 1862 and 1867, for "the preparation and publication at a moderate price and under gratuitous professional control of Reports of Judicial Decisions of the Superior and Appellate Courts in England". All the official reports connected with proceedings in the High Court are now produced by this Council which is now known as the Incorporated Council of Law Reporting for England and Wales. The composition of the Council nowadays is two members who are nominated by each of the four Inns of Court and the Law Society together with three members by co-option and the law officers.

Reports are produced annually for the Queen's Bench, Chancery, and Probate, Divorce, and Admiralty divisions as well as for the Appeal Courts. In addition to these, which are bound annually into volumes, the courts used to have the assistance of certain other weekly reports such as *The Times Law Reports*, the *Law Journal*, the *Weekly Notes*, and the *Solicitors Journal*. During the period 1948–53 the recommendations of a committee which had sat in 1940 under the chairmanship of Mr. Justice Simonds, all these came to an end. However, the *All England Reports*, which were first published in 1936, have been and still are available, these reports being compiled and edited by barristers. In 1953 the *Weekly Notes* were replaced by the *Weekly Law Reports*, a publication which is also subject to editorship by barristers, whilst reports of a fairly wide scope still continue to be issued with the *Justices of the Peace and Local Government Review* and *Knight's Local Government and Industrial Reports*.

SHORTHAND NOTES

We will refer briefly to the daily shorthand notes that are taken in court in order that a full note may be available if required of actions in the High Court.

First, it must be noted that proceedings which take place in chambers are normally private. Should a shorthand note be taken, a transcript of it cannot be used without the consent of the judge. In the event, however, of a judge adjourning any application into open court, the proceedings will then become public, unless the hearing is "in court as chambers".

In all civil actions in the High Court and courts of record a record of the proceedings is taken. The form this record takes, is usually an official shorthand note of any evidence given orally in court, the summing up by the judge (if there is a jury), and any judgment. The taking of shorthand notes is paid for out of public funds.

A judge, however, has power to direct that no official shorthand note need be taken, and in the event of an appeal, should one have been taken he has power to intimate that the official note need not be transcribed, but that his own note will suffice for the purposes of the appeal. The judge has a complete discretion as regards making an order relating to the transcribing of evidence whether of any particular witness or witnesses, or in toto.

Should an appellant need a transcript for the purpose of an appeal he has to pay for it himself in the first instance, but the cost incurred will be included in the costs of the appeal unless otherwise ordered. In the event, however, that the judge or the Court of Appeal should be satisfied that the costs of a transcript would be an excessive burden on an appellant, and are satisfied also that there is reasonable ground for an appeal, a certificate may be issued certifying that the transcript should be supplied at the expense of public funds.

CHAPTER 8

Palatine Court—Liverpool Court of Passage

Chancery Court of the County Palatine of Lancaster—Liverpool Court of Passage.

THE Supreme Court of Justice together with the assize courts which are held in the various circuits throughout England and Wales are of paramount importance in the administration of civil justice. But to complete the picture it is necessary to refer briefly to two other courts which still exercise jurisdiction, namely the Lancaster Palatine Court and the Liverpool Court of Passage.

CHANCERY COURT OF THE COUNTY PALATINE OF LANCASTER

The jurisdiction of this court was founded in the year 1351 when Edward III granted by charter to the then Duke of Lancaster for his lifetime, a court of chancery, a chancellor, and such other *jura regalia* in the county of Lancaster as pertained to a county palatine. Similar charters were granted to successive Dukes of Lancaster until 1399 when Henry IV severed the duchy from the Crown, and since that time the County Palatine of Lancaster has remained as a separate inheritance in the possession of the sovereign.

As a result of this the County Palatine of Lancaster still has a court of its own which is now known as the Court of Chancery of

Lancaster. There is in addition an Attorney-General of the County Palatine and Duchy of Lancaster. The jurisdiction of this court is now regulated by a number of statutes, whilst the procedure of the court is regulated by rules which have the effect of assimilating the procedure in the Palatine Court to that of the High Court of Justice.

The jurisdiction of this court within the County Palatine is the same as that of the High Court of Justice in its Chancery Division (Chancery of Lancaster Act, 1890, section 3), and is therefore unlimited as to amount. An action commenced in the Palatine Court which is not within the ancient chancery jurisdiction of that court may be transferred to the High Court by order either of the Chancery Court of Lancaster or of the Court of Appeal. Similarly, actions that are assigned to the Chancery Division (except appeals) and certain actions assigned to the Queen's Bench Division may be transferred to the Lancaster Palatine Court (sections 1 and 5, Court of Chancery of Lancaster Act, 1952); and this transfer may take place at any stage of the proceedings.

Until the Supreme Court of Judicature Act, 1873, came into force, the County Palatine had its own court of appeal, but that statute transferred the appellate jurisdiction of that court to the Supreme Court of Justice. An appeal from the Palatine Court now lies to the Court of Appeal, and thence to the House of Lords (Appellate Jurisdiction Act, 1876, section 3 (1)).

Whereas formerly the judicial functions of this court were exercised by the Chancellor of the Duchy and County Palatine, this appointment is today a political one. The qualification necessary to hold such office is that of a barrister of not less than 10 years' standing. The holder of the office has to take the judicial oaths and holds office during good behaviour, and is not allowed to practise as a barrister during the tenure of his appointment. Further, the holder of the office must have his permanent abode within such distance of the cities of Liverpool and Manchester as the Lord Chancellor may direct (section 14 (1), Administration of Justice Act, 1928).

LIVERPOOL COURT OF PASSAGE

The jurisdiction of this Court originated from charters granted by Charles I and William III. It would appear that the name was chosen as an indication that the court would deal with causes that arose out of imports and exports passing through the city.

The jurisdiction of the Court in personal actions where the defendant resides or carries on business within the jurisdiction of the court is unlimited as to amount, provided that no such action can be commenced where only part arises within the jurisdiction, if the county court has cognizance thereof; the sum involved does not exceed £20; and the defendant does not reside or carry on business within the jurisdiction. The Court can also try actions of ejectment where the lands or premises are situated in the jurisdiction and their value does not exceed £100. In addition the Court can also deal with moneylending matters, hire purchase transactions, and civil proceedings by or against the Crown. The powers of the Court as regards the making of orders are similar to those of the High Court of Justice.

The Passage Court is presided over by a judge who must be a barrister of not less than 7 years' standing. His powers are similar to those of a judge of the High Court, and the holder of the office is precluded from practising as a barrister in connection with any proceedings arising in the Court of Passage or at the Quarter Sessions for the city.

The court officials consist of a registrar who may be either a practising barrister or a solicitor of not less than 5 years' standing, and who is appointed by the corporation, together with a deputy registrar having the same qualifications. There is too a serjeant-at-mace of the city who is also appointed by the corporation, and whose powers regarding the execution of process out of the Court of Passage are similar to those of a sheriff of the superior courts. The serjeant-at-mace appoints the bailiffs and officers who assist him in his duties and, if so required, he has to give security to the Court of Passage both in respect of himself and of his officers.

The procedure of the Court is regulated by the Rules of the Liverpool Court of Passage, 1934, as amended by later rules. In effect these rules virtually provide the same procedure to the Court of Passage as that for the Queen's Bench and Admiralty divisions of the High Court. Here, again, if the High Court or a judge deem it desirable, actions may be removed from the Court of Passage to the High Court. Actions based on contract, where the claim endorsed on the writ is less than £10, or if the amount has been reduced to less than £10 by payment or other reason, may by order of the judge or registrar be transferred to a county court. The rules of the court also allow the judge or registrar to refer matters to the registrar or to a special referee.

Orders made or directions given by the registrar in interlocutory matters are subject to an appeal to the judge; but, on other than interlocutory matters, appeals from the registrar lie to the Divisional Court of the High Court.

Non-residence of a party within the jurisdiction of the Court of Passage can render an order unenforceable. Such an order, however, becomes enforceable when it is made by virtue of an order of the High Court and a receipt and an affidavit are produced to this effect.

CHAPTER 9

High Court Practice and Procedure

The issue of proceedings — Interlocutory proceedings — Applications to the master (O., 32, R.S.C.)— Interlocutory Injunctions (O. 29) — Joinder of causes of action and parties (O. 15, R.S.C.) — Infants and mentally disordered patients — Steps in common law action: Writ of summons; Service of writ (O. 10 and O. 11); Defendant's appearance (O. 12) — Order 14 — Pleadings (O. 18) — Statement of claim — Defence and Counterclaim: Defence; Counterclaim (O. 15, r. 18, and O. 18) — Reply and defence to Counterclaim (O. 18, rr. 14 and 18): Reply; Defence to counterclaim; Close of Pleadings (O. 18, r. 20) — The defendant's case: Striking out (O. 18, r. 19); Further and better particulars; Defence and counterclaim (O. 15, r. 2); Third parties (O. 16); Security for costs (O. 23); Payment into court (O. 22); Tender (O. 18, r. 16 and O. 22) — Discovery of documents (O. 24) — Summons for directions (O. 25) — Setting down (O. 34) — Lists of actions (O. 34, rr. 4–7).

THE ISSUE OF PROCEEDINGS

Before an action is started there will generally have been correspondence, and perhaps even discussions, between the legal advisers to the prospective protagonists; and frequently attempts are made to compromise the dispute without recourse to litigation.

Litigation is, and should be, the last resort when all else fails, and should only be embarked upon with a full understanding of what is involved in an action in the High Court. It is a comparatively simple step to start an action; but costs on both sides mount as the action proceeds, and once started, a decision to withdraw can be expensive.

It is therefore of the utmost importance to decide how much the costs on either side are likely to be before starting an action. In the more usual type of action, such as an action for damages for personal injury caused by a motor vehicle ("Running Down" action), or for personal injury resulting from accidents in factories, an experienced solicitor will be able to give a fair estimate. But in cases where difficult points of law are involved, no one can predict with certainty, either the result of the action or its likely cost, because of the possibility of an appeal to a higher court.

Among the many factors which have to be considered at this stage, are the value of the matter or the amount at stake; who is or are the possible defendants; what is their financial standing, and is it such as to meet an adverse judgment including the plaintiff's costs. Whether they may be insured against the contingency which has given rise to the claim, what the plaintiff can afford to stand in the way of costs, and of course, what evidence, documentary and verbal has the plaintiff to support his case, also what are the prospects of success, are all most important considerations. It should be remembered that most workmen belong to trade unions and are usually entitled to the support of their union in litigation connected with their employment. This may include the provision without charge to the member of solicitors engaged by the union, and of counsel. Alternatively, the financial position of the plaintiff may be such that he is entitled to legal aid, as to which see Chapter 12.

Advice at this stage is generally in the hands of a solicitor, although he may in a difficult case, or if the client wishes, take the opinion of counsel. Before passing to the various stages of an action, a few words should be said about the persons who may sue or be sued, and certain other matters which have to be considered before the writ is issued.

The time within which actions may be commenced is subject to the limitations laid down by the Limitation Acts, 1939 and 1963. Section 2 (1) of the former Act imposed a time limit of 3 years in cases where damages are claimed in respect of personal injuries (including disease or impairment of a person's physical or mental condition), or in respect of a person's death. This period was extended by section 1 of the 1963 Act, in cases where the court has granted leave in respect of an action for damages for negligence, nuisance, or breach of duty where the damages claimed by the plaintiff for any nuisance or breach of duty are in respect of personal injuries to the plaintiff or any other person; the following requirements having also to be fulfilled:

(*a*) that the material facts of a decisive character relating to the cause of action were outside the knowledge of the plaintiff until a date after the end of the 3-year period or not earlier than 12 months before the end of that period; or

(*b*) in either case was a date not earlier than 12 months before the date on which the action was brought.

INTERLOCUTORY PROCEEDINGS

For the legal practitioner there is no effective substitute for the White Book which contains the Rules of the Supreme Court, (hereinafter referred to as R.S.C.) for points of practice and procedure in all the divisions of the High Court and the Court of Appeal. The lawyer's task is not so much to know what the law is, but to know where to find it and how to apply it. This section is intended therefore only as an introduction to the subject and not as a comprehensive guide. As the majority of civil actions in the High Court are started in the Queen's Bench Division, the procedure in that division will be concentrated on.

The culmination of every action is the trial itself. That is, when the parties and their witnesses attend in open court, give their evidence on oath, and receive judgment. But before the trial itself there are many steps which have to be taken and these are known as "interlocutory proceedings". Each action commenced is assigned to one of the masters, and he will decide what procedural steps should be taken, and how the action will be tried. These proceedings take place in chambers and are subject to appeal usually to the judge in chambers, and thence to the Court of Appeal, and ultimately to the House of Lords.

The principal purpose of these proceedings is to ensure that the issues between the parties are clearly defined, that the parties have made full and frank disclosure of all the information to which the other side is entitled; and that the action is fit and ready for trial.

But there is a secondary and equally important function served by the interlocutory proceedings. As the action proceeds the parties and their legal advisers will discover more about the other side's case, and will be able to assess to some extent its strength and its weakness, which will often lead to a relaxing of the firm resolve to fight to the bitter end. Many are familiar with the phrase "settled out of court", and the figures speak for themselves. Of actions started in the Queen's Bench Division only about 2–3 per cent ever get to trial; the rest are settled, often as a result of facts which have emerged during the interlocutory stage.

APPLICATIONS TO THE MASTER (O. 32, R.S.C.)

The master exercises all the jurisdiction of the judge in chambers with few exceptions, such as criminal matters, grant of injunctions where in dispute, and appeals from district registrars. The usual mode of application for an order is by summons, which is a printed form which the applicant must complete and indicate the order required. He must then take it to the appropriate office, which will be the Central Office for actions in the High Court, and the District Registry for actions proceeding in that registry, where it will be sealed and issued.

Further, the applicant must then serve the summons on his opponent at least two clear days before the return date (date of hearing) given in the summons. In most cases these summonses will be attended by solicitors, and if counsel is briefed on one side, the other side must be notified and the summons will be transferred into "Counsel's List" which is taken at 1.30 p.m. in the "Bear Garden", as it is called, in the High Court, unless a special appointment is made. The summons for directions and the Order 14 summons are in different categories and will be dealt with later in this section.

Not every procedural step requires the leave of the master, but where it is required the R.S.C. will so indicate, and also the mode of application. Some applications, generally those which are purely formal, or do not affect the rights of the other party, such as a defendant's application to issue a third party notice after the service of his defence, do not require notice to be given to the plaintiff nor any attendance, and leave may be obtained *ex parte* by leaving an affidavit deposing to the facts relied on, and the other necessary documents in the Master's Secretary's Department. Finally, once an action is in the list for trial, such applications as an application to put back the date of trial must be made to the Judge in charge of the list in open court, and such applications are not usually viewed with great favour. An affidavit is a statement of facts sworn to before a solicitor of the Supreme Court who is also a commissioner for oaths, and may include exhibits, i.e. correspondence, etc., which also have to be marked by the Commissioner at the time when the affidavit is deposed to.

INTERLOCUTORY INJUNCTIONS (O. 29)

No chapter on civil practice and procedure would be complete without making mention of this important aspect of the court's powers. So highly regarded is the power to grant an injunction before the trial that it can only be exercised by a judge unless the parties agree to the making of the order, in which event a master may deal with it.

The jurisdiction to grant interim injunctions stems from the equity practice of the old Chancery Court. It is now exercised by all divisions of the High Court by virtue of section 45 of the Judicature Act, 1925, and O. 29, R.S.C. The value of the jurisdiction lies in the fact that a litigant will frequently require relief from the court urgently. An award of damages may be insufficient to compensate him for the injury he is suffering or about to suffer. He may either wish to prevent someone else committing a wrongful act, or to make him perform an act which he should perform, and the delay consequent upon awaiting trial will deprive him of such specific remedy.

For example, he may wish to prevent a neighbour from building so as to trespass on his property, or to prevent a custodian of his goods from disposing of them, or to make someone perform an act he should perform. In such cases he may issue his writ, and in the Queen's Bench Division apply by summons supported by affidavit to the judge in chambers for an injunction, either to restrain the defendant from doing the act complained of, or in a mandatory form to order him to do something. In cases of extreme urgency he may apply to any judge of that division before the writ is issued, but the judge will then, if he grants the injunction, restrict its operation until the first hearing of the summons.

In the Chancery Division the application is made by notice of motion to a chancery judge. In many cases the grant or refusal of an interim injunction will dispose of the real issue between the parties. Hence the jurisdiction to grant is used sparingly, and it is always made a condition of the grant that the successful applicant undertakes to compensate his opponent for any loss sustained by reason of the injunction, should it appear to the court later that it should not have been granted. Not infrequently such an application leads to the giving of cross undertakings by the parties: by the defendant to discontinue his acts complained of, pending the trial, and by the plaintiff to compensate the defendant if he should fail in his claim.

Where such an undertaking is made by a defendant in the face of the court disobedience thereto may be punished in the same way as disobedience to an order granting an injunction or to any other order of the court, namely by the court committing the offender to prison for contempt or by imposing a fine (O. 52).

Under O. 29 the court also has power to order perishable property which is the subject matter of a dispute to be sold, samples to be taken, and property in issue to be preserved pending the trial.

JOINDER OF CAUSES OF ACTION AND PARTIES (O. 15, R.S.C.)

It may be extremely difficult for plaintiffs to decide from among a number of possible defendants, which is liable to him in law, and he may also have a number of different causes of action which he would like to include in the one writ. Order 15 is intended to define the circumstances in which a plaintiff and a defendant respectively may join parties and causes of action in the one proceedings in order to avoid multiplicity of actions about the same subject matter, and a multiplicity of parties where an action brought by or against one party representing the other will bind the others. Order 15 also applies in a situation where a party dies and his executor wishes to continue the action.

A plaintiff may without leave join in one writ against the same defendant several causes of action, provided that he claims, and the defendant's liability is alleged to arise, in the same capacity in respect of all the causes of action. He cannot, however, sue the defendant both in his personal capacity and in a representative capacity. Further, two or more persons may join in one action as plaintiffs or defendants with the leave of the court, or where some common question of law or fact arises between them; or where all rights to relief, claimed in the action arise jointly, severally, or in the alternative; or arise out of one transaction or a series of transactions. But a number of plaintiffs and defendants cannot be joined in the one action, where each plaintiff is alleging a separate cause of action against one defendant only.

Under this order the court has wide powers to order separate trials, to order joinder of persons not joined in the action, to correct misjoinder and to order actions to be conducted by representatives of numerous parties.

INFANTS AND MENTALLY DISORDERED PATIENTS

Infants and mentally disordered patients receive special protection from the courts in litigious matters. The procedure is governed largely by O. 80. They cannot sue except by a person appointed to act for them, who is called a "next friend", and they cannot defend or appear in an action except through a "guardian *ad litem*", who must have consented in writing to act as such.

Moreover, persons under disability (as they are called) who claim or recover damages, or whose claims are compromised or settled, must obtain the master's prior approval of the terms. Monies recovered will usually remain in court and be invested for the benefit of the person having disability; for an infant until he reaches the age of 21 years.

STEPS IN COMMON LAW ACTION

Writ of Summons

There are four ways in which a High Court action may be commenced: either by writ of summons (or writ as it is usually called); by originating summons; by petition; or by way of motion. The majority of actions are commenced by writ. The originating summons, as its name suggests, originates an action and it is quite distinct from the summonses used to make applications in interlocutory proceedings. It is used principally when the only, or principal, question to be decided is the construction of a statute, deed, will, or contract, or where the real issue is one of law, not fact. The circumstances in which its use is apt are set out in O. 5, rr. 2 and 3, R.S.C., and procedure is governed by O. 28. Its main advantage is that the procedure is more economical than that by way of writ. A petition is used in most matrimonial causes, bankruptcy, and in applications to wind up limited companies. A motion is required in some cases, for example, for an appeal against the decision of a tribunal brought under section 9 of the Tribunals and Inquiries Act, 1958, and O. 55, R.S.C.

The writ is in a form laid down by O. 6, and the requirements are also set out therein. The form is obtainable from the Central Office in London or from a district registry by which its reference number will be filled in with the plaintiff's initial, year, and number, viz. 1966 C. No. —. It has to be completed by the plaintiff or his legal advisers, who must (1) fill in the names of the parties in full in the title, or if this cannot be done, give the surname and status of the person, e.g. male, married woman, *feme sole*, and also state any representative character concerned, e.g. "executor of the estate of X deceased"; (2) name the division in which the action is brought, e.g. Queen's Bench Division; (3) give the name and address of the person or firm issuing the writ; and (4) unless a statement of claim is indorsed on or delivered with the writ, state briefly the nature of the plaintiff's claim, viz. "The plaintiff's claim is for damages for breach of a contract in writing dated the 8th December 1966".

The writ must be completed in duplicate and taken to the appropriate office (Central Office or district registry), where it will be witnessed on behalf of the Lord Chancellor, sealed, and issued, and stamp duty must be paid. One copy will be retained and filed by the court and the other given to the plaintiff or his solicitor for use in serving the defendant.

A writ must be used for any claim in tort (other than trespass to land), fraud, damages for breach of duty, statutory or at common law, breach of promise of marriage, or infringement of patent. Once issued it remains in force for 12 months, but if the defendant has not been served with it within that time, it may be renewed with leave of a master for a further period of 12 months, and so on from time to time, upon good reason being shown why it has not been served, e.g. that the defendant is out of the jurisdiction. A writ remains in force for a year from the date of its issue, i.e. it expires the day before the anniversary of its issue.

Service of Writ (O. 10 and O. 11)

The basic rule for service of the writ is far more strict than that for service of other documents, because of the consequences which may follow if it is disregarded. It must be served personally on each defendant sued, by leaving a copy with him and showing him the original if required.

If a defendant's solicitor agrees in writing to accept service and the writ is served on him, that is deemed to be good personal service and the writ must be indorsed accordingly; but it is still open to the defendant to challenge its validity if he has given no instructions to his solicitor to accept service for him. The person serving the writ must complete the indorsement of service.

Some of the provisions relating to service overseas and O. 11 have already been mentioned in chapter 6, pp. 127 and 128, and other provisions covering cases where personal service is obviously impracticable or there are special circumstances are dealt with in O. 10. In the case of an infant, service has to be effected on his parent or guardian *ad litem* and, in the case of a mentally disordered patient upon his guardian; limited companies may be served at their registered office, and departments of state have solicitors appointed to accept service on their behalf. If for any good reason, such as deliberate evasion by the defendant, personal service cannot be effected, a master has power in his discretion to order under O. 65, r. 4, R.S.C. that service may be effected in any way which is likely to bring to the defendant's notice the writ and claim against him. This may be service by post, or even by newspaper advertisement, but the master's discretion to order what is called "substituted service" will be exercised sparingly, and only upon satisfactory proof being given on affidavit that the defendant is deliberately avoiding service.

Defendant's Appearance (O. 12)

The defendant's "appearance" to the writ is no more than the completion and signing of a formal document in duplicate by his solicitor or himself, and the sending or delivery of the same to the court office from which the writ was issued. The formality is, however, an important one, as if the defendant fails to enter his appearance within 8 days of service of the writ, including the day of service, the plaintiff may sign judgment against him in "default of appearance" (O. 13).

Where leave has been obtained to serve the process out of the jurisdiction, a longer period is normally allowed for entry of appearance (O. 11). The time for appearance may be extended by agreement between the parties or by the master upon good cause being shown by the defendant.

Once a defendant has entered an unconditional appearance, he is deemed to have waived any irregularity of service and to have accepted the jurisdiction of the English court. If he wishes to object to service or jurisdiction, he must apply to the master for leave to enter a "conditional appearance", i.e. appearance under protest (O. 13, r. 7) and, if leave is granted, apply to have the writ or service, or both, set aside.

If the claim is for a liquidated sum, e.g. "£1000, the price of goods sold and delivered", or "£1000, money lent", the plaintiff may, if the defendant is in default, sign final judgment for the sum claimed and costs, upon producing an affidavit of service to the Central Office. A plaintiff cannot recover interest unless the agreement so provides or the statute allows it.

If the claim is for unliquidated damages or for detinue of goods, he may enter interlocutory judgment for damages to be assessed, or in detinue for delivery up of the goods or their value to be assessed, and the action will then proceed, usually before the master, upon the basis that liability has been established but that the amount due still has to be proved. If the plaintiff's claim is for possession of land only, he may also obtain final judgment in default, provided that the action is not a mortgage action, and he files an affidavit to that effect.

To meet cases where injustice would be caused to the defendant by allowing a judgment in default to stand, the master has power to set it aside upon terms which will usually include a provision that the defendant should pay the costs thrown away in any event.

ORDER 14

The procedure laid down by this order is of vital importance to lawyer and litigant alike. It provides a speedy and relatively cheap means of obtaining judgment in cases where the plaintiff's right to relief is clear, and it goes a long way towards preventing a defendant using the machinery of the courts to avoid or delay payment of his just debts.

The special procedure is open to a plaintiff in all actions, other than claims for libel, slander, malicious prosecution, seduction, breach of promise of marriage, or claims based on an allegation of fraud. Where a statement of claim has been either indorsed on the writ served, or served upon the defendant, *and* the defendant has entered an appearance, the procedure permits judgment to be asked for a given sum in respect of part of a claim, and it also permits a defendant to ask for and obtain summary judgment on his counterclaim. Similar procedure is open to a plaintiff in the Chancery Division when he is claiming specific performance (O. 86).

By a general indorsement of his claim on the writ the plaintiff gives no more than the bare bones of his claim. To make use of this procedure he is required to set out his claim in much more detail. This he may do, either by indorsing a statement of claim, as it is called, on the writ itself or by serving it separately. Further reference will be made later to the statement of claim under the title "Pleadings", but at this stage it is sufficient to say that it must contain sufficient particulars to let the defendant know the case which he has to meet.

Having taken these steps, and the defendant having entered appearance, the plaintiff may then apply to the master for summary judgment against the defendant. This application is made by summons supported by an affidavit setting out the facts on which he bases his claim, and deposing to his belief, if the claim is for a liquidated sum, that there is no defence to it; or if unliquidated, that there is no defence save as to the amount of damages.

The summons and a copy of the affidavit and any exhibits thereto, must be served on the defendant at least 4 clear days before the action date that appears on the summons. If the defendant intends to contest the application upon issues of fact, he will usually have to depose to the facts upon which he relies in an affidavit, and deliver the same to the plaintiff before the hearing; although he may in exceptional circumstances attend and give evidence. If he wishes to rely only on points of law, they may be argued without having to swear to an affidavit.

The Queen's Bench masters have very wide powers under this order. It is for the defendant to satisfy the master that he has a prima facie defence to the claim, or that part of it which is in dispute; alternatively, he must show that he has a counterclaim, the amount of which should be set off against the plaintiff's claim. The position of the parties would, of course, be reversed if the defendant were seeking summary judgment on a counterclaim.

On the hearing the master may give the plaintiff judgment for the whole of his claim, or part thereof, or may give leave to defend the claim as a whole or in part. He may give leave to defend unconditionally, or he may put the defendant on such terms as a condition of leave to defend as he thinks just, e.g. security for costs or payment of monies into court. He may also order a stay of execution of judgment given against a defendant until after the trial of a counterclaim.

While the procedure is of great value, plaintiffs should not make use of it except in cases where the evidence is overwhelmingly against the defendant. The procedure could operate harshly, and even unjustly, on a defendant unless the masters exercised their discretion to order judgment sparingly. In particular, the imposition of terms such as payment into court, or security for costs, could have the effect of depriving a financially embarrassed defendant of the right to defend a perfectly proper issue.

Hence the masters use their discretion sparingly in favour of a plaintiff, and in practice if the defendant raises a "triable issue", the master is obliged to give leave to defend unconditionally. A further hazard a plaintiff may have to face is, that if he uses this procedure, well knowing that the defendant is relying on a contention which would entitle him to unconditional leave to defend, he may be ordered to pay the defendant's costs forthwith. If, after the hearing of the application, matters are still left to be tried, the master will give directions as to trial, and the parties must be prepared for this. Appeal from the decision of a master lies to the judge in chambers, and on the appeal fresh evidence may be heard.

PLEADINGS (O. 18)

In every action commenced by writ in the High Court the parties are required to set out in written, typed or printed form, the precise nature of their respective cases. These documents are termed "pleadings", and are of vital importance in a civil action. The art of drafting pleadings is one of the major preoccupations of common law junior counsel; although solicitors and even litigants themselves can undertake the task if they so wish. The author of the pleading, however, cannot remain anonymous, as he has to sign the document and withstand any criticism by the court of his workmanship and skill.

Success in pleading requires knowledge of the law relating to the dispute, experience in the branch of litigation which is dealt with, an understanding of the essential facts of the case, as well as skill in the use of words. The principal pleadings are the statement of claim of the plaintiff, the defence, or defence and counterclaim of the defendant, and the reply and defence to counterclaim, if a counterclaim is made.

The above-mentioned pleadings may all be served on the other side without leave within the requisite period, but leave of the master is required to serve any subsequent pleadings. Service can be effected by the medium of ordinary post, or by leaving the document in question at the address which has been given by the other party for service.

The parties must set out in a clear and concise form all the material facts upon which they intend to rely, but *not* the evidence by means of which these facts will be proved. A party is bound by his pleading and will not be allowed to raise allegations of fact not pleaded, nor to set up a new cause of action at the trial without leave; and leave will be given rarely at that stage, and then only on stringent terms as to costs.

Before the trial either party may, before the pleadings are closed, amend once without leave, but he must otherwise obtain the master's leave, and will normally have to bear his own costs and those of his opponent occasioned by the amendment (O. 20).

The formal requirements of every pleading in the action are set out in O. 18, r. 6, and will not be repeated here, as they can be seen from the specimen pleadings in actions for breach of contract and damages for negligence as set out at the end of Chapter 10 which deals with trial in the High Court. (They are all the particulars, other than those contained in the numbered paragraphs.)

It is, moreover, a requirement of O. 18, r. 6, that pleadings which contain any number of allegations must be divided into paragraphs numbered consecutively, and that figures, dates, and numbers must be given in figures.

A fundamental principal of pleading is that one must not take one's opponent by surprise. All barristers will know that one is fully entitled, and indeed, morally obligated to communicate to one's fellow barrister, if a pleading which bears his signature is not understood and if it is intended to apply to the court in respect thereof.

As a general rule a party is not strictly required to plead matters of law, but he may do so, and frequently does so, in cases where he is relying on part of a statute or regulations imposing duties, such as those imposed upon employers and others in respect of persons working in docks and ships, by the Docks Regulations made under the Factories Acts. As will appear presently, a defendant is in some cases bound to plead statutory defences.

Apart from its essential purpose of telling one's opponent the case he has to meet, it should be remembered that the pleading is the first introduction to the judge of the case which he has to try; and a clear and well laid out pleading is more likely to impress him favourably.

Apart from the fact that the party who puts his opponent to unnecessary expense by denying facts which he could clearly have admitted, it is good pleading to make admissions wherever this can be done without damaging one's case, as it adds force to the denials. If a pleading lacks sufficient particularity for the other side to answer it, he is entitled to request in writing "further and better particulars" before he serves his own pleading. This should be done initially by letter, and if the request is not complied with, a summons to the master may be issued. Apart from a real difficulty in seeing the nature of the case, such requests should be left until the summons for directions stage, which is dealt with in a later section.

STATEMENT OF CLAIM

The plaintiff's claim should be set out in the logical sequence of events, so that one can see at once who the parties are, the nature of their relationship in law, e.g. master and servant, buyer and seller, landlord and tenant; the duty or contract alleged to have been broken; particulars of the breaches alleged, and any injury and damage caused thereby. Damage is to be divided broadly into two categories, namely general damage, which flows naturally from the breach and need not be specially pleaded, and special damage which only arises in the particular circumstances of the case and must be pleaded in detail.

DEFENCE AND COUNTERCLAIM

Defence

If the plaintiff has served a summons under O. 14 the defendant's time to serve his defence, and counterclaim (if any) is extended until the hearing of the summons. If he is given leave to defend he will usually be allowed 14 days by the master's order. Otherwise a defendant who has entered an appearance will have 14 days from the time limited for appearance (8 days), or from service of the Statement of Claim, whichever is the later. He may, if he requires further time obtain it by agreement with the plaintiff or from the master on a time summons.

It is not enough for a defendant to make an omnibus denial of the statement of claim. The defence must deal with each allegation of fact separately. He may either traverse (deny) the allegation, or admit it, but he must not be evasive. For instance if the plaintiff alleges that the defendant owes him £1000, the defendant should not plead "The defendant denies that he owes the plaintiff £1000", because this leaves open the possibility that he owes the plaintiff some other sum; so that he should add words which make this clear, such as "or any sum at all".

Any allegation of fact which is not specifically traversed is deemed to be admitted, except for allegations of damage which are deemed to be traversed unless expressly admitted. The defendant may also "confess and avoid", which means that he may admit some or all of the facts alleged, but set up fresh facts which excuse him from liability, viz. "the defendant admits that the plaintiff paid him £1000, but the same was the price of a motor car sold and delivered by the defendant to the plaintiff on the 10th July 1950."

The defendant *must* plead some defences in law, viz. performance, release, waiver, statutes of limitation, fraud, illegality. He must also plead to an action for possession of land, the defence on which he relies, and not simply plead that he is in possession of the land. He may, without counterclaiming, seek by his defence to "set-off" against, i.e. diminish or extinguish the amount of the plaintiff's claim, by the amount of any sum, whether ascertained or not. But if he is claiming a sum which is or may exceed the plaintiff's claim, he must counterclaim.

Counterclaim (O. 15, r. 18 and O. 18)

A counterclaim may be described as a "sword" whereas a set off is a "shield", the former being a weapon of attack, and the latter one of defence. The defendant may counterclaim in respect of any claim, relief or remedy he alleges he has against the plaintiff. If he succeeds and the plaintiff also succeeds, the sum awarded to one may be set against the sum awarded to the other, judgment being given for the balance. He may join as defendant to his counterclaim a person or persons other than the plaintiff, where he alleges that such person is liable with the plaintiff, in respect of his counterclaim. The master, however, always has a discretion to order separate trials where the multiplicity of causes of action or parties may cause delay or inconvenience. In all other respects the pleading of the counterclaim is subject to the general rules of pleading and in particular those relating to the statement of claim.

REPLY AND DEFENCE TO COUNTERCLAIM
(O. 18, rr. 14 and 18)

Reply

If there is no counterclaim, a reply is rarely needed, because all facts which are not admitted in the defence are deemed to be denied or, as it is termed, "issue is joined" between the parties. The plaintiff may, however, serve a reply where he wishes to meet facts set up by way of confession and avoidance in the defence, or where he wishes to admit some allegation in the defence in order to save costs.

He must *not* in his reply set up any new claim or raise fresh facts inconsistent with those contained in his statement of claim. "Departure", as it is called, is forbidden, and if he wishes to alter his claim or any of the facts in his statement of claim he must do so by amending that pleading.

The first paragraph of the reply should contain the joinder of issue, viz.: "Save as hereinafter admitted, and save in so far as the Defence consists of admissions, the plaintiff joins issue with the defendant thereon". In the subsequent paragraphs the plaintiff should deal with the matters he wishes to admit or traverse specifically.

Defence to Counterclaim

Where a counterclaim has been made the plaintiff will have to serve in one document a reply and defence to the counterclaim. The reply should join issue as above, omitting any reference to the plaintiff's admissions if none are to be made. The defence to the counterclaim is subject to the general rules of pleading already mentioned, and in particular, those applicable to a defence.

Close of Pleadings (O. 18, r. 20)

Pleadings are deemed to be closed 14 days after service of the defence if no further pleadings have been served, or 14 days after service of any reply, or reply and defence to counterclaim. It is the duty of the plaintiff's solicitor to take out the summons for directions within one month of the close of pleadings.

THE DEFENDANT'S CASE

Just as the plaintiff's legal advisers will have considered all the practical and legal implications of commencing proceedings against the defendant, so the defendant's advisers should have been considering his situation. As a general rule litigation is not resorted to until negotiation has failed, and by the time that the writ is issued the lawyers should have a fair idea of the issues that are involved.

Every case raises different questions, the following being only a few of those that are encountered most frequently.

(1) Does the statement of claim disclose a proper cause of action or is it a case where an application to strike out the writ and statement of claim would be likely to succeed?
(2) Has the defendant a defence to the claim, wholly or in part, or a right of set-off or counterclaim against the plaintiff?
(3) Is there any third party to whom the defendant may be entitled to look for an idemnity or contribution in respect of the plaintiff's claim?
(4) Is it a case where the court would order the plaintiff to give security for costs?
(5) Should the defendant make a payment into court or plead tender?
(6) Is the statement of claim pleaded with sufficient clarity to enable the defendant to answer it, or should further and better particulars be requested?

In addition to these questions, the defendant and his legal advisers will have to consider the following basic questions: How much is at stake? How much is the action likely to cost? How much can the defendant afford to risk? What prospects are there of recovering any costs or other monies from the plaintiff if the defendant wins?

The question of legal aid enters into this aspect of the matter, as will be seen when we come to consider the whole question of costs in Chapter 12. If the plaintiff is in receipt of legal aid, this fact will of itself serve to give the defendant a fair idea of his financial standing and vice versa. Further, the defendant himself may be entitled to legal aid.

Any legal adviser who fails to take this aspect of litigation into account, and to warn his client of the possible hazards, is doing him a great disservice. In every action one side has to lose, and the normal consequence of losing is that the loser pays not only his own costs, but also those of the winner. Even in a relatively straightforward Queen's Bench action these may well amount to a total of £400 or an even larger sum.

The questions mentioned above may now be examined more closely.

Striking Out (O. 18, r. 19)

An application to strike out an opponent's indorsement of claim on the writ or pleading rarely succeeds, and should therefore not be embarked upon lightly. The grounds for such an application are that the pleading:

(*a*) discloses no reasonable cause of action or defence; or
(*b*) is scandalous, frivolous or vexatious; or
(*c*) may prejudice, embarrass or delay the fair trial of the action; or
(*d*) is otherwise an abuse of the process of the court.

Under this order the court has jurisdiction to bring to an end summarily untenable claims and defences; to prevent the processes of the court from being used for improper purposes, and generally to ensure that the rules of pleading are observed. Except in cases under (*b*) or (*d*) it is generally wise to give an opponent a chance of putting his pleading in order by amendment before making an application to strike out. It is, indeed, a rule of etiquette at the bar that a fellow barrister must be warned before such an application is made.

Further and Better Particulars

If a party's pleading lacks sufficient particularity to show his case clearly, or in enough detail, the other side may apply for further and better particulars. Except where the pleading is so defective that it cannot be understood or dealt with, such applications are dealt with on the summons for directions.

In the event that an earlier application to the master is intended, the particulars should first be requested in writing, as failure to give an opponent this opportunity may cause the applicant to be mulcted in costs. Such an application may be made together with, and as an alternative to, an application to strike out.

Defence and Counterclaim (O. 15, r. 2)

The form of pleading has already been considered, and this section is concerned only with the preparatory steps. At the earliest possible moment the defendant's legal advisers should obtain statements, preferably in writing, dated and signed, from the plaintiff and his potential witnesses, and inspect all relevant and material documents. The value of any oral evidence lessens as time progresses and recollection dims, and witnesses are therefore frequently asked in cross-examination when they were first asked to recall the events they have described.

They must also consider whether any of the special defences mentioned under "Pleadings", such as infancy, are open to the defendant. The final step will be to marshal the facts and decide what defence and counterclaim, if any, is open to the defendant, and to advise him accordingly. It cannot be emphasized too strongly that proper groundwork at this stage is of the utmost importance.

Third Parties (O. 16)

This term embraces all parties other than the plaintiff and the defendant who are brought into the action by means of third party procedure. Third party procedure was created by the Judicature Acts, and is now consolidated by section 39 (1) (*b*) of the Judicature Act, 1925. Its purpose, like that of joinder of parties and causes of action, is to prevent multiplicity of actions being brought over the same subject matter of dispute between a number of interested parties.

This section covers all cases in which a defendant is entitled to indemnity or contribution, and includes a co-defendant in the same action. It now also extends to nearly every case in which the third party's wrongful act is alleged to have caused the damage in respect of which the plaintiff is suing the defendant; for example, the supplier of goods to a retailer who is being sued by a customer for defects of quality, or a master stevedore whose negligent loading of a ship has caused or contributed towards an accident to a dock labourer in respect of which he sues his employer for damages.

An application for leave to issue a third party notice giving notice of the defendant's claim is usually not necessary, provided that the defendant issues it after entering appearance, and before serving his defence. But, where it is necessary, application may be made to the master *ex parte*, by leaving the notice and an affidavit in support with the master's secretary.

The notice must set out the nature of the claim against the defendant, the nature and grounds of the defendant's claim against the third party, or the questions or issues to be dealt with as between them. It must be served together with a copy of the writ and any pleadings. Once the third party has been served he becomes a party to the action, and stands in the same relation to the defendant as the defendant stands to the plaintiff, and he may in turn bring in other persons as further parties to himself in precisely the same way.

If the third party enters an appearance the defendant must issue a summons for directions as between himself, the plaintiff, and the third party, and serve it on them. At the hearing of the summons the master will decide whether the notice is in order. If it is, he may order judgment to be given against the third party, or dismiss the defendant's application, and terminate the action against the third party, or give directions as to the trial of the issues between the parties, and how the trial shall be conducted, and the part to be taken therein by the third party.

Should the third party default, either in entering an appearance or in serving a defence, he will be deemed to have admitted any claim stated in the third party notice, and he will be bound by any judgment or decision given in the action, so far as it affects the claim against him.

As between co-defendants in negligence claims, a simplified form of notice and procedure is available, whereby one defendant can claim contribution from the other. This is sufficient to invoke the jurisdiction of the court to apportion blame, and the liability in damages of the defendants.

Moreover, O. 16, r. 10 contains a useful provision whereby any party sued as third party, or as one or more tortfeasors (wrong-doers) liable in respect of the same damage, to make contribution, may make a written offer of contribution to the other or others. Should the offer be rejected, it may be brought to the judge's attention at the trial, after liability and amount of the award have been decided, and the judge may take it into consideration when he is determining the question as to what costs should be paid, both as to which party should pay them, and also as to what proportion should be so payable.

Security for Costs (O. 23)

The court has power in certain cases to order a plaintiff on his claim or, exceptionally, a defendant on his counterclaim, to lodge in court security for the other side's costs. The most common instances are where a plaintiff is resident outside the jurisdiction, or in the case of an insolvent limited company, or where a nominal plaintiff sues for the benefit of someone else, who is believed to have insufficient means to pay the other side's costs if he loses.

In the event of making such an order it will normally be included as one of the conditions, that no further steps may be taken by the party under order until security is given, and this has to be done within a set time limit.

The application should be made as soon as possible, first by letter, and only then, if rejected, by summons to the master. Once an order has been made, applications for further security may be made if the original security ordered appears to be inadequate. This jurisdiction is, however, exercised sparingly because of the possible injustice it might cause to litigants. The insolvency or poverty of a plaintiff is no ground for requiring him to give security for costs except in the two cases mentioned above.

Payment into Court (O. 22)

In any action for debt or damages a defendant may at any time after he has entered an appearance, pay money into court, either in full satisfaction of the plaintiff's claim, or if there are several causes of action, in respect of any one of them.

He must give to the plaintiff notice in writing of such payment, in the prescribed form, and must specify the causes of action to which it relates. If a defendant who is counterclaiming pays money into court, he must also state which parts of his counterclaim he is setting off against the plaintiff's claim, and which he is taking into account in calculating such payment. A plaintiff may do likewise, if he wishes to pay into court in respect of a counterclaim.

A plaintiff in respect of his claim, or a defendant in respect of his counterclaim, cannot accept money in court in partial satisfaction of a cause of action; but if he decides to accept it, he may within 14 days upon giving notice to the other side, take the money out of court without leave; and thereupon the cause of action to which the payment relates is discharged, and he is entitled to his costs thereof. The exceptions to this rule are infants, mentally disordered patients, and widows suing for damages in respect of the death of husbands where their claim is coupled with a claim by an infant. Monies recovered for these classes are administered by the court, and only paid out with the court's leave during incapacity.

In the event, however, of failure to accept within 14 days, the party so failing will have to obtain the master's leave in order to take the money out of court, and will usually have to pay any costs incurred by the other side after the 14 days have expired. The fact that money is in court, and the amount thereof, is not disclosed to the judge or the jury until the issues of liability and the quantum (amount) of damages have been decided, except in the case of tender. These provisions are of vital importance to both plaintiffs and defendants, because of the effect they have on costs.

As from the date of payment in, the person to whom the offer of payment is directed is in peril as to costs, since, if he carries on the action and in the result is awarded no more than the amount in court, he will usually be ordered to pay all the other side's costs as from the date of payment into court.

In cases of simple debt and other liquidated claims, the system works well on the whole. But it is questionable whether it assists the cause of justice in actions for damages for personal injuries, or death caused in traffic or industrial accidents. Nearly every defendant in this class of case is covered by insurance, and those who have practised in this type of work will know the difficulty of advising a plaintiff whose claim may be worth in the region of £1000, of the risk in costs which he runs if he rejects a payment into court by the insurance company of £800. As a matter of simple arithmetic he could be risking £300–£400 in costs for a possible additional gain of about £200.

The advantages of this to the insurance company are obvious; but they are not so obviously fair to the plaintiff who may well be hard pressed for money and therefore in no position to gamble.

Tender (O. 18, r. 16 and O. 22)

There are only two exceptions to the rule that payment into court may not be disclosed. Firstly, in the case of tender in actions of debt or liquidated damages. Should a defendant, before the action is brought, have tendered what he believes he owes to the plaintiff, and this offer has been refused, he may state this openly in his pleading, and pay the amount into court.

Secondly, section 2 of the Libel Act, 1843, and section 2 of the Libel Act, 1845, afford a defence to an action for libel contained in a public newspaper or other periodical publication in certain circumstances and permit the defendant to make a payment into court "by way of amends". This payment in may also be disclosed.

The plaintiff cannot take money paid into court with a defence of tender, without the master's leave, and if he elects to do so, he will usually have to pay all the defendant's costs.

DISCOVERY OF DOCUMENTS (O. 24)

After the close of pleadings the parties will have to prepare for the trial. The first step which has to be taken by each side is the mutual disclosure of all documents relevant to the issues to be tried. This practice is one derived from the old Chancery Court procedure.

Under the existing procedure the first step is automatic; each party must, within 14 days of the close of pleadings, serve on the other side a list in the prescribed form of all documents he has, or formerly had, relating to the matters in issue. Each party will then give notice of such documents as he wishes to inspect, and he will then be given an opportunity of inspecting and copying them.

Discovery can, however, be dispensed with, or limited to classes of documents, either by agreement or by order of the master. Order 24, r. 2, expressly provides that in running down actions defendants will not be required to give discovery unless the master orders otherwise.

Should either party so wish, he may by notice require his

opponent to verify his list by affidavit. He will do so, however, only if he suspects that the list is incomplete, or that his opponent is being less than frank. Moreover the master has an overriding power to order full and fresh disclosure and, if he is satisfied that a party is being deliberately perverse or obstructive, he may order the action to be dismissed or the defence to be struck out, or even commit the defaulting party to prison or make such other order as may be just.

SUMMONS FOR DIRECTIONS (O. 25)

Until recent times it was permissible for parties to proceed piecemeal with applications for directions before trial. Under the modern procedure they must only in exceptional circumstances make applications to the master before the summons for directions. The summons must usually be taken out within one month of the close of pleadings to be returnable to the master in at least 14 days and served on the opposite side. Should the plaintiff fail to do this, the defendant may either do so himself or apply for the action to be dismissed.

The summons is a printed form containing some thirty paragraphs in which are set out the directions which are usually required by plaintiffs and defendants in most actions, including the place, mode and estimated length of trial, and the time within which the action must be set down for trial. The usual mode of trial will be by a judge alone, or by judge and jury.

The plaintiff must indicate any direction he does not require by crossing through the number which precedes that paragraph. If he wishes to request any further and better particulars of his opponent's pleading, or administer interrogatories, he should serve the relevant documents on him or his solicitor. Similarly, should the defendant want any directions to be given other than those set out in the plaintiff's summons, he must serve on the plaintiff a counter notice specifying them.

Apart from the trial itself, this is generally the most vital and crucial stage of any action. It is frequently the first time that the parties' legal advisers meet in relation to the action. Sufficient of the cards are by now probably disclosed to get some idea of strength and weakness, and, not least important, from this moment onwards costs are going to mount up as serious preparation for trial takes place. Not unexpectedly, therefore, it is at this stage that many an action is settled.

The master will usually give all the directions to the parties which he considers necessary up to trial at the one hearing, but he may adjourn some to a later date.

Interrogatories are rarely used in ordinary actions, but they are worthy of mention. They are a series of questions in writing that are put to an opponent and which are required to be answered on affidavit. The questions must be directed to matters strictly relevant to the issues in the case. They must not be prolix, and must be capable of being answered simply. What are called "fishing" interrogatories are not permitted.

Assuming that all necessary directions have been given and have been complied with, the next stage will be that of setting down for trial.

SETTING DOWN (O. 34)

It is the duty of the plaintiff or his solicitor to set down the action for trial. If he fails to do so within the period fixed by the master's order made on the hearing of the summons for directions, the defendant may do so himself, or he may apply to the court to dismiss the action for want of prosecution.

The party setting down the action must deliver to the proper officer, by post or otherwise, a request that the action be set down for trial at the place specified for the trial in the master's order. He must also deliver therewith two bundles (one of which will become "the record" of the court), and the other for the judge's use, consisting of copies of the writ, all pleadings including any affidavits ordered to stand as pleadings, all requests or orders for further and better particulars given, all orders for directions and, if legal aid has been granted, the certificate.

The documents must be bound in chronological order and the record bundle must be stamped to denote payment of the fee for setting down, and bear the names, addresses, and telephone numbers of the solicitors for the parties or, where a party is acting in person, like details in respect of himself.

The proper officer for the purpose in relation to actions to be tried in the Royal Courts of Justice in London is the Chief Associate of the Crown Office for Queen's Bench actions, and for Chancery actions, it is the cause clerk of the Chancery Registrar's Office.

The party setting down is obliged to notify the other parties that he has done so within 24 hours of his so doing, and he must also notify them of any communication he receives from the clerk of the list as to the date of the hearing, or any date before which the action will not be tried. Further, all parties to an action are under a duty to inform the clerk of the lists without delay of any settlement or likely settlement or withdrawal, and to withdraw the record if a settlement takes place.

The parties are also under a similar duty to inform the proper officer of any assignment, change or devolution of their respective interests or liabilities. If an action remains in any list for 1 year marked as abated or as ordered to stand over generally, it will be struck out of the list unless the order specifies otherwise.

LISTS OF ACTIONS (O. 34, rr. 4–7)

Lists of High Court actions for trial in London are kept in the Royal Courts of Justice and similar lists are kept at assize towns. Every Queen's Bench action set down for trial will appear in one of the following lists, namely: the jury list; the non-jury list (trial by a judge alone); the short cause list (cases estimated to last 2 hours or less, to be tried by a judge alone); and, in London only, cases to be tried in the commercial list; the revenue list (tax matters); and the special paper list (references from arbitration). In London the Queen's Bench lists are kept in the Crown Office and the Chancery lists in the Registrar's Office. In the assize towns they are kept by the district registrars.

The great majority of all actions in the High Court of Justice in London are set down in the non-jury list. Initially, they will simply appear in the list in the order of setting down, and they will remain there unless one or more of the parties applies to the clerk of the lists to fix a date for hearing. This he may do by obtaining an appointment from the clerk and notifying the other parties of his intention to apply. On such an application, if the parties cannot agree a date, the clerk will fix one for them. Any dissatisfied party has a right of appeal to the judge in charge of the non-jury list.

Once, however, a date has been allocated and the action placed in the non-jury list, only the judge himself in charge of this list can alter it, and he will only do so if some very good reason is shown. One of the best testing grounds for a young barrister is to appear before the judge in charge of the list upon such an application. Trying to "wrap up" his application in words which will persuade the judge to grant an adjournment is an invaluable experience.

Lists would, of course, be virtually useless unless they were sufficiently promulgated. Without them solicitors engaged in litigation could not keep their clients advised nor arrange their work, and barristers' clerks could not decide what briefs to accept. Accordingly a list of non-jury actions to be tried in London is published weekly and supplied to those who pay for this publication. This list will show all non-jury actions which are likely to be tried in the following week, non-jury fixtures which have been fixed for hearing during that term, and all other non-jury actions that have been set down. It is called the "Pending List of Non-jury Actions".

In addition, a "Daily Cause List" is published and distributed; as its name suggests, it is daily. This list is of necessity not compiled until late in the preceding day, when those in charge of the lists can see what is left over from that day's work—the part heard case being the bugbear that tends to thwart the efforts of all who are concerned in compiling lists and making fixtures for the hearing of specific cases. The list will show all actions and causes due to be heard in the Royal Courts of Justice the next day, and will also contain in a section entitled "Warned List" other non-jury Queen's Bench actions which are likely to be tried, not the following day, but possibly the day after or within a day or so.

These lists are open to the general public to see, and can be found both inside and outside the Royal Courts of Justice and even in some of the nearby refreshment places.

CHAPTER 10

Trial in the High Court

Final preparations — Briefing counsel — Parties to an action — Opening by plaintiff — Submission by defence — Conduct of defence and counterclaim — Summing up and judgment — Running-down actions — Costs — Payment into court — Trial by jury — Right of appeal — Forms of pleadings: (a) In an action for sale of goods; (b) In an action claiming damages for negligence.

THE reader has been taken through many of the possible proceedings that may occupy a litigant's consideration prior to the actual trial itself from the issuing of the writ down to the final setting down of an action for trial. It is proposed in the present chapter to make a short reference to the conduct of the trial.

FINAL PREPARATIONS

It has first to be pointed out that the trial of an action can be regarded either as the final hearing in open court or as the entire proceedings from the moment that the writ is issued. It is in the former sense that the word trial is used in this chapter. One of the most common forms of action tried in the Queen's Bench Division of the High Court in modern times is that in respect of personal injuries caused by negligence, and generally known as "running-down actions", since the majority of them arise out of accidents in which motor vehicles have been involved. Another common type of action concerns the sale of goods—transactions which may involve quite a variety of legal liabilities and a number of parties.

The final preparations for trial throw a great responsibility on to the solicitors who are acting on behalf of the parties to a High

Court action, since any lack of care or foresight on their part in the final steps prior to the actual trial itself may have the direst consequences for their client. Once a trial has been set down for hearing a solicitor must make absolutely sure that he has warned all the witnesses that it is proposed to call on behalf of his client and also to see that all the necessary correspondence and exhibits that are relevant to the claim are available for the court.

BRIEFING COUNSEL

Both parties to an action have, through the medium of the interlocutory proceedings, made as thorough an investigation as is legally permissible of their opponent's case. Their respective strengths or weaknesses will now be known to each other, and the stage is set for the trial to take place. As already indicated, the solicitors on both sides will have prepared all the requisite documents and taken statements from all the witnesses whom it is intended to call on behalf of their respective clients.

The climax of all this preparation results in the delivery of a brief to the counsel who has been chosen to appear in court on behalf of the client. It should, however, be noted in passing that a lay client has always the right to appear on his own behalf and conduct his case in court himself if he so chooses. Since the great majority of cases that are dealt with by the High Court have counsel appearing on both sides, it is necessary to consider shortly how a solicitor ought to instruct counsel in his brief.

The main purpose of the brief to counsel is to ensure that all the important factors which may weigh in favour of or against his client are set out fully in the instructions that appear in the brief. These instructions apart, the brief will also include copies of the statements or "proofs" as they are called, of all the witnesses that it is proposed to call, together with a copy of all the relevant correspondence and documents; copies will also be made available for the use of counsel of any exhibits that are required in order to support his client's case, or to meet those of his opponent.

In the majority of actions both parties will in all probability be represented by one counsel, that is to say, a member of the junior bar. In larger or more complicated matters, however, it may well be that either one, or even both sides, will be represented by two counsel, that is to say, a leader or Q.C. as well as a junior. It will be appreciated that there is no hard and fast rule as regards representation in court. Many factors have to be considered, the main one being that a sharp eye has to be kept on the costs that are incurred on behalf of the client. The two main items of expense in relation to an action in the High Court are in respect of the work done by the solicitor, and the fees which he has agreed for the services of counsel. Whether to incur the additional expense of two counsel as opposed to one becomes a most important factor for a solicitor to determine on his client's behalf. He may well have to advise that, since the opposition are engaging the services of two counsel, it may be unwise for his client not to do so.

PARTIES TO AN ACTION

The two main parties to an action are, of course, the plaintiff and the defendant; and as has already been seen, when there is a counterclaim to be decided, this in effect constitutes the hearing of two actions at one and the same time. It may well, however, not rest here since actions not infrequently involve the adding of a third party to the proceedings. For instance, if a vendor is sued for damages for the defective quality of goods that he has supplied, he may well himself have a legal right to claim damages from the person who supplied the goods to him. Hence, whilst A sues B for damages in respect of defective goods supplied to him by B, B in turn sues C for supplying him with the defective goods which he sold to A. In such a case, since the cause of action is common to all three parties, instead of two actions—A. *v.* B and B. *v.* C.—the two possible actions are joined together and can be set down for trial at the same time. C thus becomes a third party to the action.

Similarly, in cases in which negligence is involved, a plaintiff may have a possible right of action against more than one person.

He may sue them all as defendants or he may select the one against whom he considers he has the best chance of success. In the first case the defendant who is sued may bring in as third parties any persons from whom he claims contribution or indemnity in respect of any damages he may have to pay the plaintiff. In the latter case, co-defendants can achieve the same result by serving each other with simple contribution notices.

OPENING BY PLAINTIFF

We have already seen that actions are allocated to the respective divisions of the High Court. The final allocation occurs when the action is put down for hearing in the list of cases to be tried by the Hon. Mr. Justice X in Court Y on the blank day of blank. On the completion of the case that immediately precedes it, the associate who sits in court with the judge will call the case on for trial. It is thus that the case of *Smith* v. *Jones* starts on its final and all-important phase. In the meanwhile, however, the court usher will have ascertained for the benefit of the judge the name or names of the counsel who are engaged in the case, together with any lists of law reports and law books that counsel intend to refer to during the course of the hearing of the case, and the reports and books themselves. By so doing the usher will have made sure that copies of any cases that are cited by counsel will be immediately available to the judge. It is the duty of counsels' clerks to see that such lists are made available in good time.

To take a very simple example, we will assume that Smith is suing Jones to recover a sum of money which he, Smith, claims that Jones promised to pay him in respect of goods supplied to him, Jones has entered a defence and counterclaim to the effect that the goods as supplied were utterly worthless and that he, Jones, has suffered damage as a result of passing on the goods to other persons who are suing him in respect of their totally defective character.

The action will be commenced by counsel who is briefed on behalf of Smith proceeding to open his client's case. He will outline the facts to the judge pointing out that goods to the value of £1000 were sold to Jones on a particular date and that he, Smith, has not received any money from Jones in settlement of the transaction. During the course of his opening counsel will refer the judge in particular to the pleadings in the action, and since Jones has put in a defence and counterclaim, he will at the same time deal with this aspect of the case. Another important duty of counsel in opening the case will be to make sure that he refers the judge to all the relevant documents that are contained in the bundle which will be before the court. It is most important that counsel in his opening should try to clarify the issues that the judge will eventually be asked to determine. A well-opened case will not only assist the judge, it may also result in giving him a favourable opinion of the plaintiff's cause of action, which counsel for the defence may find it hard to dislodge.

Having thus put the broad outline of his client's case before the judge, plaintiff's counsel's next task will be to call his witnesses one by one and to examine them on the proofs of evidence which have been supplied to him with his brief. Here again, a good advocate will nurse his witnesses in such a way that he ensures that they only give such evidence as is strictly required of them. All witnesses cannot, of course, be kept strictly under control, but it is a factor to be borne carefully in mind. Each witness before he is examined has to take the statutory oath—that the evidence he gives is the truth, the whole truth and nothing but the truth. Should a witness desire to affirm, either because he has no religious belief or because taking an oath is contrary to his religious belief, he will be permitted to do so.

It will then be the turn of counsel for the defendant to cross-examine each witness for the plaintiff, and in the course of this process he must put the defendant's case to the witnesses and endeavour to challenge the evidence which they have given on behalf of the plaintiff, so that their truthfulness, accuracy, or reliability may be tested. Cross-examination is an art and a difficult one to master. The novice is often tempted to put the extra question which almost invariably turns out to be the one that produces the last answer he wanted. As a general rule, it is better to ask only those questions to which he knows the answer already. Plaintiff's counsel always has the right to re-examine his own witnesses, and he will do this if he thinks that by so doing he can repair any damage that has been done to their evidence by the cross-examination. The judge can ask witnesses questions if he desires to clarify any point, but this right is usually exercised sparingly. Plaintiff's counsel will then close his case.

SUBMISSION BY DEFENCE

Should it transpire that defending counsel takes the view at this stage of the trial that the defendant really has no case to answer on the plaintiff's claim, it is open to him to make a submission to the judge with the intention of persuading him that the plaintiff has not succeeded in establishing even a prima facie case to be answered. Such a submission may be founded either on law or on fact. A submission of this kind will only be made in a clear-cut case as the judge may put counsel to his election; that is to say, he may ask counsel if he intends to rely on his submission or to call evidence. If counsel chooses the former, he cannot call witnesses to rebut the plaintiff's case if his submission fails. The risk is generally too grave a one to take. In any event, plaintiff's counsel will be given an opportunity to reply before the judge will deliver his ruling. Should that ruling turn out to be in the defendant's favour, then judgment on the claim will be pronounced forthwith in his favour and the action will proceed no further unless there is still a counterclaim to be tried.

There remains the question of costs. Apart from any unusual circumstances arising, a successful party is normally entitled to his costs as of right. It has to be remembered, however, that all costs in High Court actions are subject to taxation. Thus, a successful party, although he is awarded the costs of the action, may still find himself having to subsidise the sum so allowed out of his own pocket in order to recoup his solicitor and counsel for their services. Assuming, however, that no submission is made at this stage on the defendant's behalf, the trial will then proceed in the normal manner.

CONDUCT OF DEFENCE AND COUNTERCLAIM

It now becomes the duty of counsel appearing on behalf of the defendant to place the full facts on which the defendant relies before the court, and in carrying out this duty he may have a dual role to play. If the defendant in addition to entering a defence to the plaintiff's claim has also put in a counterclaim on his own behalf, the court will require to be fully informed both in regard to the defence and as to the counterclaim. Defendant's counsel will, therefore, make his opening speech covering this ground, and will then in his turn proceed to call his witnesses who will be subjected to cross-examination by plaintiff's counsel, and in due course if he so desires it, to re-examination on his part. The judge will by this time have become fully seised of the nature of the defence and counterclaim, since apart from the fact that both will have been the subject of pleadings in the action, the cross-examination of the plaintiff's witnesses will have served to indicate the main grounds on which these are based.

All the evidence relative to the action having now been adduced before the court, including the disclosure of any documentary evidence that the parties wish to bring to his notice, it now only remains for counsel on either side to make their final speeches. In this connection, the benefit of the last word is an expression that may well be familiar to persons who are not lawyers. To advocates, however, it is a matter of considerable importance, and a really eloquent and persuasive address made just before the judge has to deliver his judgment and summing up may result in a victory which might not otherwise have been achieved.

We have already seen that plaintiff's counsel has the advantage of opening and presenting his client's case before counsel for the defendant has an opportunity to perform a similar task on his client's behalf. It might, therefore, be thought that this initial advantage held by the plaintiff would be offset by the defence having the last word prior to the judge's judgment and summing up. In fact, however, counsel for the defendant has to make his final speech as soon as he closes his own case, and before plaintiff's counsel makes his final speech.

The latter is thus in a position to comment on any portion of defending counsel's speech, and is in a strong position to take full advantage of having the benefit of the last word. It is evident, therefore, that a heavy responsibility rests on the shoulders of the defendant's counsel, since his task is to present his client's case in as favourable a light as possible, bearing in mind all the time that any deficiencies on his part will doubtless be seized on by his opponent in his final speech.

SUMMING UP AND JUDGMENT

Counsel on both sides have now completed their tasks and it becomes the judge's turn to fill in the final stage of the trial; that is, to sum up the facts and to deliver his judgment. Comparatively rarely, usually in cases which have involved intricate legal arguments, a judge may adjourn the trial at this stage in order to deliver his judgment at some later date. This will enable him to take due time in preparing his summing up, and when the adjourned date of the hearing is reached he will in all probability deliver his judgment in a written form, which he will read out in court.

Where, however, the action that he has been trying is one of pure fact, and presents no difficult features, the judge will usually deliver his summing up and judgment forthwith. The summing up consists of a concise analysis of the evidence that has been given during the course of the hearing together with the reasons which have induced the judge to arrive at his final decision. Thus it is the last sentence of the summing up, as this is very often when the final verdict is declared, that in effect amounts to the judgment concerning the matter at issue. The parties will now know their fate and the judge will deliver his judgment in favour either of the plaintiff or of the defendant or otherwise, as the case may be.

Reverting therefore once more to the case of *Smith* v. *Jones*, it will be seen that there are three possible results that may emerge as a result of this particular trial. Firstly, the judge may be satisfied on the evidence adduced by Smith, that the goods which he sold to Jones were, in fact, of perfect quality, and accordingly judgment will be delivered in favour of Smith for the full amount of his claim for payment of £1000 in respect of the goods which he delivered to Jones, and dismiss the counterclaim. Secondly, the judge might find as a fact, that the goods were partially defective and therefore not worth the full amount which Smith is claiming in respect of them, in which event he would reduce the sum claimed by Smith *pro rata* in accordance with the extent to which he found the goods to be defective and possibly also find for Smith on the counterclaim in part. Whilst the third possibility is the other extreme, when the judge is satisfied by the evidence adduced before him on behalf of Jones that the goods are, in fact, worthless, and in this case he will enter judgment for Jones on the claim and also on the counterclaim if satisfied that the damage suffered by Jones's customer also flowed from Smith's breach of contract.

RUNNING-DOWN ACTIONS

Having given a short example of an action involving the sale of goods, it is now proposed to make a brief reference to one of the other common types of action with which the Queen's Bench Division is concerned, namely running-down actions. Another common type of action relates to industrial injuries. Running-down actions are most frequently ones in which plaintiffs seek to obtain damages in respect of injuries and loss which have been suffered by them consequent on accidents in which motor vehicles have been the cause of the injuries. Speaking generally, the conduct of these actions follow the same lines as those already illustrated in connection with sale of goods actions.

There are two main issues which have to be determined, first and foremost the liability or otherwise of the defendant. Should the plaintiff fail in his endeavour to establish negligence on the part of the defendant, his action will fail, however grave his injury, and judgment will be delivered in the defendant's favour.

Assuming, however, that the plaintiff is able to make good his claim with regard to the defendant's liability, there then arises the all-important question of the quantum of damages that he can recover as against the defendant. This matter may well prove to be a difficult one for the judge to determine, since the consideration of personal injuries frequently involves taking into account the evidence of conflicting medical opinions. The value of the motor vehicle which belongs to the plaintiff, and which has suffered damage, will in all probability present no problem. The gravamen of the action will lie in the amount of damages which the plaintiff ought to be entitled to recover from the defendant in respect of personal injuries and loss, past and future, suffered by him as a result of the defendant's negligence. In this respect a factor that has to be borne in mind by the judge is the wage earning one—not only having regard to the loss of wages due to his immediate incapacity, but also having due regard to the possibility of a permanent reduction in his wage-earning capacity.

COSTS—PAYMENT INTO COURT

The trial being over and judgment duly delivered, the associate will then draw up an order which will include the judgment of the court set out in precise terms, together with any order that has been made with regard to costs. Reference has already been made in Chapter 2 to the question of costs in connection with bills of costs delivered by solicitors, and further reference will be made to this subject in Chapter 12. It is only necessary, therefore, to refer very briefly to this matter here.

It has already been pointed out that the costs incurred in litigation in the High Court may amount to a considerable sum, a sum which will of necessity be much greater should an unsuccessful party to an action be ordered to pay his opponent's costs in addition to his own.

As already mentioned in Chapter 9, there is, however, one important step that is open to a defendant should he feel uncertain of ultimate success, and by means of which he may be able to minimise the risk in costs that may ultimately be incurred by him in the event of the failure of his defence. This consists in the payment of money into court, which may take place either during the interlocutory proceedings that precede the trial in court, or at any time prior to the actual date of the hearing of the action. Thus, if Jones should be of the opinion that Smith may well be awarded £750 in the action in which he is claiming £1000 for goods delivered and he, Jones, pays that amount into court, in the event of the judge deciding that £750 or a lesser amount is all that Smith can recover in the action, Jones will not be liable in respect of any costs incurred by Smith on or after the day on which he made his payment into court: and indeed, Smith will generally be ordered to pay any costs incurred by Jones since that date.

TRIAL BY JURY

The illustrations which have been given both relate to actions tried by a judge in what is known as the non-jury list. Of recent years the tendency has been for fewer and fewer cases to be tried by a judge and jury, whilst the majority of actions are set down for hearing by a judge alone. The facilities, however, still exist, and it is still possible for a litigant to choose this method of trial in a limited class of cases, the most usual of which are in libel and slander. One slight variant takes place in the conduct of such a trial: where the plaintiff is represented by leading counsel, the action is commenced by junior counsel for the plaintiff opening the pleadings to the jury. In other words, he reads out the pleadings, statement of claim, defence and, if there is one, the counterclaim.

Such a trial then proceeds on similar lines to a non-jury action, except for the fact that the judge in his summing up will put certain specific questions to the jury for their determination. The judge throughout the trial will remain the sole arbiter as regards points of law, whilst the jury will be the sole judges of the issues of fact.

RIGHT OF APPEAL

A right of appeal lies from the judgment in an action tried by a judge alone, or that of a judge and jury, to the Court of Appeal. The ultimate court of appeal is the House of Lords, and leave to appeal may be given either by the Court of Appeal or by the House of Lords.

FORMS OF PLEADINGS

(1) In an action for sale of goods:
- (*a*) Statement of claim.
- (*b*) Defence and counterclaim.
- (*c*) Reply and defence to counterclaim.

(2) In an action claiming damages for negligence:
- (*a*) Statement of claim.
- (*b*) Defence.

Specimen Pleadings in Action for Breach of Contract

IN THE HIGH COURT OF JUSTICE 1967 S. No. 1
QUEEN'S BENCH DIVISION

Writ issued the 2nd day of January 1967.

BETWEEN: JOHN SMITH *Plaintiff*
and
DAVID JONES *Defendant*

STATEMENT OF CLAIM

1. By an oral agreement made on the 10th October, 1966, between the Plaintiff and the Defendant the Plaintiff agreed to sell to the Defendant and the Defendant agreed to buy from the Plaintiff 1000 yards of cloth at a price of £1 per yard.
2. The Plaintiff duly delivered the said cloth to the Defendant but the Defendant has failed to pay therefor the said price or any part thereof.

And the Plaintiff claims: £1000

(*Signed*)

IN THE HIGH COURT OF JUSTICE 1967 S. No. 1
QUEEN'S BENCH DIVISION

BETWEEN: JOHN SMITH *Plaintiff*
and
DAVID JONES *Defendant*

DEFENCE IN COUNTERCLAIM

Defence

1. The Defendant admits that he entered into an oral agreement with the Plaintiff on the 10th October 1966 for the purchase of 1000 yards of cloth at £1 per yard but he denies that the said agreement is fully or accurately set out in Paragraph 1 of the Statement of Claim.
2. It was an express condition of the said agreement, alternatively the Plaintiff expressly warranted that the said cloth would in quality and description correspond with a sample produced by the Plaintiff and shown to the Defendant beforehand.
3. The Defendant admits that the Plaintiff delivered to him 1000 yards of cloth and that he failed to pay any sum for the same.

   For the reasons stated hereinafter he denies that he is indebted to the Plaintiff in the alleged or any sum.
4. The said cloth was not in accordance with the said sample and was of an inferior quality and description. By reason of such inferiority it was worthless and useless to the Defendant, alternatively it was worth £750 less than if it had accorded with the said sample.
5. If, which is not admitted, there is any sum due from the Defendant to the Plaintiff, he will seek to set off against such sum, if any, so much of his Counterclaim herein as will be sufficient to satisfy the same.
6. Save as hereinbefore expressly admitted each and every allegation in the Statement of Claim is denied.

(*Signed*)

Counterclaim

7. The Defendant repeats Paragraphs 1 to 5 inclusive of his Defence.
8. At and prior to the making of the said agreement the Defendant made known to the Plaintiff that he had previously entered into a contract with one Brown for the sale at the price of 25 shillings a yard to the said Brown of 1000 yards of cloth of the same quality and description and that he was buying the said cloth expressly for the purpose of fulfilling that contract.
9. The Defendant upon receiving the said cloth delivered it to the said Brown in purported performance of his said contract but the said Brown rejected the said cloth as not being of the quality and description agreed.
10. By reason of the matters aforesaid the Defendant has lost £250.

    And the Defendant counterclaims £250.

(*Signed*)

REPLY AND DEFENCE TO COUNTERCLAIM

Reply

1. Save insofar as the Defence consists of admissions and save as hereinafter admitted the Plaintiff denies each and every allegation contained therein and joins issue with the Defendant thereon.
2. The Plaintiff admits that the agreement between the Defendant and himself was for the sale of the said cloth by sample but he denies that the said cloth or any part thereof was otherwise than in accordance therewith or that he is guilty of the alleged or any breach of the said agreement.
3. Further or alternatively it is denied that the said cloth is either worthless or useless or worth less than £1000, the price agreed therefor.

Defence to Counterclaim

4. The Plaintiff repeats paragraphs 1 to 3 inclusive of his Reply herein.
5. The Plaintiff denies that he knew as alleged or at all any of the matters set forth in paragraph 8 of the Counterclaim at the time of the said agreement between himself and the Defendant and he makes no admissions either as to the agreement alleged between the Defendant and the said Brown or as to any of the other matters alleged in the said paragraph.
6. If, which is denied, the Defendant has lost £250 or any sum as alleged or at all the Plaintiff denies that such loss has been caused by the alleged or any breach by him of the said agreement.

(*Signed*)

Specimen Pleadings in Action claiming Damages for Negligence

IN THE HIGH COURT OF JUSTICE 1967 S. No. 7
QUEEN'S BENCH DIVISION

Writ issued on the ...... day of ...... 19.......

BETWEEN: JOHN SMITH *Plaintiff*

and

TOM JONES *Defendant*

STATEMENT OF CLAIM

1. At about 8 a.m. on the 10th October 1966 the Plaintiff was driving his Humber motor-car, registration number PO440C along Piccadilly, London W.1 in the direction of Piccadilly Circus when the Defendant so negligently drove and controlled his Ford motor lorry registration number PPP42C along the said road in the same direction that it collided with the rear of the Plaintiff's said motor-car whereby the Plaintiff's said motor-car was severely damaged and the Plaintiff has been caused personal injury, loss and damage.

Particulars of Negligence

The Defendant was negligent in:

1. Driving too fast.
2. Failing to keep a proper look-out.

3. Failing to observe that the traffic lights at the junction of Piccadilly and Berkeley Street were red against him.
4. Failing to keep a safe and proper distance between his vehicle and the Plaintiff's motor-car.
5. Failing to stop, slow down or turn aside so as to avoid the said collision.

Particulars of Personal Injury

The Plaintiff sustained laceration of the face and head necessitating the insertion of 22 stitches, severe bruising, concussion and shock. He was detained in hospital as an in-patient for 7 days and thereafter he was by reason of his said injuries unable to return to work for 11 weeks.

Particulars of Special Damages

Loss of earnings at a net average of £20 a week for 12 weeks	£240	0	0
Damage to Humber motor-car	£175	0	0
	£415	0	0

And the Plaintiff claims damages.

(*Signed*)

IN THE HIGH COURT OF JUSTICE 1967 S. No. 7
QUEEN'S BENCH DIVISION

BETWEEN: JOHN SMITH *Plaintiff*
and
TOM JONES *Defendant*

DEFENCE

1. The Defendant admits that on the date alleged he was driving his said motor lorry in Piccadilly towards Piccadilly Circus when it collided with the Plaintiff's said motor-car.
2. Save as aforesaid the Defendant denies that the said collision and such injury, loss or damage (if any) as the Plaintiff may prove to have suffered, were caused in the manner alleged or by reason of the alleged or any negligence (which is denied) on his part.
3. Further or alternatively the said collision and the Plaintiff's injury, loss and damage (if any) were caused solely or alternatively contributed to by his own negligence in:
   (1) Failing to keep a proper look out.
   (2) Driving his said motor-car from its parked position by its nearside kerb outside Green Park Underground Station into the stream of traffic when by reason of the approach and proximity of the Defendant's vehicle it was unsafe for him to do so.
   (3) Giving no prior signal or warning of his intention to draw away from the said kerb.
   (4) Giving the Defendant no opportunity of avoiding the said collision.

4. No admissions are made to any of the alleged injuries, loss and damage.
5. Save as hereinbefore expressly admitted each and every allegation in the Statement of Claim is denied as fully as though the same were set out separately herein and traversed seriatim.

(*Signed*)

CHAPTER 11

Tribunals and Inquiries

INTRODUCTION

We have explained in the preceding chapters how civil actions are tried and decided in the ordinary courts of law. In this chapter it is proposed to consider the field of administrative law which lies outside the original jurisdiction of the ordinary courts.

By administrative law we mean, broadly speaking, the whole field of social legislation. Parliament has found itself increasingly involved in this field since the middle of the nineteenth century and more particularly since the end of the Second World War. For example, the Government has by statute provided such services as national insurance, health, housing and education, and controlled the acquisition, development, and use of land. Parliament has given itself powers to regulate the day-to-day activities of the community, and machinery has had to be provided to deal with disputes and questions which occur inevitably from time to time between the government authority and individuals affected by the powers, and with claims of persons to benefit from public services or public funds. The principal methods of resolving disputes is by administrative tribunals, and this chapter is concerned principally with describing them.

Firstly, the statute which creates the powers of regulation may provide for the setting up of a tribunal to try and decide claims and disputes in the particular field which the state regulates. Such a tribunal is generally independent of the Government and will follow the judicial process in arriving at its decision. Its decision will thus be a truly judicial one and the meaning of this will be explained later.

Secondly, the statute may provide that the ultimate decision lies with the Minister of the Government department concerned. In this case, the statute usually provides that the individual who is aggrieved is entitled to have his objection, claim or appeal, heard at an inquiry presided over by a person appointed by the Minister before the final decision is made. In this case the decision is termed a quasi-judicial one. The distinction between judicial and quasi-judicial decisions was considered by the Committee on Minister's powers in their report which was published in 1932.

The definitions which were given in the report are so clear and authoritative that they are quoted below, thus:

> A true judicial decision pre-supposes an existing dispute between two or more parties and then involves four requisites:
>
> (1) the presentation (not necessarily orally) of their case by the parties to the dispute;

(2) if the dispute between them is a question of fact, the ascertainment of the fact by means of evidence adduced by the parties to the dispute and often with the assistance of argument by or on behalf of the parties on the evidence;

(3) if the dispute between them is a question of law, the submission of legal argument by the parties; and

(4) a decision which disposes of the whole matter by a finding on the facts in dispute and an application of the law of the land to the facts so found, including where required a ruling upon any disputed question of law.

A quasi-judicial decision equally pre-supposes an existing dispute between two or more parties and involves (1) and (2) but does not necessarily involve (3) and never involves (4). The place of (4) is taken by administrative action. In the case of the quasi-judicial decision the finality of (4) is absent. Another and different kind of step has to be taken; the Minister has to make up his mind whether he will or will not take administrative action and, if so, what action. His ultimate decision is quasi-judicial and not judicial because it is governed, not by a statutory direction to him to apply the law of the land to the facts and act accordingly, but by a statutory permission to use his discretion after he has ascertained the facts and to be guided by considerations of public policy.

As a general principle, the process of ministerial decision accompanied by an inquiry or hearing is adopted where the ultimate decision may have to be based wholly or partially on policy. Such matters as housing and land development, for instance, may involve questions of government policy, public finance, public opinion and even expediency. Further, they are fields in which the central government has delegated some responsibility for making decisions to local government and therefore lend themselves to the quasi-judicial process.

The main purpose of creating a tribunal is to provide an independent body to decide disputes in a limited and specialized field where the questions which have to be decided do not have a direct effect on government policy and a truly judicial decision is possible and desirable.

The next official inquiry into the working of tribunals and ministerial inquiries was undertaken by the Committee on Administrative Tribunals under the chairmanship of Sir Oliver Franks (the Franks Committee). This Committee's terms of reference were limited to the "constitution and working" of tribunals and the "working" of ministerial decisions where the procedure includes the holding of an inquiry or hearing. It was therefore not concerned with the purely administrative powers of Ministers. The Committee's report was published in 1957. It separated its findings on tribunals and ministerial inquiries, but in practice they overlap and it is therefore convenient to consider the effects of its recommendations. The Committee accepted that there should be "special procedures" to give binding decisions, apart from decisions made by the ordinary courts, but stressed that these special procedures should have the characteristics of "openness, fairness and impartiality" in the same way as the courts of law. It concerned itself mainly with suggestions as to ways in which these three objects could best be achieved.

The principal recommendations on which action has been taken are as follows:

(1) *The Tribunals and Inquiries Act*, 1958

This statute established a Council on Tribunals, the members of which are appointed by the Lord Chancellor. Its functions are supervisory and advisory, its members work part-time and it has a full-time secretariat. Its duty is to consider the activities of the tribunals which are specified in the Act and such other matters concerning tribunals as the Lord Chancellor may refer to it and to consider and advise on rules of procedure for the specified tribunals.

In relation to ministerial inquiries the Council has a more limited function. It has to consider and report on matters concerning tribunals referred to it by the Lord Chancellor which it considers to be of special importance. In practice the Council has had more to do with inquiries than tribunals because of public dissatisfaction with decisions made in that way.

(2) *Legal representation*

The Committee recommended that legal representation should be permitted and that hearings should be the rule. These views have been largely accepted.

(3) *Reasons for decisions*

This is perhaps the most important recommendation of the Franks Committee which has been implemented. In the case of tribunals it was usually the practice for reasons to be given for a decision, but in the case of inquiries this was not so. The inspector would hold the inquiry and make his report to the Minister and all that the interested parties would receive in due course was an announcement of the Minister's decision.

Rules have now been made for two of the most important classes of inquiry, namely, appeals to the Minister against the decisions of local planning authorities refusing planning permission and against compulsory purchase orders. These rules ensure that the individual concerned is given not only a fuller and franker disclosure of the reasons for the Minister's decision, but also a statement in advance of the points which will be relied on by the authority.

(4) *Other measures*

The Act did not provide a right of appeal as of course, but in general a right of appeal on points of law now exists where it did not before. Similarly, the Act did not implement the recommendations as to the appointment of chairmen of tribunals and independent inspectors to preside over inquiries. In many cases chairmen of tribunals are selected by ministers from panels of independent persons appointed by the Lord Chancellor. Inspectors are still not independent; they remain the employees of the ministry and this is still a source of dissatisfaction.

A general picture of the part played by tribunals and ministerial inquiries respectively has now been given. It is important to remember that they are quite distinct. Ministerial decisions and inquiries will be considered in the following section and then it is proposed to consider some of the more important tribunals.

MINISTERIAL DECISIONS AND INQUIRIES

In considering this subject it is important to remember that a minister is the head of a Department of State. As such he is responsible to Parliament for the administrative acts and decisions of his department although he may have no personal knowledge of them. His department is primarily concerned with administering the powers and duties with which he is entrusted. It is only when these have an impact on other bodies or private citizens that the need arises for an inquiry to be held. Such an inquiry is conducted by an officer of the ministry, usually termed an inspector, who is qualified in the particular field with which the inquiry is concerned, e.g. an architect or surveyor in planning appeals. But it must be stressed that the inspector does not decide the matter. His duty is to hear the evidence and report back to the minister with his findings of fact and recommendations. The decision rests solely with the minister, and he is in no way bound to accept his inspector's recommendations.

In nearly every case which leads to a public inquiry there may well have been discussions and correspondence between government department and a local authority. Before 1958 the private citizen would probably have known nothing about these, although the inspector would have had access to the files and may well have perused them.

Inevitably there has been strong suspicion among the public in general, and more particularly among those who felt they had been wronged, that far too much went on behind the scenes, and that decisions were being affected by matters not disclosed at the inquiry, which they had had no opportunity of dealing with. This dissatisfaction led to the setting up of the Franks Committee. The terms of reference of the Franks Committee and the nature and scope of its report have already been considered in the introduction to this chapter. Unfortunately, its inquiry did not extend to inquiries appointed voluntarily by a Minister or to maladministration by government or local government officers.

The two main fields in which the final decision is reserved to a

Minister of the Crown and he is required by law to cause a public inquiry to be held are the compulsory acquisition of land by the government and other authorities and the control of the use of land by town and country planning authorities.

COMPULSORY PURCHASE

Statutory powers to acquire land compulsorily for a variety of public purposes have been given to many public authorities. For example, a local authority may acquire it for housing or schools or a Minister may acquire it for a highway. The procedure for compulsory purchase is conditional in the Acquisition of Land (Authorization Procedure) Act, 1946. The first step is for the acquiring authority to make a compulsory purchase order. Notice of the order must be served on every owner, lessee, and occupier of the land, and advertized in the local press. If no objection is made or all objections are withdrawn, the minister may confirm the order, but if an objection is made he must cause a public local inquiry to be held or give an opportunity to the objector to be heard in private. The inquiry is conducted by an Inspector employed by the ministry and the proceedings resemble a trial except that they are less formal. The inspector does not announce his decision. He reports to the minister, who will, in due course, give his decision and the reasons therefor in writing. Legislation which will give inspectors powers of actual decision in minor matters is now pending.

TOWN AND COUNTRY PLANNING

The procedure in relation to planning appeals is somewhat similar. The Minister of Housing and Local Government is responsible for securing and executing a national policy for the development and use of land. The local planning authority, who are the county councils and county borough councils have powers delegated to them to grant or refuse planning permission and they in turn may delegate some of their powers to borough, rural, district, and urban district councils.

If planning permission is refused by the local planning authority or granted subject to conditions to which the applicant objects, the applicant may appeal to the Minister, who will appoint an inspector to preside over a public inquiry into the dispute. As in the case of compulsory purchase procedure, the inspector will report to the Minister, who will make the final decision.

TRIBUNALS

The number of tribunals at work in this country exceeds 1000 and may even exceed 2000. The complexity of the problem of tracing a common denominator can be judged by the fact that each is exercising its powers in a limited field with a particular object in view and deriving its jurisdiction and powers from statute and regulations made thereunder. Generalization is difficult and often dangerous and the only safe method of determining the powers and duties of each tribunal is by reference to the statute which creates it.

As we have already seen, there are some permanent tribunals which exercise jurisdiction over specialized matters and are presided over by High Court judges and which for all practical purposes may be regarded as part of the High Court. To the two already mentioned, namely the Court of Protection and the Restrictive Practices Court, there should be added the Patent Appeal Tribunal and the Registered Design Appeal Tribunal.

Of similar status, although not presided over by a High Court judge or forming part of the High Court, are the Lands Tribunal and the Transport Tribunal. Both are presided over by legally qualified chairmen, and appeal from their decisions lies to the Court of Appeal.

Other tribunals of a permanent nature are the Industrial Court, the industrial tribunals, the agricultural land tribunals, the rent tribunals, tribunals set up under the National Insurance Act, 1946, and the National Insurance (Industrial Injuries) Act, 1946, the war pensions appeals tribunals, and one of the most recently constituted, the Criminal Injuries Compensation Tribunal.

A description is given in the following sections of some of the tribunals which occupy an important position in our system of administrative law.

Land

THE LANDS TRIBUNAL

An example of a permanent tribunal of high judicial status which has become of increasing importance in recent years is the Lands Tribunal. This was created by the Lands Tribunal Act, 1949. The main purpose of the statute is to establish a new tribunal in place of its official predecessors, who were arbitrators and umpires unversed in law, to determine disputed questions relating to the valuation of land and to the amount of compensation to be paid for the compulsory acquisition of land by government departments and local or public authorities and similar matters. A tribunal for the United Kingdom, except Scotland, called "The Lands Tribunal" was set up (section 1 (1) Lands Tribunal Act, 1949). Section 1 (3) of that Act sets out the references to be dealt with by this tribunal and further defines its jurisdiction.

The members of the Lands Tribunal are appointed by the Lord Chancellor. They consist of a president in addition to such number of and such other members as the Lord Chancellor may decide to appoint. All the appointments to the tribunal are subject to Treasury consent. The qualification for the president is that he must be a person who has either held high judicial office under the Crown or has been a barrister of at least 7 years' standing. As regards the other members of the tribunal such number as the Lord Chancellor may decide must be barristers or solicitors of similar standing, and the remainder persons with experience in valuation of land, generally qualified surveyors. The purpose of the mixed appointments is to ensure that the tribunal can deal with both the legal and technical aspects of its jurisdiction. The Lord Chancellor is further empowered, subject to Treasury consent, to appoint and remunerate the other officers and servants of the tribunal.

The jurisdiction of the tribunal can be exercised by any one or more of its members, and the president has the power to select a member or members to deal with a particular case or class or group of cases (section 3).

The tribunal's jurisdiction has been added to by various statutes. It now includes the whole of the jurisdiction which was formerly exercised by the panel of official referees (section 1, Lands Tribunal Act, 1949). Appeals from local valuation courts in rating matters set up under the Local Government Act, 1948, were transferred to the Lands Tribunal before the provisions of that Act had come into force.

The jurisdiction of this tribunal has been even further enlarged by other modern statutes, perhaps the most important of which are the Town and Country Planning Acts. Under these Acts the tribunal deals with questions of compensation for planning decisions, or for the revocation or modification of planning permissions already granted.

The procedure of this tribunal is prescribed by rules made by the Lord Chancellor under section 3 of the Lands Tribunal Act, 1949 (Lands Tribunal Rules, 1963, S.I. 1963, No. 483).

Proceedings are set in motion by means of a reference in writing in a prescribed form. This has to be sent to the registrar of the tribunal within the time limit laid down by the rules. The reference having thus been initiated, the rules provide for application to be made for directions of an interlocutory nature. Such applications also have to be made in writing to the registrar and must state the grounds of the application.

A party who objects to such an application has the right, within 7 days of receiving a copy of it, to send a written objection to the registrar. In considering the application the registrar has to have regard to the convenience of the parties and the desirability of limiting costs; he must also communicate his decision in writing to each party. Further, if so required, the registrar must refer an application to the president for decision.

Lands tribunals sit at such places as the president may from time to time determine and it is the duty of the registrar to send to each party to the proceedings notice informing him of the place and time of the hearing, at least 14 days before the appointed date. The permanent offices of the tribunal are in London. At the hearing only one expert is normally allowed to be called by either side. Application may, however, be made either by means of interlocutory proceedings or at the hearing itself for the right to call additional expert evidence. The claimant begins and the other parties are heard in such order as the tribunal may determine. Parties may appear and be heard in person or they may be legally represented at the hearing.

Evidence may be given orally or by affidavit, and the examination may be on oath or affirmation. Apart from certain statutory exceptions the tribunal must conduct its proceedings in public, and it may inspect the land under consideration if so requested. In this latter event it must give notice of its intention to do so and the expert witnesses are entitled to attend.

The president if present will preside. If there is a disagreement the decision is by majority. A casting vote is available to the person presiding in the event that the members should be equally divided.

A decision of the Lands Tribunal is final subject to the right of appeal to the Court of Appeal of any person who is aggrieved by a decision due to errors in law. For this purpose an aggrieved person has 6 weeks from the date of the decision in which to lodge notice in writing to the registrar requiring the tribunal to state a case. On receipt of the case stated the aggrieved person must lodge it within 21 days with the proper officer of the Court of Appeal. The powers of the Court of Appeal are, either to amend the case, or to order it to be sent back to the tribunal for amendment. Powers to order costs or to tax and settle costs are given to the tribunal by virtue of section 3 (5) of the Lands Tribunal Act, 1949.

Agricultural Land Tribunals

By section 73 (1) of the Agriculture Act, 1947, an agricultural land tribunal was set up for each area in England and Wales by order of the Minister of Agriculture and Fisheries. There are eight such areas, and a statutory duty is placed on these tribunals to determine all matters referred to them under the Agriculture Act, 1947, or the Agricultural Holdings Act, 1948. The original function of the tribunals was to hear appeals from the decisions of the Minister and county agricultural executive committees. Since 1958 when the committees were disbanded and the powers of the Minister to control farmers curtailed, the principal functions of the tribunals have been to control the eviction of tenant farmers by landlords, and to deal with questions of compensation for improvements and disturbance of tenure and with matters arising under the Land Drainage Act, 1961.

Each tribunal has a chairman and deputy chairman who are appointed by the Lord Chancellor, who have to be either barristers or solicitors of not less than 7 years' standing. Two other members are appointed for each reference from panels representing the interests of tenant farmers and the owners of agricultural land respectively. The Minister also has power to direct that two assessors selected by him from a panel nominated by the President of the Royal Institution of Chartered Surveyors should be appointed to assist the tribunal.

The proceedings before these tribunals are regulated by order of the Minister (section 73 (3) of the 1947 Act). The order covers the forwarding of relevant documents to the secretary of the tribunal, the service of notices, legal representation, procedure in default of appearance, examination of witnesses, and inspection of land, etc., by the tribunal.

The tribunal sits in public and the parties to the proceedings may appear in person or they may be represented by lawyers or by other persons such as surveyors or union officials. The procedure followed is similar to that of the Lands Tribunal but it is rather less formal and appeal on questions of law is to the High Court.

Rent Tribunals

The First World War led the central government to intervene between landlords and tenants of some classes of dwelling-house in order to fix reasonable rents and to prevent the eviction of tenants without a court order. A great weight of complicated and frequently incomprehensible legislation has resulted and the rent tribunals are one part of the machinery which has been evolved for these purposes. These tribunals had their birth in the Furnished Houses (Rent Control) Act, 1946, and they were intended to fix fair rents for dwellings let furnished or with services such as heat, light, or attendance provided to a substantial extent. Such tenancies had hitherto escaped the net of Rent Act control and provided a useful loophole for landlords who wished to take advantage of the shortage of housing to raise rents.

The Act authorized the Minister of Housing and Local Government to establish a rent tribunal in a district where satisfied either on representation by or after consultation with the local authority that it should be applied to that district (section 1).

In such a case the Minister would then constitute a tribunal for that district and either party to a contract concerning a dwelling in the district that came within section 2 of the Act could refer it to the tribunal. The tribunal's duty was to hear the reference and fix a reasonable rent which would then be registered with the local authority.

The constitution of the tribunal was laid down in the 1946 Act, which provided for a chairman and two other members to be appointed by the Minister. The schedule to the Act also provided for the appointment of a clerk and other necessary officials as well as providing for the payment of salaries and allowances subject to Treasury approval. Initially, no particular qualifications were required for the chairmen or members, but by the Tribunals and Inquiries Act, 1958, the Minister is required to appoint chairmen from a panel set up by the Lord Chancellor and the practice is for chairmen to be lawyers. No qualification is required for the other members.

These tribunals have had a somewhat up-and-down career due largely to the fluctuations in official policy towards housing. For example, their jurisdiction was increased by the Landlord and Tenant (Rent Control) Act, 1949, and by the Housing, Repairs and Rent Act, 1954. By the Rent Act, 1957, dwelling-houses with rateable values of over £40 in London and £30 elsewhere were released from statutory control subject to certain safeguards for sitting tenants, and furnished tenancies of such houses were also decontrolled. This removed a large part of the tribunal's work.

The pendulum swung back once more with the passage of the Rent Act, 1965. This Act creates a new type of rent restriction over what are called "regulated tenancies". Section 1 (4) provides for the assessment and registration of "fair rents" by rent officers. Under sections 22 and 25 rent officers and deputy rent officers are to be appointed by the clerk to the local authority, and rent assessment committees are to be appointed in areas where the Minister brings into operation the scheme for registration set out in Part 2 of the Act. Control is re-introduced over all dwellings where the rateable value in Greater London is £400 or less and £200 elsewhere.

Section 39 of the Act amends the 1946 Act substantially and continues it in force. The jurisdiction of the tribunals is extended to dwellings within the above rateable limits but the Minister has power to vary these limits nationally or locally, thus paving the way for a possible ouster of jurisdiction of any rent tribunal in future in favour of the new machinery of rent officer and committee.

Further, the Act increases the periods of security of tenure which tenants could be given by tribunals under the 1946 and 1949 Acts from 3 to 6 months and it enables extended security to be given even where the original application is made after service of a notice to quit on the tenant. The Act extends the effect of the 1946 and 1949 Acts to the assignees of the original parties to the letting and it also enables a landlord to obtain a reduction or cessation of a period of security where the tenant is guilty of certain acts or omissions, e.g. nuisance or annoyance. Finally, it prevents the overlapping of the jurisdictions of the rent tribunals and the machinery of rent registration set up under Part 2 of the Act.

Appeal from the decision of a rent tribunal on a point of law lies to the High Court.

Transport

THE TRANSPORT TRIBUNAL

Another permanent tribunal of high status is the Transport Tribunal. It was created by the Transport Act, 1947, under which a public corporation known as the Transport Commission was also set up and empowered to take over road haulage and the railways, and to exercise control over road passenger transport. Reference should be made to sections 72–81 inclusive and the tenth schedule of the Act for the tribunal's powers.

In 1953 the powers of the commission were diluted when much of the publicly owned road haulage business was returned to private ownership, but the tribunal remained in being and still exercises important functions.

The Transport Tribunal inherited the jurisdiction of a number of earlier tribunals. Firstly, there was the Railway and Canal Commission which, as its name suggests, was concerned principally with the provision of proper rail services by the railway companies. This was a court of record presided over by a High Court judge, and appeal from its decisions lay to the Court of Appeal.

Secondly, there was the Railway Rates Tribunal, which was also a court of record presided over by a lawyer of distinction. The right of appeal also lay to the Court of Appeal. This tribunal was concerned with the establishment and control of rates of payment for the carriage of goods by rail. Thirdly, there was the High Court's jurisdiction over tolls.

Fourthly, by far the most important part of the jurisdiction of the Transport Tribunal is vested in that section which hears appeals against the grant or refusal of road haulage licences to carriers of goods, and deals with the limitations, terms, and conditions imposed on grant of a licence. This jurisdiction was taken over from the tribunal set up under the Road and Rail Traffic Act, 1933 to hear such appeals.

Like the Lands Tribunal, the members of the Transport Tribunal are appointed by the Lord Chancellor. The tribunal consists of a president who is a lawyer of standing and other members who are experienced in commerce and transport, so that it is suited to dealing with both the legal and the practical aspects of transport. It is a court of record, and counsel must appear robed before it.

The tribunal has two divisions, one of which deals principally with the regulation of fares for passenger transport in London, and the other with appeals from traffic commissioners in relation to road haulage licences.

Apart from fares in the London area, the tribunal has no jurisdiction over the licensing of public service vehicles for the carriage of passengers. This side of transport is under the control of traffic commissioners appointed by the Minister of Transport. Applications are heard in public, and parties and other persons interested may be legally represented. The system is an administrative one, and appeal against the grant or refusal lies to the Minister.

Applications for the grant of licences to carry goods by road vehicles are also made to the traffic commissioners, and the paramount consideration for the grant or refusal is the interests of the public. Interested persons can, however, object or support, and there can be legal representation. Appeal lies from the commissioners to the road haulage appeals division of the Transport Tribunal, and from there to the Court of Appeal.

Practice and procedure in the appeal division is similar to that in the Lands Tribunal. There is a registrar who performs similar functions to those of a High Court master, and the proceedings are governed by rules, at present the Transport Tribunal Rules, 1965. The registrar deals with interlocutory matters, and appeal from his decision lies to the tribunal itself.

Industry

Since the establishment of conciliation boards by the Conciliation Act, 1896, it has been increasingly recognized that workers' wages and conditions of employment are matters of vital concern to the nation as well as to the employers and employees concerned. Except for the period from 1940 to 1951 when the national emergency led to the temporary setting up of a National Arbitration Tribunal with powers of compulsion over both sides, the machinery for the settlement of industrial disputes has rested largely on the principle of collective bargaining and mutual consent. Industrial disputes may still be resolved by conciliation boards but other machinery now exists.

This tribunal was disbanded in 1951 and the position now is that it is left substantially to employers and employees to fix terms of employment and to settle their disputes, although encouragement is given to them to make use of the machinery which exists for arbitration and negotiation.

Industrial Court

An important part of this machinery is the Industrial Court which was established under the Industrial Courts Act, 1919. The same Act also provided for the appointment by the Minister of *ad hoc* courts of inquiry to inquire into industrial disputes as and when the need arose. It should be noted that the court is not intended to displace the ordinary processes of conciliation, but rather to add to them. Thus, a dispute may not be referred to the court unless there is either no machinery for the settlement of disputes in the trade or industry, or such machinery as exists has been tried and failed, or as under the Terms and Conditions of Employment Act, 1959, mentioned below. Further, the Minister has no power to refer a dispute unless the parties to it consent.

The Industrial Court is a standing court and consists of persons appointed by the Minister of Labour. Some members of the court are independent persons, some represent employers, others represent workmen. In addition one or more members are women (section 1 (1) Industrial Courts Act, 1919). The Minister directs one of the independent persons to act as president or chairman as the case may be (section 1 (4)).

A "trade dispute" within the court's jurisdiction is defined in section 8 of the Act as any dispute or difference between employers and workmen or between workmen and workmen connected with the employment or non-employment, or the terms of employment or with the conditions of labour of any person. "Workman" is defined as meaning any person who has entered into or works under a contract with an employer. It must be noted, however, that not all work done by A for B is done under a contract of employment. Much work is done by independent contractors. The distinction between the independent contractor and the employee is an important and difficult one. Important because it may affect the common law rights of A against B: it may also affect his right to receive industrial injury benefit under the National Insurance (Industrial Injury) Acts. Difficult because the line of distinction sometimes is a fine one.

The Minister of Labour's powers as to reference of disputes to the Industrial Court are laid down in section 2 of the Act. These powers include the right to refer disputes to arbitration. The full powers are by reference:

(*a*) to the Industrial Court; or
(*b*) the arbitration of one or more persons appointed by the Minister; or
(*c*) to a board of arbitration consisting of one or more persons representing the employers concerned, and an equal number of persons representing the workmen with an independent chairman nominated by the Minister.

The Industrial Court's procedure is laid down in the Industrial Court (Procedure) Rules, 1920 and 1924. The court may act, subject to the consent of the parties, even if a vacancy exists in its numbers. If the members are unable to agree, the matter is decided by the chairman. The court is further empowered to call in assessors to assist it. Subject to the court's permission, the parties may be represented by solicitor or counsel.

The Minister can, also, refer any matter relevant to a trade dispute to the court as a court of inquiry appointed by him (section 4 (1), Industrial Courts Act, 1919), or for advice. Such a court of inquiry may consist either of the chairman and other persons appointed by the Minister or of one person. The duty of the court in this case is to inquire into the matters referred to it and then to report to the Minister.

The practice has arisen whereby *ad hoc* rules of procedure are often appended to the court's terms of reference. Section 4 (5) of the 1919 Act further empowers the court to require any person who may have any knowledge of the subject matter of the inquiry to furnish a statement in writing, or where necessary to attend in order to give evidence on oath.

Another and most important part of the jurisdiction exercised by the Industrial Court is that which concerns terms and conditions of employment in a particular trade or industry, and which therefore affect a large body of workmen and employers.

The Terms and Conditions of Employment Act, 1959, provides that if (*a*) terms and conditions of employment are established in any trade or industry or any section thereof either generally or in any particular district, which have been settled either by agreement or award, and (*b*) the parties to the agreement or to the award are or represent organizations of employers and workmen respectively, forming a substantial proportion of the employers and workmen in that trade or industry or part thereof, and such workmen are of the description to which the agreement or award relates, and (*c*) any employer engaged in such trade or industry whether a party to the award or agreement or not, is not observing the terms or conditions in respect of any such workman: claims may be made in writing to the Minister to establish that the employer is in breach.

The Minister may then endeavour to settle the claim himself but if all else fails he may refer it to the Industrial Court. The court, if satisfied that the above three provisions are met, and unless it is satisfied that the terms and conditions of employment observed by the employer are not less favourable than those provided by the agreement or award, must then make an award requiring the employer to observe the recognized terms or conditions. Thereafter, the terms of the award become an implied term of the agreement between the employer and the class of workers concerned from such date as the court directs, but it must not be a date earlier than the date when the employer was first informed of the claim.

Terms and conditions of employment have been established by industrial agreement or award in many industries and trade. The result is that an employer may well find himself bound by the terms of an award or an agreement to which he was not even a party.

Wages Councils

The Trade Boards Acts, 1909 and 1918, provided for the establishment of trade boards in certain trades and industries. The main functions of the boards were to fix minimum rates of pay and to compel the employers to pay them.

The members of the boards were appointed by the Minister of Labour. Some members were independent persons and an equal number were appointed from among persons nominated by employers and trade unions and workers' organizations generally.

The Wages Councils Act, 1945, altered the name of the boards to Wages Councils. These councils inherited the functions of the trade boards. Their members are appointed by the Minister as before. A council's main duty is to investigate questions of pay, holidays, and holiday payments, and to endeavour to resolve such questions by agreement. If agreement cannot be reached, the employers and workers' representatives vote but if agreement still cannot be reached, the independent members may vote. The council will submit the result to the Minister as a proposal. The Minister may send it back to the council for further inquiry or consideration or he may confirm by order.

Once a statutory order has been made, the employer is liable in law to pay not less than the wage specified. If he does not do so, any workmen of the class described may recover the amount underpaid from his employer. The employer may also be prosecuted.

Fifty-one wages councils are now in operation in England and Wales. In addition, minimum wages are fixed by statute in a number of industries such as coal-mining and agriculture.

Industrial Tribunals

The Industrial Training Act, 1964, provides for the establishment of industrial training boards for the training of persons for industry. The Act also provides that levies may be made on employers to meet the expenses of the boards. Appeals against assessment to levies are made to industrial tribunals established under this Act.

These industrial tribunals also have jurisdiction to decide questions under the Contracts of Employment Act, 1963; the Redundancy Payments Act, 1965, the Selective Employments Payments Act, 1966: and the Docks and Harbours Act, 1966. They also have the jurisdiction previously vested in referees and boards of referees to deal with questions of compensation for loss of employment or loss or diminution of emoluments or pension rights under a number of statutes.

The Contracts of Employment Act, 1963, requires employers to give their employees written particulars of certain terms of their contract of employment and to give a specified minimum period of notice to terminate employment. On a reference by an employee an industrial tribunal may decide what terms should have been included in the written particulars of the contract in order to safeguard thc cmployees' rights.

The Redundancy Payments Act, 1965, imposes an obligation on employers to make redundancy payments to employees who are dismissed by reason of redundancy or laid off or kept on short time.

A fund called the redundancy fund has been set up under the management of the Minister of Labour. Employers have to pay weekly contributions to the fund for each employee. Employers who make redundancy payments are entitled to a rebate out of the fund. If an employer refuses or fails to meet an employee's claim wholly or partially, and the Minister is satisfied that the employee is entitled to payment, the claim must be met out of the fund and the employee's rights and remedies against the employer vest in the Minister.

To qualify under the scheme male employees must be under the age of 65 and female employees under 60. They must also have been continuously employed by the employer for at least 104 weeks before the date when the employment ends. An employee may lose his right to payment if he has been dismissed justifiably for misconduct or he has unreasonably refused an offer of re-employment by the employer or alternative employment or, in some cases, where he goes on strike during the currency of a notice to terminate his employment.

A dismissal is due to redundancy where it is attributable wholly or mainly to the fact that: (1) the employer has ceased, or intends to cease, to carry on the business for which the employee is employed or to carry it on where he was employed, or (2) where the requirement of that business for employees to carry out work of a particular kind or to carry it out where he was employed have ceased or diminished or are expected to do so. The industrial tribunals deal with the many difficult questions which arise under this Act, such as the right of an employee to receive redundancy payment and the amount thereof. A common point of dispute centres around the question whether the dismissal was due to redundancy.

The industrial tribunals also have jurisdiction over questions arising out of an employer's right in certain cases to receive a refund of selective employment tax paid pursuant to the Selective Employments Payments Act, 1966, and to decide disputes about the meaning of "dock work" under the Docks and Harbours Act, 1966.

The president of the industrial tribunal is appointed by the Lord Chancellor and must be a barrister or solicitor of no less than 7 years' standing. Each tribunal consists of a chairman and two other members. Either the president or a person selected by him from a panel of persons having like qualifications who have been appointed by the Lord Chancellor presides as chairman. The other members are selected by the president from two panels appointed by the Minister of Labour. One panel represents employers' organizations, the other represents employees' organizations.

Applications to the tribunal are made by originating application in writing. A copy of the application has to be sent to the respondent, who must enter an appearance within 14 days. The tribunal may make interlocutory orders as to discovery, further, and better particulars and similar matters. The time, date, and place of hearing is fixed by the president. Representations may be made in writing. A party may appear in person or by counsel or solicitor or by a representative of an employer's organization or trades union. The procedure for giving evidence and addressing the tribunal follows that of the ordinary courts, and the tribunal's decision is by majority vote. Costs are not usually awarded against any party.

The procedure for an appeal against an assessment to an industrial training levy is made by notice of appeal in writing to the tribunal. A copy of the notice must be sent to the industrial training board. The hearing is usually held in private, the procedure being otherwise the same as that for an originating application.

An appeal lies to the High Court from any decision of an industrial tribunal on a point of law.

National Joint Industrial Councils

The national joint industrial councils play an important and valuable part in the settlement of industrial disputes. They owe their existence to the report of the Whitley Committee which was published just after the First World War, and they are therefore generally referred to as Whitley councils. Each council embraces a whole industry. The members are drawn from trades unions and employers in the industry and they meet regularly to discuss their problems. The Whitley councils have no statutory basis or authority but any agreement they reach has great weight within the industry it represents and with the government. In some industries machinery has been set up to resolve dispute by arbitration but, apart from this, the main function of the Whitley councils is to settle their differences by discussion and agreement.

Public Service

ELECTRICITY AND GAS ARBITRATION TRIBUNALS

We now come to a brief consideration of two tribunals which owe their existence to the essential requirements of our modern civilization, both for domestic and industrial purposes, namely electricity and gas. Turning in the first place to electricity a tribunal which is called the Electricity Arbitration Tribunal was established by section 31 of the Electricity Act, 1947. Its principal function is to decide questions arising out of the acquisition of electricity undertakings and the compensation to be paid therefor.

Section 63 of the Gas Act, 1948, established a similar tribunal for the gas industry. This tribunal deals with questions arising from the acquisition of gas undertakings and compensation.

Each tribunal consists of a legally qualified president and two other members, one of whom has experience in business, and the other experience in finance. All three members are appointed by the Lord Chancellor.

The tribunals are courts of record with official seals and any order made by them is enforceable in England and Wales as if it were an order of the High Court.

The tribunal is empowered to, and if so ordered by the Court of Appeal is required to state in the form of a special case for determination by the Court of Appeal, any question of law arising before it.

Rules of procedure may be made by the tribunals with the approval of the Lord Chancellor. The Minister of Fuel and Power has a right to be heard in all proceedings before the tribunals, and on a case stated by or on appeal from them.

Social Security

Legislation

A subject which has lent itself readily to the use of special tribunals is that of "social security". In the immediate post-war period there was a spate of legislation concerned with the provision of free medical and other services and the payment of benefits to persons who had children, to sick persons, to injured workmen and to others. The first of such enactments was the Family Allowances Act, 1945, which provided for the payment of benefits in respect of some children. In the following year three further Acts were passed, namely the National Health Service Act, the National Insurance Act, and the National Insurance (Industrial Injuries) Act, to be followed in 1948 by the National Assistance Act. These statutes provided the modern foundation on which our system of State welfare has been built.

In the succeeding years further statutes were passed, until in 1965 and 1966 the whole field of social security came under review by Parliament. In 1965 three important statutes were passed. The National Insurance Act, 1965, consolidated the law relating to national insurance; the National Insurance Industrial Injuries Act, 1965, consolidated the law relating to national insurance in respect of industrial injuries, and the Family Allowance Act, 1965, performed a like function in respect of family allowances.

In the following year Parliament passed two further statutes, the National Insurance Act, 1966, and the Ministry of Social Security Act, 1966. The former statute amends both the National Insurance Act, 1965, and the National Insurance (Industrial Injuries) Act, 1965. In substance it provides firstly that, with the exception of certain "special questions" which arise in relation to industrial injuries, all questions arising in connection with claims for, or awards of, benefits under the Industrial Injuries Act are to be decided in the same manner and by the same persons or bodies as under the National Insurance Act, 1965. Secondly, the Act consolidates a number of senior appointments under the earlier statutes. It provides for the appointment by the Queen of a Chief National Health Commissioner to hold office for the purposes of both the National Insurance and the Industrial Injuries Acts, whereas there had been hitherto two offices of commissioner although the offices were customarily held by the same person. The Act also provides for the appointment of a number of National Insurance commissioners to deputise for and assist the chief commissioner. Those persons who formerly held office as commissioner and deputy commissioners under the earlier acts are deemed to hold the new appointments.

The Ministry of Social Security Act, 1966, dissolved the Ministry of Pensions and National Insurance which formerly had the responsibility for National Insurance and Industrial Injury benefit. It also dissolved the National Assistance Board. The Act created a new appointment of Minister of Social Security, and to this Minister were transferred the functions of the former Ministry, except that some of the functions of the former National Assistance Board are now exercised by a newly constituted body known as the Supplementary Benefits Commission.

National Insurance

The National Insurance Acts, 1946–66, provide for the payment of weekly contributions for national insurance and for the making of claims for benefit, and the payments of benefit in matters such as sickness, unemployment, retirement, maternity or death.

Questions arising under these Acts have to be determined by either (*a*) the Minister of Social Security, or (*b*) an insurance officer, local tribunal, or the commissioner, or (*c*) by the High Court on appeal.

The decision of the Minister has to be sought in such matters as ascertaining the class of insured persons a claimant is in; the entitlement to increased benefit; whether a person has satisfied the contribution conditions for benefit; and whether a person is entitled to family allowances.

Such matters may be referred to the Minister by an insurance officer for decision. Local tribunals may direct them to be referred to an insurance officer for reference to the Minister, and the Minister may appoint a person to hold an inquiry into the matter and report to him before he gives his decision. On questions of law the Minister may refer the matters to the High Court for decision and any person aggrieved by the Minister's decision on a point of law may appeal to the High Court, where the decision is final.

The Minister also has wide powers to review his decisions and to alter an award in the light of new facts brought to his notice, or if he is satisfied that the decision was given in ignorance of, or was based upon, a mistake as to some material fact.

The effect of these Acts is that claims for benefit have to be submitted first to an insurance officer who, if he does not decide the claim himself, must refer the matter to a local tribunal for that purpose or, where appropriate, to the Minister.

A right of appeal to a local tribunal lies from any decision of an insurance officer which is adverse to the claimant, and notice must be given in writing within 21 days of the insurance officer's decision. Where, however, an insurance officer certifies that the sole ground of his decision is a decision given by the Minister, leave to appeal has to be given by the chairman of the local tribunal.

The local tribunal consists of three persons, one member being drawn from a panel representing employers and insured persons, other than employed persons, one from a panel of insured employed persons, and a chairman. Since 1959 the chairman has had to be appointed from the Lord Chancellor's panel. The other members of these panels hold office for such period as the Minister may direct. A chairman's period of office is laid down by his letter of appointment, but he may resign by giving written notice to the Lord Chancellor.

Unless the chairman for special reasons makes a direction to the contrary, hearings before these tribunals take place in public. Reasonable notice of the date and place of hearing has to be given to the claimant and to all interested persons. At the hearing the claimant, the insurance officer and the Minister are entitled to be heard. When considering its decision the tribunal has to order all persons, with the exception of its clerk, to withdraw. The decision has to be in writing and must include the grounds for its findings on material questions of fact. A majority decision prevails, and if necessary the chairman has a casting vote.

An appeal from a local tribunal, which has to be brought within three months of the tribunal's decision being given, lies to the chief national insurance commissioner, who has the standing of a High Court judge, and it may be heard by him or one of the national insurance commissioners. The qualification for all commissioners is that they must be barristers or, in Scotland, advocates, of not less than 10 years' standing.

An appeal to the commissioner lies at the instance of an insurance officer, the claimant or certain other groups of persons, such as the claimant's union, provided that he is and was a member when the question at issue arose.

An appellant has the right to claim an oral hearing and the commissioner must grant such a request unless he is satisfied that he can determine the appeal without such a hearing. Further, the hearing must be in public unless otherwise directed by the commissioner, on the grounds that intimate personal or financial circumstances are likely to be disclosed or that a question of public security is involved.

If the commissioner nominated to hear the appeal considers that it raises a point of law of special difficulty he may direct that the appeal be heard by a tribunal of three commissioners in which case there may be a majority decision. Where there is a question of fact of special difficulty the commissioner may require the assistance of a special assessor or assessors specially qualified, who will be selected from a panel appointed for that purpose, and the commissioner may also refer questions to a registered medical practitioner.

In conclusion, it should be noted that wide powers exist under the Acts for the review of the decisions of commissioners, local tribunals and insurance officers, and that any decision given on review is subject to appeal as in the case of an original decision. Much of the practice and procedure is governed by regulations made pursuant to the Acts.

Industrial Injuries

Before the National Insurance (Industrial Injuries) Act, 1946, came into force, claims by workmen for compensation for injuries due to their employment were dealt with by the county courts under the Workmen's Compensation Acts. Alternatively, the injured workman could sue his employer in the ordinary courts for damages if his injury was caused by the employer's negligence or breach of duty.

The latter course is still open to the workmen, but for injuries which have occurred since the 1946 Act came into force, industrial injuries insurance has replaced workmen's compensation.

The nature and scope of the industrial injuries insurance scheme will be considered in more detail later in this section. At this point it may be helpful to describe it in general terms. The scheme is one of compulsory state insurance. Employers and employees are required to pay contributions in addition to those paid for national insurance. Benefits are payable to employees who suffer personal injury, disease or death due to employment, and provision is made for deciding disputes concerning claims for benefit and other related matters.

The National Insurance (Industrial Injuries) Act, 1946, provided that as from the appointed day all persons employed in insurable employment had to be insured also against personal injury caused by accident arising out of, and in the course of, such employment. The appointed day was 5 July 1948.

The Act further provided that any person who was so insured was insured also against any disease or any personal injury not so caused provided that it was a disease or personal injury prescribed by the Minister in relation to the person and due to the nature of his insurable employment and developed on or after the appointed day.

The decision as to whether or not a disease or injury should be prescribed in relation to any insured persons rested with the Minister, who had to be satisfied, firstly that it ought to be treated, having regard to its causes and incidence and any other relevant considerations, as a risk of their particular occupations and not as a risk common to all persons, and, secondly, that it was such that, in the absence of special circumstances, the attribution of particular cases to the nature of the employment could be established or presumed with reasonable certainty. These provisions have been re-enacted in the National Insurance (Industrial Injuries) Act, 1965. The Minister has by regulation prescribed a considerable number of diseases and injuries; many relate to poisoning by various substances, such as lead and arsenic, while others relate to diseases such as dermatitis and tuberculosis, to name but a few.

Until the National Insurance Act, 1966, was passed there were appointed for the purposes of the National Insurance (Industrial Injuries) Acts insurance officers, local appeal tribunals, commissioners, and deputy commissioners to adjudicate upon industrial injury claims in a similar way to claims brought in respect of national insurance benefits. The powers and duties of the Minister in respect of industrial injury benefit were similar also, and the rights of appeal from his decisions the same.

National Insurance Act, 1966

This Act repealed much of the National Insurance (Industrial Injuries) Act, 1965, and transferred the functions and duties of the former commissioners, tribunals, and insurance officers appointed under that Act to decide industrial injuries questions to the National Insurance Commissioners, local tribunals, and insurance officers appointed under the National Insurance Acts, 1965 and 1966. They were empowered to decide industrial injuries questions with the exception of certain "special questions" and those reserved to the Minister to determine in accordance with the provisions of the National Insurance Acts, 1965. It follows that with certain exceptions which are referred to hereafter, the tribunals and the procedure in relation to industrial injury claims are the same as those for national insurance.

One of the questions which has to be determined by an insurance officer, local tribunal or commissioner is whether the claim results from an industrial accident or disease as defined at the beginning of this section. But in addition to this type of question there are further questions of a medical nature which are "special questions" calling for medical adjudication, as illustrated below.

The medical boards and medical appeal tribunals constituted under the earlier Acts have been retained to deal with these questions. Medical boards are appointed by the Minister and consist of two or more medical practitioners, one of whom is appointed as chairman. Medical appeal tribunals are also appointed by the Minister and consist of a chairman and two general practitioners.

An insurance officer must refer to a medical board any "disablement question", i.e. a question as to whether an accident has resulted in a loss of faculty and, if so, at what degree and for what period the disablement should be assessed. If a claimant is dissatisfied with the decision of the medical board he may appeal to the medical appeal tribunal, and on points of law an appeal lies to the National Insurance Commissioner at the instance of the claimant or his union or the Minister. Leave to appeal to the commissioner has to be obtained either from the medical appeal tribunal or from the commissioner.

Family Allowances

The Family Allowances Act, 1965, provided that claims for allowances under this Act should be made to the Minister. The Act also provides that:

(*a*) questions as to the right to an allowance in respect of any person for any family; or (*b*) questions which by virtue of the schedule to the Act fall to be determined by the Minister in his discretion, arising under the Act,

should be determined in the same way and by the same processes as are applicable to claims for benefit under the National Insurance Act.

Accordingly, reference to the section on National Insurance should be made.

National Assistance

The National Assistance Acts replaced the poor law.

The National Assistance Act, 1948, covered that part of the field of social security which was not dealt with by the other Acts, namely the provision by the state of financial and other assistance to persons in need whose needs were not met by National Insurance or by other means. The scheme was administered by the National Assistance Board.

Under the Ministry of Social Security Act, 1966, the National Assistance Board was abolished; the new Ministry of Social Security was set up and a new scheme of supplementary pensions and supplementary allowances was created. These replaced national assistance. The Act also made provision for the payment of non-contributory benefit in certain cases.

The Act created the Supplementary Benefits Commission, a body corporate with a common seal, which consists of a chairman, deputy chairman, and not more than six other members appointed by the Minister, including at least two women. It is the function of the commission acting through the Ministry and other employees to determine whether any person is entitled to benefit under the Act and the amount of such benefit. A person claiming or in receipt of benefit under the Act may appeal to the Appeal Tribunal against any decision of the commission or against a refusal of the commission to review a decision. On appeal, the Appeal Tribunal's decision is conclusive.

Appeal tribunals are appointed by the Minister for districts throughout the country. Each tribunal consists of a chairman and two other members. One such member must be a person who appears to the Minister to represent work-people. It must act in accordance with rules laid down by the Minister. Any question which arises on an appeal as to whether a person's own requirements are to be disregarded because of his activities in relation to a trade dispute must be referred by the appeal tribunal to a local tribunal established under the National Insurance Acts. Reference should be made to the earlier section which deals with local tribunals.

National Health

The National Health Service Act, 1946, inaugurated "free" medical and dental treatment by hospitals and like establishments, and by medical and dental practitioners and others who belong to the scheme. Provision is made for complaints by patients against practitioners to be made to executive councils which have been set up in areas throughout the country. These councils are composed in part of persons representing the various bodies and professions concerned with the health service, such as the local health authority, doctors, dentists, pharmacists, and, in part, of persons appointed by the Minister. A complaint has first to be considered by a committee of the council, presided over by a lay chairman who will report its findings and recommendation, if any, to the council.

If the executive council decides that the practitioner should be deprived of the right to practise within the National Health Service, the matter has then to be referred to the National Health Service Tribunal for consideration. This tribunal consists of a chairman who must be a barrister or solicitor of at least 10 years' standing who is appointed by the Lord Chancellor, and two other members appointed by the Minister of Social Security, one a member of the same profession as the person against whom the complaint has been made, and the other a lay person. The final right of appeal against this tribunal's decision lies to the Minister, but only if the decision is adverse to the professional person. A decision by the tribunal against removal of the professional person from the National Health Service is final. The appellate procedure is thus part judicial and part administrative.

If the complaint is rejected by the executive committee, or the doctor, dentist, or other member of the service, is held to be blameworthy, but not to an extent which justifies his dismissal from the Health Service, either party has a right of appeal to the Minister. The ultimate decision in this instance is therefore administrative, as it is the Minister who decides and not a tribunal.

The processes described above should not be confused with those performed by bodies such as the disciplinary committee of the General Medical Council under which a practitioner may be disciplined and removed from the medical register for misconduct. There are similar bodies for dentists, nurses, and many other branches of the medical profession, as for other professions, and their ultimate sanction is to expel the offender from practice under the banner of their organization, not only from practice within the Health Service.

Supervision by the High Court

The jurisdiction of the High Court in relation to the activities of ministers and tribunals stems from two principal sources. Firstly, the divisional court of the Queen's Bench Division has inherent common law power to examine the extent and mode of exercise of powers of inferior courts and tribunals and even a Minister when he acts judicially or quasi-judicially. The power may be exercised by the orders of prohibition, certiorari and mandamus or by injunction or declaration. As a general rule, this control can only be exercised if the activity in question is judicial or quasi-judicial as defined in the introduction to this chapter. It is, moreover, limited to cases of excess of jurisdiction, ultra vires, error of law on the face of the record and denial of natural justice. This aspect of judicial review will be considered more fully in the next section.

Secondly, there may be a right of appeal to the High Court against the decision of a Minister or tribunal. The right to appeal is quite distinct from the right to ask for a review by the High Court. As a matter of general principle there is no right of appeal from the decision of a Minister or tribunal unless the statute or statutes which establish the particular tribunal or other machinery for acting or making decisions or some other enactment expressly give a right of appeal. Since the Franks Report a number of statutes have given persons aggrieved by decisions of tribunals and ministers a right of appeal, but the right is limited to appeal against errors of law.

Control by Review

In cases of review the court is not concerned with the merits of the decision. The review is of the way in which the decision has been reached. The grounds upon which the High Court may use its powers of review may be summarized as follows.

Firstly, excess of jurisdiction and the ultra vires doctrine may be considered together. The powers of ministers and tribunals in the sphere of administrative law are for the most part derived from statute and these powers can only be exercised to the extent and in the manner laid down by the statute. If the powers do not exist or they have been exceeded, the reviewing court may declare anything done pursuant thereto null and void and quash it.

An act may be null and void because it has been performed by a person who is not authorized to do it, or because an essential fact which has to exist to establish the jurisdiction of the Minister or tribunal is found not to exist. Similarly, it may be found either that the tribunal or person making an order or decision is not properly constituted or appointed, or that a statutory power which has been given for one purpose has been used for another and unauthorized purpose. Lastly, an action or decision may be vitiated by mala fides, e.g. where there has been bad faith in the exercise of a discretionary power.

Secondly, error on the face of the record. This presupposes that there is a "record". The error must be ascertainable by looking at the record only. The "record" includes any documents which initiate the proceedings, pleadings, if any, and the adjudication, but it will not include evidence or reasons unless they have been incorporated in the record.

Lastly, the rules of natural justice. The courts of law operate on the principle that justice must not only be done, it must be seen to be done, and they require other persons or bodies exercising judicial or quasi-judicial function to observe the same principle.

There are two basic rules: first, that a person is entitled to know the case against him and be given the opportunity to answer it. Second, that a person be given a fair hearing: he is entitled to have an impartial and unbiased tribunal to consider his case.

Powers of Review

Prerogative Orders

The three prerogative orders with which this section is concerned are prohibition, certiorari, and mandamus. They take their names from the ancient prerogative writs which were abolished by the Administration of Justice (Miscellaneous Provisions) Act, 1938. The purposes for which each may be used remains substantially those of the writs but the Act has simplified the procedure for their use.

Prohibition and Certiorari

The writs of prohibition and certiorari originally formed part of the process by which the High Court restrained inferior courts of law from exceeding their powers. Prohibition restrained the inferior court from proceeding to hear matters in excess of jurisdiction. Certiorari lay to bring the proceedings of the inferior court before the High Court for inquiry into their legality and regularity, and if appropriate, to quash any order which had been made. In the course of time their operation has been extended to control the proceedings of bodies other than the law courts. If any person or body having legal authority to decide questions which affect the rights of citizens and also having a duty to act judicially, acts in excess of their legal authority they are subject to the jurisdiction of the divisional court exercised by these orders. Certiorari will issue where a body has acted ultra vires or in excess of jurisdiction, where there is an error of law on the face of the record or where the rules of natural justice have not been observed.

Mandamus

Mandamus lies to command persons, bodies and inferior courts to perform public duties which are imposed on them by law. It is not limited to the performance of judicial acts. The applicant for mandamus must have a sufficient interest in the performance of the duty to justify his application and must have requested its performance and had his request refused. The Court has a discretion whether or not to grant mandamus and will not do so if there is an equally suitable alternative method of enforcement. A respondent who disobeys an order of mandamus may be proceeded against for contempt of court.

Declaration

A person may bring an action in the High Court by which he asks the court for an order declaring the legal rights of the parties. The applicant must, however, have an interest in the subject matter to which the declaration relates as the Court will not answer hypothetical questions. The Court has a discretion to grant or refuse a declaration. A declaration cannot be enforced but it is a useful method of ascertaining the legal position where there is a genuine dispute as to the law and the respondent is a responsible person or body who is likely to accept the law once it is stated authoritatively.

Injunction

A person may also bring an action in the High Court by which he claims an injunction. An injunction is an order that the party to whom it is addressed shall do or refrain from doing the act referred to in the order. The grant of an injunction is discretionary and will generally be refused where some other equally effective remedy is available, or damages would compensate the applicant adequately or the injunction sought is mandatory, i.e. it requires the performance of an act, and the act is one which the Court cannot enforce effectively.

An injunction will not be granted to a private person to restrain a breach of public law unless he can show that the breach either interferes with his private rights or causes him special damage. An injunction may be granted to restrain a breach of contract or a tortious act. It may also be granted to prevent the commission of an ultra vires act by a public body. An injunction will not be made against the Crown.

Tribunals and Inquiries Act, 1958, Section 11

Before 1958 a number of modern statutes which dealt with questions which were subject to review by tribunal or inquiry contained provisions designed to exclude or limit the inherent supervisory powers of the High Court. Section 11 of the Tribunals and Inquiries Act, 1958, rectified this retrospectively by enacting that any provision in a statute passed before 1 August 1958 which purported to exclude any of the powers of the High Court should not have effect so as to prevent the High Court making orders of certiorari or mandamus.

Appeal to the High Court

Section 9 of the Tribunals and Inquiries Act, 1958, gives to any party to proceedings before any one of the tribunals which are specified in the Act a right of appeal in point of law.

The statute gives the appellant two alternative courses; he may either appeal to the High Court or he may require the tribunal to state and sign a case for the opinion of the High Court. The statute leaves the question of procedure to be dealt with by rules of the Supreme Court.

The procedure on appeal is governed by O. 55, R.S.C. and the procedure in respect of case stated by O. 56. An appeal is brought by notice of originating motion specifying the grounds. The notice must be served on every party to the proceedings and on the chairman of the tribunal, Minister, government department, or other person concerned, and service must be effected and the appeal entered within 28 days of the date when notice of the decision has been given to the appellant. Any one of the specified tribunals may of its own motion or at the request of any party to the proceedings state a case for the opinion of the High Court upon a point of law which arises in the course of the proceedings before it.

Further, if the tribunal refuses to state a case, an aggrieved party may apply to the High Court for an order that the tribunal do so. The application is made by notice of originating motion stating the grounds, the question of law involved and any reasons given by the tribunal for its refusal. The notice must be served as in the case of an appeal and the motion entered for hearing, but the time limit is 14 days from receipt of notice of the tribunals' refusal. The case must be signed by the chairman of the tribunal or such other person who had the conduct of the proceedings and served on the person at whose request, or upon whose application to the Court, it was stated; or where the tribunal has acted of its own motion, it will be served upon such parties as the tribunal considers appropriate.

The party on whom the case is served must within 14 days lodge it in the Crown Office and Associates' Department of the High Court, together with a notice of motion, and serve on every other party to the proceedings a copy of the notice of motion and the case and serve on the chairman of the tribunal a copy of the notice. The High Court has power to draw inferences of fact from the facts stated in the case and may amend the case or send it back to the tribunal for amendment.

Among the many tribunals specified are rent tribunals and those concerned with the retention of medical and other personnel within the Health Service. Such rights of appeal also extend to certain decisions of the Minister of Housing and Local Government in town and country planning matters and to decisions of the Minister of Transport on appeal from the Traffic Commissioners.

REVIEW OF ADMINISTRATIVE ACTS

The Ombudsman or Parliamentary Commissioner

The last hundred years or so has seen in England the growth of elaborate social services regulating much of the citizens' daily activities. The average citizen tends to regard the state as a leviathan apart from himself and its officials as similarly remote creatures. One hears the word "they" commonly used when referring to some government activity. The traditional methods of control of the misuse of power appear to be insufficient. The powers of review of administrative decisions by the courts of law are strictly limited and, in the view of a number of people, the procedure is too unwieldy, too slow and too costly for any ordinary person to challenge a decision in this way. Further, the courts have shown themselves unwilling or unable to interfere with purely administrative decisions, so that there is a vast field of legislative and executive discretion which is shielded from judicial scrutiny.

The Franks Committee's Report in 1957 covered only those areas of ministerial decision where the decision was preceded by a hearing before a tribunal or an inquiry. Hence, the Council on Tribunals has no power of supervision or review over a wide area of executive discretion which is not subject to any appeal procedure and, until recently, was not subject to any supervision except that of Parliament itself and the press. As to the former, electors might complain to their member of parliament who might raise the matter at question time in the House of Commons or upon adjournment debates, but time for these measures is limited, and the M.P. might have difficulty in obtaining access to the department's files. Thus it was thought that the best solution was for an independent person to be appointed to investigate grievances, whilst preserving the relationship between M.P.s and electors by channelling all complaints through M.P.s.

Most people have heard of the Ombudsman: The office is of Scandinavian origin, the first appointment being made in Sweden in 1809, followed in Denmark in 1953 and more recently in Norway. New Zealand followed suit in 1962, and Canada and Australia are now considering making similar appointments. The functions of the Scandinavian Ombudsman are extremely wide. For example, the Danish Ombudsman, who is an entirely independent person is under the duty of supervising all state administration.

On 1 April 1967 the Parliamentary Commissioner Act, 1967, came into force. This Act provides for the appointment by the Queen of a Commissioner to be known as the Parliamentary Commissioner for Administration. The first commissioner has been appointed and has assumed his functions, which are similar to those of the Ombudsman, though more limited in their scope. He is an independent person concerned to investigate complaints of maladministration in administrative actions of departments of the central government or other authorities to which the Act applies.

The public have no right of direct access to him; complaints must be made in writing to a Member of Parliament, not necessarily the complainant's own, and referred by the member to the commissioner. Unless the commissioner is satisfied that there are special circumstances, a complaint must be made to an M.P. within 12 months from the day on which the complainant first had notice of the matters alleged in the complaint. His field of inquiry is limited. He cannot for example investigate complaints relating to local government authorities, the nationalized industries, the police, the armed forces or local bodies of the health service. These fields and in particular local government are those in which private grievances arise most frequently and there is still therefore a wide area where the citizen has no easy or effective means of ventilating his grievances. There is, however, power to extend the commissioner's field of inquiry later, and it may well be that this will happen in due course.

Unless the commissioner is satisfied that there are circumstances which justify an aggrieved person in not resorting to a court of law or tribunal, he will not investigate any actions in respect of which the complainant has or has had a remedy or right of relief in such court or tribunal. He has no power to order any action to be taken. His function is to investigate grievances with the aid of his staff and to recommend action if necessary. He has access to departmental files and power to question any person concerned with the case and to question witnesses and he can in the last resort certify to the High Court that a person who is obstructing the investigation without lawful excuse is in contempt.

Experience in other countries has shown that the mere fact that machinery exists to investigate grievances and to lift the veil which surrounds the activities of government departments has a salutary effect and that the mere initiation of an investigation is generally sufficient to ensure that any genuine grievance is remedied. In any case where the commissioner investigates he will send a report of the result of his investigations to the member of parliament, to the principal officer of the department or authority concerned and to any other person alleged to have taken or authorized the action complained of, and if he is satisfied that injustice has been caused to the complainant by maladministration which has not been or will not be remedied, he may also lay a special report before both Houses of Parliament.

If he decides not to investigate he will report his reasons to the M.P. Once a year the commissioner is required to lay a general report before Parliament.

Tribunals of Inquiry

In conclusion, however, some mention should be made of the tribunals which are set up from time to time to inquire into allegations of misconduct or maladministration. Inquiries are made often into such matters by royal commissions, departmental committees and parliamentary committees but for the most part these excite little public interest.

Occasionally, however, there is a public scandal in which allegations of misconduct, maladministration, or neglect are made against ministers or other persons in public life. In these circumstances a tribunal may be set up under the Tribunals of Inquiry (Evidence) Act, 1921, to inquire into the matter. Such a tribunal can only be constituted on the resolution of both Houses of Parliament. It is an *ad hoc* tribunal appointed to inquire into a specific matter and is customarily presided over by a High Court judge. Familiar examples are the Lynskey Tribunal in 1948 which inquired into the alleged activities of Mr. Sidney Stanley and certain members of the Government; the Bank rate inquiry in 1958, the Vassall inquiry in 1963, and the most recent, the Aberfan inquiry.

Such a tribunal has all the powers of the High Court in respect of witnesses. The tribunal can compel persons to attend and give evidence, and has the full powers of the High Court to fine or to commit to prison for contempt of court, as happened to certain journalists as a result of the Vassall inquiry. The procedure of the tribunal is inquisitional rather than accusatory. There is no trial as such, no parties, and all witnesses are witnesses of the tribunal. The tribunal is usually represented by the Attorney-General and other counsel with him. They call the witnesses, and it is in the discretion of the tribunal to decide what other persons may be permitted to appear and be heard and to what extent cross-examination is allowed.

The function of the tribunal is not to adjudicate; it is simply to inquire and find the facts and report these to Parliament.

CHAPTER 12

Costs of Litigation — Legal Aid

Magistrates' courts — Quarter sessions — County courts — Actions remitted from High Court: Security for costs; Taxation — High Court of Justice: Security for costs; Taxing masters; Allocatur — House of Lords: Taxation of costs; Legal aid; Financial conditions — Legal advice — Matters not involving litigation — Cost to Exchequer — Solicitors and counsel — Functions of the Law Society — Regulations — Legal Aid Act, 1964.

ALTHOUGH it has been necessary to refer in earlier chapters to the question of costs, this subject is considered to be of sufficient importance to warrant a chapter on its own. It is therefore proposed to deal with this subject in so far as the civil jurisdiction of the various courts is affected. At the same time the opportunity will be taken of referring to the provisions of the Legal Aid and Advice Act, 1949, as amended by the Act of 1960 together with the Legal Aid Act, 1964.

MAGISTRATES' COURTS

Turning first to the jurisdiction of magistrates' courts in relation to the awarding of costs, reference has already been made in Chapter 4 under the sub-title of Civil Debts to the powers of magistrates in this respect (see p. 85). These powers may be briefly summarized as follows. A magistrates' court on the hearing of a complaint has a discretion to award costs to be paid either by a defendant to a complainant or vice versa subject to the limitation that such costs must be just and reasonable. It is equally important to note that the power to award costs ought not to be exercised vindictively.

In hearing a complaint, however, unless the defendant is given the opportunity of asking for the complaint to be withdrawn, the magistrates will have no power to order the complainant to pay the defendant's costs. A magistrates' court also has power to make an order on complaint for the payment of any money recoverable as a civil debt. Their power of committing a defaulter to prison is, however, restricted by the provisions which are laid down in section 73 of the Magistrates' Courts Act, 1952, and section 27 of the Criminal Justice Act, 1967. The overriding necessity is that the court must be satisfied before committing any person to prison, that that person has the means to pay the full amount or instalment which is in question. There is also the further restriction which is contained in Rule 42 of the Magistrates' Courts Rules, 1952, to the effect that notice has to be given to the defendant before a committal order can be enforced.

It will be readily appreciated that it is not possible to give any idea of the amount of costs that may be awarded by a magistrates' court. There are naturally many different factors that have to be taken into account, and the magistrates will exercise their discretion in accordance with the particular circumstances which may arise in relation to any case with which they are dealing.

It should, however, be pointed out that when dealing with ejectment proceedings under the provisions of the Small Tenements Recovery Act, 1838, there would appear to be no power given to the magistrates to award costs. In the circumstances the provisions of section 55 of the Magistrates' Courts Act, 1952, do not therefore apply to such proceedings.

QUARTER SESSIONS

Speaking generally, courts of Quarter Sessions have a complete discretion as to the awarding of costs on the hearing and determination of appeals from petty sessional courts. This general power includes the right to amend an order or judgment of the justices on such terms of costs as the court shall think fit (Summary Jurisdiction Act, 1879, section 31).

Since in general solicitors have no right of audience at Quarter Sessions, and the majority of appeals are conducted with the appearance of counsel on both sides, the costs which are incurred by an unsuccessful appellant in an appeal to Quarter Sessions are of necessity higher than those which are normally imposed by magistrates' courts. Here again, however, no specific sum can be mentioned as each appeal is considered on its own particular circumstances. Any costs which are awarded by a court of Quarter Sessions take the form of an order of the court, and in the case of a successful appellant are payable by the respondent to the appeal to the appellant. On the other hand, an unsuccessful appellant has to pay any costs so ordered to the respondent. The court has no power to enforce the payment of such costs, and they are recoverable as a civil debt. It quite frequently happens, therefore, that a respondent to an appeal does not find it worth while to spend further money in chasing such an award.

In addition to its general power of awarding costs certain statutes give quarter sessions the right to order costs. The two most important of such statutes are the Betting, Gaming and Lotteries Act, 1963, where the power to award costs is given to Quarter Sessions by virtue of the provisions of paragraph 21 of the first schedule; and the Licensing Act, 1964, section 24 of which lays down similar powers.

Before passing on to the consideration of costs in relation to the higher courts, it should be noted that magistrates carry out their duties under certain statutory safeguards which protect them against being made personally liable for the payment of costs. The principal provisions for the indemnity of justices of the peace in relation to costs that are incurred in proceedings brought against them in respect of anything done or omitted in the exercise of their office are now contained in section 27 of the Administration of Justice Act, 1964. Section 25 of the Licensing Act, 1964, and paragraph 22 of the first schedule to the Betting, Gaming and Lotteries Act, 1963, respectively, make provision for the payment out of local funds of costs incurred by magistrates in relation to appeals to Quarter Sessions to which they have been made a party.

COUNTY COURTS

Costs, in so far as they may be incurred in actions in county courts, have been referred to in Chapter 5 under the sub-heading "Costs" on pp. 109, 110. It is only necessary, therefore, to remind the reader in the present chapter of the broad principles which are involved.

In a general sense, the costs of proceedings in a county court are in the discretion of the court. This discretion has, however, to be exercised in the same manner and on the same principles as that of the High Court, and must therefore be exercised judicially.

Solicitors' charges and disbursements are regulated by different scales of costs which vary according to the amount at issue. Since full reference has been made to these scales on p. 110 it would be redundant to refer further to them at this point.

Fees payable to counsel, subject to certain restrictions, are allowable within the limits that are set in the appropriate county court scales. These include refresher fees in respect of cases which are either not completed in a day or are adjourned for want of time or on payment of the costs of the day.

Costs on scale 1, however, do not cover fees for counsel unless the judge or registrar certifies that the case is fit for counsel. Where costs are on scale 3 or 4 the judge may certify for the employment of more than one counsel.

Such sum as the judge or registrar thinks reasonable may, subject to certain prescribed maxima, be allowed in respect of the attendance of witnesses who give evidence as to facts or who produce documents. In addition, reasonable travelling and hotel expenses may be allowed, and if a case lasts for more than one day the allowances in respect of attendance are payable in respect of each day that a witness is required to attend court.

ACTIONS REMITTED FROM HIGH COURT

Where actions have been remitted to the county court from the High Court, unless the High Court has made an order as to costs in relation to proceedings prior to remission, costs of the whole proceedings are dealt with by the county court judge (see section 76 of the County Courts Act, 1959). So far as costs prior to remission are concerned, the county court, where applicable, must give effect to the provisions of section 47 of the County Courts Act, 1959, which relate to the costs of actions commenced in the High Court but which could have been commenced in the county court.

Security for Costs

By O. 58, r. 9 (5) of the Supreme Court, the Court of Appeal may, in special circumstances, order that such security as may be just shall be given for the costs of an appeal. As a general rule the Court of Appeal will not require security for costs where leave to appeal has been given unconditionally or where inability to give security would deprive an appellant of a vested right determinable only by the Court of Appeal. If reasonable grounds for appealing are shown and there are no special circumstances, an order for security for costs will not be made against an assisted person. Where, however, it is proved to the court's satisfaction that the appellant has disposed of his property in order to avoid paying the respondent's costs, an order for security will be made.

Taxation

The remuneration which a solicitor is entitled to claim in respect of contentious business carried out by him in a county court is regulated by the provisions of the Solicitors Act, 1957, sections 59–73. Where the amount of a bill of costs relating wholly or partly to contentious business done in a county court does not exceed £500 a county court can order taxation.

When such an order is made the solicitor must lodge his bill within 14 days of the order being made. Such a bill is known as "a solicitor and client bill". The registrar in a county court acts as taxing master, subject to review by the county court judge, and he has to give 3 days' notice of the time and place fixed for the taxation.

The amount allowable in respect of any item relating to proceedings in a county court in a solicitor and client bill of costs is not allowed in excess of the amount which could have been allowed in respect of such an item in a party and party bill of costs in those proceedings.

In cases where legal aid has been given, any assisted person's costs are payable out of the legal aid fund, and the amount to be so paid is ascertained by taxation in accordance with the ordinary rules that apply as between solicitor and client.

Any party who is dissatisfied by a taxation of costs by a registrar may apply within 2 days to him to reconsider the taxation, specifying the items to which objection is made. The registrar must then reconsider his taxation and, if so required, state his reasons in writing thereon.

HIGH COURT OF JUSTICE

Security for Costs

Generally, security for costs may be ordered in cases where the plaintiff is in a state of poverty or insolvency; or if the appellant is a limited company and the court is satisfied that the company will be unable to pay the defendant's costs if judgment is given against them; or if the plaintiff is resident out of the jurisdiction and has no assets within it; or where the plaintiff's residence is incorrectly stated on the writ of summons, unless the latter has been an innocent mis-statement.

Taxing Masters

Usually a High Court order for payment of costs includes a direction that such costs are to be taxed, and a taxing master will then carry out the taxation. Normally this is done on a party and party basis, and on the principle that the successful party should be indemnified against any costs reasonably incurred by him in prosecuting or defending an action.

Costs that are awarded in the High Court are, however, subject to two scales—a higher and a lower scale. Normally costs are allowed on the lower scale with a discretion being reserved to the court or a judge to allow costs on the higher scale. The taxing master has, however, a very wide discretion with regard to costs. The general rule holds that he will allow all costs, charges and expenses which appear to him to have been necessarily or properly incurred. This discretion is sufficiently wide to allow him to award a sum in excess of the limit fixed by either scale.

The taxing master's discretion to allow costs operates equally with regard to his discretion to disallow them; therefore if he considers that costs have been incurred unnecessarily he can disallow any items that come within that definition. Indeed, it is his duty to look carefully into any such circumstances.

Allocatur

When costs have been finally taxed the taxing master gives his certificate or allocatur as it is known, for the amount of the costs he has allowed. This allocatur may take the form of a balance as between two sets of costs, where a party who is entitled to costs is also ordered to pay costs to his opponent.

Before the allocatur is signed any dissatisfied party may deliver to the other interested party a list of objections which must be in writing specifying the particular items together with the grounds of objection. An application has then to be made to the taxing master requesting him to review the taxation. To this the taxing master must accede in so far as the objected items are concerned, before he can issue his allocatur as regards those items.

Items not objected to are finally disposed of by the taxing master's allocatur. As to objected items, however, a dissatisfied party may within 14 days from the issue of the allocatur, apply to the judge in chambers to review the taxation, and the judge may then make such an order as he thinks fit.

Normally, the court does not interfere with a taxing master's decision on a question of fact or amount. If, however, the court is satisfied that sufficient material was not before the taxing master, or that he took matters wrongly into account, or that he failed to consider material matters, or that he acted on a wrong principle, the court will order a review. Should the court do this the review need not necessarily be by the same taxing master.

In cases where leave to appeal has been granted, an appeal lies to the Court of Appeal from the order of the judge and the appeal must be brought within 14 days.

HOUSE OF LORDS

The luxury of an appeal to the House of Lords is doubtless a matter in which a litigant will require expert advice before he will decide to undertake the risk of making himself liable in respect of further heavy legal costs.

Appeals to the House of Lords and to the Judicial Committee of the Privy Council are now regulated by the provisions of the Administration of Justice (Appeals) Act, 1934. The main purpose of that Act, which came into operation on 1 October 1934, is to restrict appeals from the Court of Appeal to the House of Lords from any order or judgment of that court to those cases in which leave to appeal is granted either by the Court of Appeal or by the House of Lords.

Not unnaturally, security for costs is a matter of prime importance in connection with such appeals, and it is the normal practice for such security to be required. To this end the Standing Orders of the House of Lords which regulate judicial business lay down that an appellant has to give security for costs in one of three ways, namely (i) by payment into the House of Lords Security Fund Account the sum of £1000, or (ii) by a similar payment of £500 together with a recognizance in respect of a further £500, or (iii) by procuring two sureties to the satisfaction of the Clerk of the Parliaments to the amount of £500, in addition to entering into a recognizance himself for a further £500.

Taxation of Costs

Where an order for costs in relation to proceedings in the House of Lords is made, the amount of such costs is determined on taxation by a person who has been appointed by the Clerk of the Parliaments to act as taxing master, and who is known as the Judicial Taxing Officer. This officer will then determine the amount of costs to be allowed and he will report to the Clerk of the Parliaments and issue a certificate for the amount so allowed. The certificate, as in High Court taxation, is known as an "allocatur".

Legal Aid

Reference has already been made in Chapter 7 under the sub-heading "Security for Costs" on p. 145 with reference to appeals to the House of Lords on behalf of poor persons. The reader is therefore introduced here to the latest statutory provisions in this respect. Section 1 and Part 1 of the first schedule to the Legal Aid and Advice Act, 1949, make provision for legal aid to be given in respect of proceedings in the House of Lords in the exercise of its jurisdiction in relation to appeals from courts in England or Northern Ireland. Although this statute received the royal assent in 1949, the above provisions have only become operative since 1960. In connection with legally aided appeals to the House of Lords, it has also to be noted that the standing order regarding security for costs specifically exempts from its provisions appellants who have been granted legal aid.

We now come to consider the statutory provisions by virtue of which legal aid and advice are made available to persons in connection with civil proceedings before courts and tribunals in England and Wales. The principal act is the Legal Aid and Advice Act, 1949, as amended by the Legal Aid Act, 1960, together with the Legal Aid Act, 1964.

The purpose of the 1949 Act is stated in the headnote: "to make legal aid and advice more readily available for persons of small or moderate means, to be defrayed wholly or partly out of moneys provided by Parliament". The fundamental distinction therefore, as the law stands at present as between legal aid granted in relation to criminal matters and legal aid granted in respect of civil matters, is that, whilst in criminal matters legal aid when granted is payable *in toto* out of public funds, in civil matters this need not necessarily be the case.

The general scope and conditions in which legal aid may be given are set out in section 1 and Part 1 of the first schedule to the 1949 Act. Representation is by a solicitor, or if necessary by counsel, subject to reasonable grounds being shown for taking, defending or being a party to any proceedings. It should be noted, however, that the regulations do not apply in connection with proceedings in which counsel or solicitor are not normally allowed to be heard.

The first point to note is that although the 1949 Act was entitled the Legal Aid and Advice Act, it was only in 1959 that a legal advice scheme was brought into operation. Legal advice may be understood to include oral advice concerning an applicant's legal rights or obligations. Such advice is to be given in the office of a solicitor who has indicated his willingness to undertake this work. Legal advice is available to any person who has attained the age of 16.

The Rushcliffe Committee had under consideration three possibilities by means of which the scheme could be put into operation, namely (i) the State, (ii) local authorities, and (iii) the legal profession. The committee chose the legal profession on the ground that it is more independent of the interests of the party involved than either the state or local authorities might prove to be.

Thus the Law Society, in co-operation with the Bar, became responsible for the operation of the scheme, which involves the division of the country into twelve areas, with each area having an Area Committee consisting of eight solicitors and four barristers. In addition to the twelve main committees there are also local committees, and under these, there are what are known as certifying committees which, as their name implies, are set up for the purpose of satisfying themselves that an applicant has a good prima facie case and a reasonable chance of success. In the event of a certifying committee refusing to grant a certificate, an applicant has a right of appeal to the area committee.

FINANCIAL CONDITIONS

Section 2 of the 1949 Act, as amended by section 1 of the Legal Aid Act, 1960, provides that legal aid shall be available for any person whose disposable income does not exceed £700 per annum; and that legal aid may be refused if he has disposable capital of more than £500, or such larger yearly figure as may be prescribed, and if it appears that he can proceed without legal aid.

Section 4 of the Act lays down the method by means of which the assessment of disposable capital and income is to be computed. A person's disposable income and disposable capital and the maximum amount of his contribution to the legal aid fund were determined formerly by the National Assistance Board, now the Ministry of Social Security (sub-section 6). Under the Ministry of Social Security Act, 1966, the National Assistance Board was dissolved as from 6 August 1966 from which date the Supplementary Benefits Commission came into being to take its place (section 3 and schedule 1).

Section 1 of the 1949 Act also enacts that a person may be required to make a contribution to the legal aid fund, and that any sums that are recovered as costs in his favour shall be paid to the legal aid fund. Further, a legally aided person's liability for costs shall not exceed an amount which is reasonable for him to pay having regard to all the circumstances.

A person's dwelling house and household furniture, together with the tools and implements of his trade, are specifically protected from seizure in execution to enforce an order for costs.

The amount of contributions to be made by an assisted person are defined in section 3 of the 1949 Act as amended by the 1960 Act. The definition is given as "a contribution in respect of income 'not greater than one-third of the amount (if any) by which his disposable income exceeds £250 a year or such larger yearly figure as may be prescribed'." A contribution in respect of capital is defined as "not greater than the amount (if any) by which his disposable capital exceeds £125 or such larger figure as may be prescribed".

Having set out shortly the main statutory effects of these two important Acts, it is not without interest to point to a few statistical features which have resulted from the working of the legal aid scheme. In this respect the following facts are disclosed in the report of the Lord Chancellor's Advisory Committee of the Law Society in relation to the administration of the scheme during the period 1963–4. It will be seen that these figures aptly illustrate the important function which the legal aid scheme now performs in relation to the administration of civil justice in this country.

During the period from March 1963 up to March 1964, which was the period then under review, applications for legal aid were received by the area and local committees from no less than 131,399 persons. This figure represents an overall increase of no less than 224 per cent as compared with the inaugural year 1959–60 when the scheme first came into operation. A further point of interest is that a very high proportion (no less than 80 per cent in 1963–64) of the applications that were granted during this period were in relation to domestic proceedings in the magistrates' courts or matrimonial cases in the Divorce Division of the High Court.

It is a further fact that while in 1959–60, of every 100 cases in the Divorce Division, an average of 62.23 per cent of the parties had legal aid, in 1963–4 this average had risen to 103 per cent.

The number of applicants who are assessed annually with regard to their eligibility for receiving legal aid now exceeds some 140,000. It would appear up to the present time that in spite of the increase in the cost of litigation during recent years, there is no evidence to the effect that the possibility that assisted persons may have to make larger contributions to the fund, has in any way deterred them from accepting offers of legal aid. Indeed, the proportion of litigants who are legally aided continues to grow substantially year by year. During the first 14 years in which the scheme has been in operation, out of a grand total of 838,815 applications, no less than 611,712 have in fact been granted legal aid.

LEGAL ADVICE

The 1949 Act envisaged that legal advice should be made available in England and Wales for any person, and outside Great Britain for any member of the Forces (section 7). The advice thus given consists of oral advice on legal questions given by a solicitor to include help in preparing an application for legal aid and in supplying information relative to determining disposable income and capital.

A person thus seeking advice may, however, be required (i) to satisfy the person from whom he seeks advice that he cannot afford to obtain it in the ordinary way, and (ii) to pay a fee of 2*s*. 6*d*. for each interview. The fee payable to a solicitor by the State is at the rate of £1 per half-hour.

A "member of the forces" is defined in sub-section 12 as meaning "a person serving on full pay as a member of the naval, military or air forces of the Crown raised in the United Kingdom".

Besides legal aid, legal advice was given to as many as 61,354 people during the 1963–4 period alone. It is interesting to compare this figure with the 12,000 who received such advice in 1960–1. It is abundantly clear, therefore, that the scheme is of assistance to an ever-growing body of persons.

MATTERS NOT INVOLVING LITIGATION

Section 5 of the 1949 Act which covers this aspect was one of the later sections to become operative, and only became so on 28 March 1960. Legal aid given under this section consists in the assistance of a solicitor, and is confined to taking steps to assert or dispute a claim where the question of being a party to proceedings before a court or tribunal does not arise or has not yet arisen.

It is still necessary, however, that a person should show that he has reasonable grounds for taking steps to assert or dispute a claim, or else legal aid will be refused. The provisions contained in section 2 of the 1949 Act as to disposable income and capital have been amended in relation to this section to read as follows: "for any person whose disposable income or disposable capital is enough to permit . . . of his making a contribution to the legal aid fund . . ."

COST TO EXCHEQUER

From the above-stated facts it becomes obvious that the cost of civil legal aid must be placing on the Exchequer an increasing burden as the years go by. In fact the cost amounted to some £1,330,000 in 1960, double the amount in 1961, and it has risen by £1,000,000 annually ever since.

The expenditure of such a large sum of public money may, however, well be justified on the grounds that the prestige of the law is enhanced. The operation of the scheme has undoubtedly resulted in many people of "small or moderate means" having been enabled to establish their legal rights which otherwise would have remained dormant, since the costs of litigation might otherwise have proved an insurmountable barrier.

SOLICITORS AND COUNSEL

Section 6 of the 1949 Act provided that panels of solicitors and barristers who were willing to act on behalf of persons who are in receipt of legal aid should be prepared and maintained. Separate panels were available for different purposes and for different courts and different districts. The purpose of the different panels is to allow solicitors to undertake legal aid work in their own particular line of practice; and to allow barristers to have their names entered on such panels as their practice made them available to appear in the courts or districts of their choice.

Sub-section 3 of this section enabled either a barrister or a solicitor who is aggrieved by any decision excluding him, either temporarily or permanently from a panel to appeal to the High Court. Power is given to that court to confirm, quash or to vary the order appealed against, thereby making their decision final. Since 19 July 1965, however, clerks of assize, clerks of the peace, and clerks to justices have been relieved of the obligation to maintain these panels in so far as counsel are concerned (see the Poor Prisoners (Counsel and Solicitors) No. 2 Rules, 1965, and the Summary Jurisdiction Appeals (Counsel and Solicitor) Rules, 1965). Consequently this subsection no longer applies to counsel.

FUNCTIONS OF THE LAW SOCIETY

As already indicated the duty is laid on the Law Society to make the necessary arrangements to formulate a scheme for operating the provisions of the Act. This has to be done with the approval of the Lord Chancellor and the concurrence of the Treasury. This function is in fact performed by the Council of the Law Society in general consultation with the General Council of the Bar.

The function of making or varying the scheme is in fact performed by a committee of the Council of the Law Society which has to include not less than three persons nominated by the General Council of the Bar and a person nominated by the Lord Chancellor.

One important function of the Law Society includes the establishment and administration of the legal aid fund, estimates of the sums required being submitted from time to time to the Lord Chancellor by the Law Society. The accounts of the fund are audited by persons appointed in respect of each financial year by the Lord Chancellor.

The Legal Aid Fund gets its money from three sources. Firstly. contributions from assisted persons; secondly, costs recovered from the other party to the action where such costs are ordered by the court to be paid; and thirdly, a government grant.

REGULATIONS

Wide powers are given under the 1949 Act to the Lord Chancellor to make regulations for the purpose of giving effect to the Act or for preventing abuses. Any regulations thus made are exercisable by statutory instrument. These powers include regulations as to taxation of costs, requirement of security for costs, provisions as to information to be furnished, provision for refusal of legal aid or advice and provisions for the recovery of sums due to the Legal Aid Fund.

The Lord Chancellor has the advantage of receiving advice from an advisory committee (see p. 256).

Sections 14 and 15 create certain offences in relation to legal aid and lay down the penalties on conviction.

Section 17 sets out a series of definitions. It is, however, only necessary to point out at this stage that "person" for the purposes of legal aid does not include a body of persons corporate or incorporate.

LEGAL AID ACT, 1964

To complete the picture of legal aid it is necessary finally to refer to the above Act the purpose underlying which was to provide a remedy for the recovery of costs incurred by successful persons in actions in which they are involved against legally aided persons.

Such persons are referred to in the Act as "the unassisted party". Section 1 enables a court to make an order for such costs to be paid out of public funds, if it is satisfied that such costs are just and equitable in all the circumstances. There are two provisos which state that no such order shall be made unless the proceedings were instituted by the party receiving legal aid, and that the court is satisfied that the unassisted party will suffer severe financial hardship unless the order is made.

Table of Statutes

49 & 50 Vict., c. 27	Guardianship of Infants Act, 1886 52, 77, 83
	Sect. 4 84
	Sect. 5 84
51 & 52 Vict., c. 43	County Courts Act, 1888 95
52 & 53 Vict., c. 10	Commissioner for Oaths Act, 1889 50
	Sect. 1 50
53 & 54 Vict., c. 23	Chancery of Lancaster Act, 1890
	Sect. 3 152
56 & 57 Vict., c. 71	Sale of Goods Act, 1893 12, 129
59 & 60 Vict., c. 30	Conciliation Act, 1896 217
9 Edw. 7, c. 22	Trade Boards Act, 1909 221
8 & 9 Geo. 5, c. 32	Trade Boards Act, 1918 221
9 & 10 Geo. 5, c. 69	Industrial Courts Act, 1919 218
	Sect. 1(1) 218
	Sect. 1(4) 218
	Sect. 2 219
	Sect. 4(1) 219
	Sect. 4(5) 220
	Sect. 8 219
10 & 11 Geo. 5, c. 33	Maintenance Orders (Facilities for Enforcement) Act, 1920
	Sect. 3 77
	Sect. 4 77
11 & 12 Geo. 5, c. 7	Tribunals of Inquiry (Evidence) Act, 1921 244
15 & 16 Geo. 5, c. 21	Land Registration Act, 1925 45
15 & 16 Geo. 5, c. 28	Administration of Justice Act, 1925 115
15 & 16 Geo. 5, c. 45	Guardianship of Infants Act, 1925 52, 77, 83, 84
	Sect. 1 84
15 & 16 Geo. 5, c. 49	Supreme Court of Judicature (Consolidation) Act, 1925 xii, 114, 116, 117, 134, 139
	Sect. 26–32 140
	Sect. 39(1)(b) 176
	Sect. 45 159
	Sect. 56 131
	Sect. 103 115
18 & 19 Geo. 5, c. 26	Administration of Justice Act, 1928
	Sect. 14(1) 152
	Sect. 16 84
20 & 21 Geo. 5, c. 32	Poor Prisoners Defence Act, 1930 51
	Sect. 1 51
	Sect. 2 52
23 & 24 Geo. 5, c. 12	Children and Young Persons Act, 1933
	Sect. 62 91, 93
	Sect. 84 91
	Sect. 86 83
	First Schedule 90
23 & 24 Geo. 5, c. 36	Administration of Justice (Miscellaneous Provisions) Act, 1933 125
	Sect. 6(1) 125

Index